MW01273454

GENERATIONAL DIVERSITY AT WORK

Over the past decade, much attention has been paid to the apparent differences in consumption preferences or workplace attitudes and behaviours across generations. Within Western economies such as the USA, UK and Australia, it is commonly assumed that there are now four generations in the workplace, namely Veterans (born 1925–1942), Baby Boomers (1943–1960), Generation X (1961–1981) and Generation Y (1982–2000).

The concept of generational differences at work is one that has recently been adopted by practitioners as a basis on which to design human resource management and career management practices. However, there has been some concern in academic circles about the validity of the notion of generations and the evidence base that supports it. There is therefore a need for new perspectives and methodological approaches to investigating generational differences at work in order to establish the validity and value of generations as an axis of diversity. *Generational Diversity at Work: New Research Perspectives* will address this need by presenting and discussing research into generational diversity that adopts a range of new theoretical perspectives or methodological approaches.

This book is designed as a first step in addressing the need to critically examine the theoretical and empirical basis for generational differences and to provide some new empirical data in this area.

Emma Parry is a Reader in Human Resource Management at Cranfield School of Management. Her research focuses on the impact of context on managing people. In particular, she is interested in the influence of national context, changing demographics and technological advances.

'This book provides an intellectually stimulating and novel approach to understanding generations and generational differences at work. It brings together an impressive array of international experts to challenge the ways we conceptualize and research generations across different cultural contexts. It will be of immense interest to academics, students and HR practitioners as the world of work becomes increasingly generationally diverse.'

Wendy Loretto, Professor of Organisational Behaviour, University of Edinburgh Business School, UK

'This edited volume from Emma Parry takes a valuable and critical look at whether, and how, generational differences contribute to understanding the effects of age differences at work. This text benefits from a broad range of perspectives on generation, as well as international dimensions. This is a must for readers on age diversity in the workplace.'

Dr John Neugebauer FCIPD, Client Director, Bristol Business School, University of the West of England, UK

GENERATIONAL DIVERSITY AT WORK

New research perspectives

Edited by Emma Parry

LONDON AND NEW YORK

First published 2014
by Routledge
2 Park Square, Milton Park, Abingdon, Oxon OX14 4RN

And by Routledge
711 Third Avenue, New York, NY 10017

Routledge is an imprint of the Taylor & Francis Group, an informa business

British Library Cataloguing in Publication Data
A catalogue record for this book is available from the British Library

Library of Congress Cataloging-in-Publication Data
Generational diversity at work : new research perspectives / edited by Emma Parry.
pages cm
Includes bibliographical references and index.
1. Diversity in the workplace--Management. 2. Conflict of generations in the workplace--Management. 3. Intergenerational relations. 4. Older people--Employment. 5. Youth--Employment. I. Parry, Emma.
HF5549.5.C75G46 2014
331.3--dc23
2013044397

ISBN: 978-0-415-81753-0 (hbk)
ISBN: 978-0-203-58406-4 (ebk)

Typeset in Bembo
by GreenGate Publishing Services, Tonbridge, Kent

CONTENTS

ILLUSTRATIONS

Figures

Tables

ABOUT THE EDITOR

Emma Parry is a Reader in Human Resource Management at Cranfield University School of Management and a Visiting Fellow at Westminster Business School. Her research focuses on the impact of context on managing people, in particular the influence of national context, changing demographics and technological advancement. Emma manages 'Cranet', a network of business schools conducting comparative research into human resource management (HRM) practices, and is a co-director of '5C', a global network that researches career experiences in different national cultures. She is also on the global team of the Center for Aging and Work at Boston College, USA. Emma has undertaken a wide range of research into HRM, for clients such as the Ministry of Defence, the National Health Service and the Chartered Institute of Personnel and Development.

Emma is the co-author of *Managing People in a Contemporary Context* (also published by Routledge). She has edited three other books and has written numerous publications in the field of HRM.

ABOUT THE CONTRIBUTORS

Dedeepya Ajith John is an Engineer from JNT University in Hyderabad, India and received her MBA from the Indian Institute of Science (IISc, Bangalore). She is also a Research Analyst with SHRM India. She is currently working on a large-scale project on multi-generational diversity along with other consulting projects in various human resource (HR) disciplines.

P. Matthijs Bal is Reader at the School of Management, University of Bath. His research interests concern the employment relationship, the aging workforce and workplace flexibility.

John R. Biggan is a Research Scientist in the Center for Healthy Living and Longevity at the University of Texas at Arlington. His research centres on better understanding the causes of age-related cognitive changes and potential interventions to combat decline.

Robert J. Blomme is Director of the Center of Leadership and Management Development and Associate Professor of Management and Organization at Nyenrode Business Universiteit, Breukelen in the Netherlands. His research and teaching cover several topics of organizational behavior, organizational theory and organizational sociology.

Franz Buscha is a Senior Research Fellow in the Centre for Employment Research at the University of Westminster. He has extensive experience in applied econometrics and evaluation methodology, applied mainly in the area of education economics.

Stacy M. Campbell is an Associate Professor of Management and Entrepreneurship in the Coles College of Business at Kennesaw State University, Georgia, USA. Her research focuses on generational differences, charismatic leadership and narcissism, and student retention in online learning.

Maria Nirmala Christine holds a PhD from the Indian Institute of Science (IISc, Bangalore) and an MPhil in Psychiatric Social Work from NIMHANS, Bangalore. She currently serves as the Practice Head – Research and Consulting at Great Place to Work.

Jeanette N. Cleveland is a Full Professor and Program Coordinator for the Industrial and Organizational Psychology doctoral program at Colorado State U (1984–2000; 2011–present). She received her PhD in I/O psychology from the Pennsylvania State U where she was employed from 2000 to 2011. For over 30 years, she has published research on older workers and work–life interface decisions.

Barbara Demel holds a doctoral degree in Organizational Behaviour and has been a Research Associate and Lecturer at the Department of Management at WU, Vienna University of Economics and Business since 2009. She is Senior Consultant in the Austrian Human Capital (HC) team at Deloitte Consulting Vienna and leads the HC area of Talent Development and Learning.

Ans De Vos is the holder of the SD Worx chair 'Next generation work: creating sustainable careers' at Antwerp Management School. Her research interests include career self-management, organizational career management, psychological contracts and managing across generations.

Lisa Finkelstein is a Professor in the social-industrial/organizational psychology area at Northern Illinois University in DeKalb, IL, USA. Her research interests including aging issues at work, mentoring relationships, stigma and humour in the workplace.

Noreen Heraty is Senior Lecturer in Human Resources Management and Development at the Kemmy Business School, University of Limerick. Her research interests include understanding the implications of age diversity in organizations, managing learning environments and cross-cultural perspectives on human resource management processes.

Elaine C. Hollensbe is Associate Professor of Management in the Carl H. Lindner College of Business at the University of Cincinnati and received her doctorate from the University of Kansas. She has research interests in identity, generations, emotion, fairness, self-efficacy in wellness and training contexts, and work–life balance.

Ilke Inceoglu is a Senior Lecturer in Organizational Behaviour and HRM at Surrey Business School, University of Surrey. Her research interests include work engagement, motivation, person–job fit and age differences at work.

Xander D. Lub is a Senior Lecturer at the Hospitality Business School, Saxion University of Applied Sciences in the Netherlands. His research interests concern the employment relationship in relation to societal changes and generational differences and he has a specific interest in psychological contracts.

Sean T. Lyons is Associate Professor of Leadership and Management at the University of Guelph in Ontario. His primary research focus is on generational differences in work values and careers. He speaks and consults regularly with organizations dealing with generational conflict.

Jean McCarthy is a Lecturer in Organizational Behaviour and Human Resource Development at the University of Limerick. She is founder and co-director of the Age in the Workplace Research Network (AWR-net), a global research associate with the Sloan Center on Aging and Work at Boston College, and a recent Fulbright Scholar at Colorado State University.

Eddy S. Ng is an Associate Professor at the Rowe School of Business at Dalhousie University in Nova Scotia. His research focuses on diversity and inclusion, including public policy on equal treatment, managing diversity for organizational competitiveness, changing work values, and career issues for women, minorities, older workers and the millennial generation.

Katherine J. Roberto is a Lecturer in the Department of Management in the College of Business Administration at the University of Texas at Arlington. Her research focuses on diversity in the workforce.

René Schalk is a faculty member of the department of Human Resource Studies at Tilburg University and holds a special chair in Policy and Aging at Tilburg University in the Netherlands. He is Extraordinary Professor at the Faculty of Economic and Management Sciences and the Workwell Research Unit for People, Policy and Performance at the Potchefstroom Campus of North West University in South Africa. His research focuses on organizations and employees, with a special interest for psychological contracts, international differences, policy issues and aging.

Linda Schweitzer is Associate Dean, Research and External and Associate Professor of Management at the Sprott School of Business in Ontario. Her research career has focused on gender, diversity and generations in the workplace, as well as alternative work arrangements and the use of technology at work.

Jesse Segers is a post-doctoral Researcher at the University of Antwerp and a Professor of Leadership and Organizational Behavior at the Antwerp Management School, where he is the Academic Director of the Future Leadership Initiative.

Yan Shen is an Assistant Professor at the Gustavson School of Business at the University of Victoria in Canada. Her primary research interests include careers, expatriation and repatriation, and developmental relationships across different cultures.

Jenny M.H. Sok is a Sociologist of Family and Education, and a Lecturer at the Hospitality Business School, Hotelschool The Hague/Amsterdam campus. Her research interests include diversity, employability and the work–home interface.

Vasanthi Srinivasan is an Associate Professor in the area of Organization Behaviour and Human Resources Management and Chairperson of the Center for Corporate Governance and Citizenship at Indian Institute of Management, Bangalore, India. She was the ICCR Chair Professor in Corporate Responsibility and Governance at the HHL Graduate School of Management, Germany. Her areas of research are diversity and inclusion, with particular emphasis on gender and multi-generational diversity.

Jean M. Twenge is Professor of Psychology at San Diego State University, the author of *Generation Me* (2007, Free Press) and the co-author of *The Narcissism Epidemic* (2010, Free Press). Her research focuses on cultural change and generational differences.

Julie Unite completed her PhD in Industrial Psychology in December 2013 from Northern Illinois University. Prior to starting her PhD, she was a practising psychologist in both Australia and the UK where she completed her Masters degree in occupational psychology. Her work and research interests include career and executive coaching, emotion and emotional intelligence in the workplace, and managing career change and transitions.

Michael J. Urick obtained his PhD from the University of Cincinnati. His ongoing research includes generational issues, leadership, conflict and identity at work.

Peter Urwin is Director of the Centre for Employment Research and Professor of Applied Economics at the University of Westminster. He has focused on the application of approaches used primarily in the field of economics, across a wide variety of subjects, with a particular focus on the issues faced by government policymakers.

ACKNOWLEDGEMENTS

I would like to thank the authors of each of the chapters in this book for their excellent contributions, without which this book would not be possible. I would also like to give special thanks to Jayne Ashley for her diligence and attention to detail in putting this text together.

1

NEW PERSPECTIVES ON GENERATIONAL DIVERSITY AT WORK

Introduction

Emma Parry

The interest in generational diversity at work has exploded since the turn of the twenty-first century. Human resource management (HRM) practitioners, consultants and media commentators are keen to promote the idea that today's workforce contains factions that differ in their values, attitudes and preferences as a result of when they were born. Indeed, it would be fair to say that HRM practitioners have eagerly adopted the notion of generations as an explanation of differences in employee attitudes and behaviour and as a means to segment the workforce when designing rewards and recognition systems. Academic interest in generational differences has predictably followed with an increasing number of scholars now writing and undertaking research about generations. Most research in this area has aimed to identify the different characteristics of each generation but, despite scepticism about the validity of generational differences at work (Parry and Urwin 2011), few academics have examined the actual conceptualization and operationalization of generations or reconsidered the perspectives popularly adopted in practice. This is perhaps surprising, as it would seem important to evaluate and develop the generational approach if HRM decisions are to be based on assumptions regarding the characteristics of generations. This book addresses this need by bringing together work from a range of scholars whose research has aimed to take an alternative approach or perspective in this growing area. The goal of this text is not to discredit past work on generational differences but rather to highlight the need for further investigation and new perspectives on this concept so that the impact of generational differences in the workplace can be more fully understood.

Generational diversity at work

The definition most commonly used for a 'generation' is that by Kupperschmidt (2000: 66): '[A]n identifiable group that shares birth years, age, location and significant life events at critical developmental stages.' In a nutshell, the idea is that individuals who were born at a similar point in time have shared similar experiences during their formative years and therefore have similar attitudes and preferences. In the Western world at least, there are generally seen to be four generations potentially in the workplace: Veterans, Baby Boomers, Generation X and Generation Y. A summary of these is shown in Table 1.1 (taken from Parry and Urwin 2011; Strauss and Howe 1991).

Considerable work has been undertaken to look at the characteristics associated with each of these four generations. For example, Veterans have been described as being loyal to employers, believing in hard work and the status quo, and having respect for authority figures (Berl 2006), as well as having core values that include dedication and sacrifice, conformity, law and order, respect for authority, patience, duty before pleasure, adherence to rules and honour (Zemke *et al.* 2000). Baby Boomers on the other hand tend to have the core values of optimism, team orientation, personal gratification, health and wellness, personal growth, an obsession with youth, work and involvement, and place emphasis on a sense of accomplishment, achievement and social recognition (Berl 2006; Carlson 2004). Generation X has been perceived as getting bored quickly, having a short attention span, expecting immediate gratification and distrusting institutions (Caudron 1997; Filipczak 1994), although other researchers have described them as self-reliant, adaptable to change and preferring to learn by assimilating information from multiple sources (Tulgan 1996). They are independent and resourceful, comfortable with diversity, value integrity and expect a balanced lifestyle (Bova and Kroth 2001). Finally, Generation Y is seen as being team oriented, cooperative and interdependent, and possessing tighter peer bonds (McCafferty 2003), as well as being particularly technologically savvy with high personal experience of Web 2.0 technology. Their core values have been reported as including optimism, confidence, achievement, sociability, morality and diversity (Zemke *et al.* 2000). It is not the purpose of this book to re-visit these characteristics or even to examine their accuracy, so I will not discuss them in detail here other than to say that these stereotypes form the basis of the assumptions on which many HRM practitioners are operating when they use generational differences as a means of segmenting the workforce (Parry and Urwin 2009).

TABLE 1.1 Definitions of generational groups currently in the workforce

Generation	*Years of birth*	*Also known as*
Veterans	1925–1942	Silent Generation, Matures, Traditionalists
Baby Boomers	1943–1960	
Generation X	1961–1981	Thirteenth, Baby Busters, Lost Generation
Generation Y	1982–	Millenials, Nexters, Echo Boomers

The state of the art

The idea of generational differences is not new. Indeed, the concept of 'generations' is grounded in the sociology literature and is most commonly ascribed to the work of Mannheim (1952), who suggested that a generation was similar to the class position of someone in society in that it is a 'social location'. Mannheim highlighted five characteristics of society that make generations possible: first, new participants in the social process are emerging; second, former participants are disappearing; third, individuals can only participate in a temporally limited section of the historical process; fourth, that cultural heritage needs to be transmitted; and fifth, that there is a continuous transmission from generation to generation. Members of the same generation have a common location in the historical dimension of the social process, due to sharing a year of birth. This limits their potential experience, meaning that they are predisposed to a characteristic mode of thought and experience. In understanding the rationale behind this book, it is important to note that Mannheim also dictated that sharing a year of birth alone is not sufficient for people to be members of the same generation. Rather they must share common experiences in order to create a concrete bond between members of a generation so that they share 'an identity of responses, a certain affinity in the way in which they all move with, and are formed by, their common experiences' (Mannheim 1952: 306).

We can see from Mannheim's theoretical description of a generation, where the idea that is commonly accepted today, that people who were born at a similar point in time share attitudes and values, has come from. However, we can also see that the description of the generations of Veterans, Baby Boomers, Generation X and Y, based on birth year alone, is not sufficient in order to satisfy Mannheim's criteria. In particular, the use of these same generational categories across different countries makes little sense – how can we expect an individual born in 1975 in Shanghai to have had the same experience growing up as one born in New York, for instance?

In a paper that I co-authored with Peter Urwin (Parry and Urwin 2011), we discussed these conceptual difficulties at length and concluded that actually, the approach to identifying generations commonly adopted in practice, and also by many scholars in their research, does not allow for a true definition of a generation, but only provides a description of different age cohorts (which of course might be useful in itself). A true definition of a generation should consider characteristics of 'social space' other than birth year, such as geographical location or gender. Indeed, previous studies have found heterogeneity within generational groups based on factors such as gender or race (Eskilson and Wiley 1999; Parker and Chusmir 1990) and research in non-Western societies has suggested that the four generations described above are not valid outside of the Western world (see for example Hui-Chun and Miller 2003, 2005; Parry *et al.* 2012). The current text also provides further evidence of this latter suggestion in Chapter 13. The failure to properly operationalize generations as conceptualized by Mannheim

(1952) is the first of two significant concerns with regard to the way that generations have been conceptualized and operationalized both practically and in research.

The second issue is more practical in nature and related to the research studies on which most evidence regarding generational differences are based. The majority of research in this area relies on cross-sectional studies that are problematic in their failure to distinguish between cohort (generational), age (maturation) and period (the time in which the research was conducted) effects (Parry and Urwin 2011; Rhodes 1983). Rhodes explained that if differences in work-related attitudes were age effects then we would expect younger adults to become more like older adults as they age. If, however, differences were due to cohort effects, we would expect these attitudes and the differences between age cohorts to remain relatively stable. Cross-sectional designs can identify differences between age groups but cannot establish whether these are due to age or cohort effects. What this means is that, despite the significant amount of work done to identify the characteristics of generational groups, not only are these findings mixed (Parry and Urwin 2011) but we cannot be sure that any differences can actually be ascribed to generational effects. Rhodes suggested the necessity to use longitudinal time-lag designs in generational research – a call that is picked up by two of the chapters in this book.

This book is not alone in highlighting the problems inherent in the study of generational diversity. Several authors have expressed the above concerns (see, for example, Giancola 2006; Parry and Urwin 2011). An understanding of these concerns is important here, however, as these form the basis and rationale for this book. Our purpose here, though, is to do more than express concern and to move the field forward with new conceptual perspectives and methodological approaches.

This book

This book has arisen as a result of ongoing conversations between a group of academics as to the validity of generational diversity as a means of segmenting the workforce. It is useful here to say a few words about how this book was conceived as this will also make clear its purpose. It is fair to say that many of us who research age diversity were initially a little dismissive of generations as a legitimate alternative to segmenting the workforce. I remember a discussion about generational diversity at a colloquium about the ageing workforce a few years ago. Several members of the group felt that this approach had no value and one even suggested that it had been created as a means to continue discriminating against individuals based on age, despite the recently introduced legislation against age discrimination in the UK. This cynicism, coupled with the operational and methodological concerns described above, has led myself and others to take a closer look at the concept of generational differences at work and to consider the best way forward in researching this area.

Specifically, *ad hoc* discussions at the Academy of Management (AOM) Annual Conference in 2010 led to more formal discussions about 'the value of generations' at a professional development workshop at the same conference in 2011. The overwhelming result of this workshop was the agreement that current approaches to studying generations were problematic and that something 'needed to be done'. A year later, some of the chapter authors from this text presented some initial research ideas in a symposium at AOM 2012 and made the decision to use these as a basis for what is now this text. We see this as very much the first step on a potentially long, but necessary, journey, to translate the notion of generations from something that merely has face validity and is useful to practitioners into a well-developed construct based on sound evidence. The chapters presented here are therefore designed specifically to move the field forward, either conceptually or empirically, and are seen as a basis for future research that we, and we hope others, will undertake.

The book is split into four main parts. Part I examines the conceptualization of generations and generational diversity at work, and contains three chapters. In Chapter 2, Segers, Inceoglu and Finkelstein consider the concept of generations alongside other perspectives on age. This chapter is useful in reminding us that generations represent only one way of conceptualizing age. Segers *et al.* suggest that generations is only one of seven substantive forms of age, along with chronological, physical–cognitive, organizational, occupational, life-events and socio-emotional age. In addition, they go on to propose that researchers should not only consider the form of age but also the point of comparison (e.g. relative or normative observations) when talking about age and the context in which an individual is operating (e.g. country, industry). Segers *et al.* therefore argue for a much more fine-grained conceptualization of age including generation as only one part.

Chapter 3 by Lub, Bal, Blomme and Schalk builds on previous work about collective memories and aims to improve our understanding of how such memories affect the psychological contract in different generations of employees. Lub *et al.* propose that both individuals and organizational contexts are affected by societal trends and events and therefore that collective memories can influence all areas of the psychological contract. The authors go on to suggest that future research on generations should focus not only on birth year but also on formative experiences and individuals' memories of these.

In Chapter 4, the final chapter in this first part, Sok, Lub and Blomme focus on one aspect of generational attitudes: those towards work–life balance. Sok *et al.* claim that different generations have different attitudes and expectations regarding work–life balance and therefore that a better understanding of generational diversity can help us to build knowledge about problems related to this area.

Part II focuses on methodological approaches to investigating generational differences. As discussed above, it has been suggested that research conducted in the extant literature has relied on cross-sectional research designs and cohort analyses that are not capable of validly identifying generational differences. Chapter 5, by Campbell and Twenge, discusses the importance of distinguishing between differences in age groups that are due to generation and chronological age and describes the use of a time-lag method in order to achieve this. Campbell and Twenge go on to discuss the findings of their previous research that has used this method in order to demonstrate its validity.

In Chapter 6, Urwin, Buscha and Parry emphasize the need to use a methodology that allows the researcher to identify generations, as described theoretically by Mannheim, rather than focusing on age cohorts as most previous research has done. Urwin *et al.* turn to historical longitudinal data in order to examine clusters of attitudes in individuals over time and therefore to identify both age and generational effects. This discussion, coupled with the previous chapter, provides a useful basis on which future researchers can build in developing methods for examining generational diversity.

Part III of this text focuses on discussing the findings of a number of recent empirical studies on generational differences. These five chapters present research that has moved the field forward rather than merely confirming or refuting previous descriptions of the characteristics of generational groups. In Chapter 7, De Vos presents research on intergenerational diversity in teams and how this diversity affects cooperation within the team. De Vos's research suggests that stereotypes about other generations did not significantly affect cooperation between generations within a team but that team processes such as team leader coaching were important in helping the team to avoid potential conflict and work together effectively.

Urick and Hollensbe present an identity-based perspective of generations in Chapter 8. Specifically, the authors present research that examines the ways in which individuals define generations and use these definitions in their identities. Interestingly, this study suggests that individuals not only adopt generational stereotypes in their own identity but also that they then reinforce these stereotypes by enacting their characteristics in organizations and basing their interactions with others on the same characteristics. This chapter provides a useful insight into how generational stereotypes might be reinforced within an organizational setting.

In Chapter 9, Roberto and Biggan also examine the stereotypes that people hold about generations and how they identify with these. This research shows that individuals not only identify with a particular generation but when interacting with other generations they promote positive stereotypes about their own generation and negative stereotypes about the other generation. Roberto and Biggan also suggest that these attitudes are not due to generational membership per se but rather to the distance between one's own generation and the generation of the subject. This chapter therefore provides an interesting relational approach to understanding generational diversity, which might help in future examinations of intergenerational conflict.

Lyons, Ng and Schweitzer look at a slightly different aspect of generational diversity with their focus on career development in Chapter 10. In particular,

Lyons *et al.* use retrospective accounts to examine generational differences in the establishment stage of individuals' careers and find that, while Baby Boomers, Generation X and Generation Y all experienced the expected challenges in their early career, the nature of these challenges differed between generations, as did the way that individuals adapted to them.

In Chapter 11, McCarthy, Cleveland and Heraty use historical attitudes data to examine, first, generational differences in job satisfaction, organizational commitment and job stress; and second, which individual and organizational factors affect generational differences in these work attitudes. McCarthy *et al.* found a number of generational differences in work attitudes, including that Generation Y reported lower job satisfaction and organizational commitment, and Generation X higher job stress than the other generational cohorts. Their research also showed that generation was the most important predictor of these attitudes over gender, job level and industry sector.

Part IV presents two research studies that examine generational differences outside of the Western context. In Chapter 12, Srinivasan, Ajith John and Nirmala examine generational differences in personal values within the Indian workplace. Srinivasan *et al.* conclude that defining generations in a transition context such as India is complex and that both significant events and socio-economic, class-based variables should be considered. More specifically, the authors suggest that historical, political, economic and social events in critical years impact the manner in which the personal values of individuals are shaped.

Our final chapter (Chapter 13), by Unite, Shen, Parry and Demel, provides a comparative study of generational differences in factors influencing career success in four countries: China, South Africa, the UK and the USA. The findings of this large-scale qualitative study show that, while there are some similarities across both generational groups and countries, there are also important differences. This indicates that national context is also an important predictor of individual level characteristics. Taken with the previous chapter, this chapter demonstrates that it is not appropriate to adopt the Western model of generations across the globe and that further research is needed to establish the characteristics of different generational groups in different countries.

With the wide variety of perspectives on generational diversity that these chapters provide, I hope that this book helps scholars, researchers and practitioners to move away from the (albeit simple) conceptualization and operalization of generational differences and realize that these are actually inadequate in order to fully understand the impact of formative experience on individual characteristics and the way that generational diversity can influence the workplace both at an organizational, team and individual level. This book serves not only to inform readers of a number of these alternative approaches but also acts as a call to scholars to undertake further research in this area so that we can achieve a more nuanced appreciation of the role that generations can play in the workplace.

References

Berl, P. (2006) 'Crossing the generational divide', *Exchange*, March/April: 73–78.

Bova, B. and Kroth, M. (2001) 'Workplace learning and generation X', *Journal of Workplace Learning*, 13(2): 57–65.

Carlson, H. (2004) 'Changing of the guard', *The School Administrator*, August: 36–39.

Caudron, S. (1997) 'Can generation Xers be trained?', *Training and Development*, 51(3): 20–24.

Eskilson, A. and Wiley, M. (1999) 'Solving for the X: aspirations and expectations of college students', *Journal of Youth and Adolescence*, 28(1): 51–70.

Filipczak, B. (1994) 'It's just a job: Generation X at work', *Training*, 31(4): 21–27.

Giancola, F. (2006) 'The generation gap: more myth than reality', *Human Resource Planning*, 29(4): 32–37.

Hui-Chun, Y. and Miller, P. (2003) 'The generation gap and cultural influence: a Taiwan empirical investigation', *Cross-Cultural Management*, 10(3): 23–41.

Hui-Chun, Y. and Miller, P. (2005) 'Leadership style: the X Generation and Baby Boomers compared in different cultural contexts', *Leadership and Organisation Development*, 26 (1/2): 35–50.

Kupperschmidt, B. (2000) 'Multigenerational employees: strategies for effective management', *The Health Care Manager*, 19(1): 65–76.

Mannheim, K. (1952) 'The problem of generations', in P. Kecskemeti (ed.) *Essays on the Sociology of Knowledge*, London: Routledge, pp. 378–404.

McCafferty, F. (2003) 'The challenge of selecting tomorrow's police officers from generations X and Y', *Journal of American Academy of Psychiatry and the Law*, 31: 78–88.

Parker, B. and Chusmir, L. (1990) 'A generational and sex-based view of managerial work values', *Psychological Reports*, 66: 947–950.

Parry, E. and Urwin, P. (2009) *Tapping into Talent*, London: CIPD.

Parry, E. and Urwin, P. (2011) 'Generational differences in work values: a review of the evidence', *International Journal of Management Reviews*, 13(1): 79–96.

Parry, E., Unite, J., Chudzikowski, K., Briscoe, J.P. and Shen, Y. (2012) 'Career success in the younger generation', in E. Ng, S. Lyons and L. Schweitzer (eds) *Managing the New Workforce: International Perspectives on the Millennial Generation*, Cheltenham: Edward Elgar Publishing, pp. 242–261.

Rhodes, S. (1983) 'Age-related differences in work-attitudes and behaviour: a review and conceptual analysis', *Psychological Bulletin*, 93(2): 328–367.

Strauss, W. and Howe, N. (1991) *Generations: The History of America's Future, 1584–2069*, New York: William Morrow.

Tulgan, B. (1996) *Managing Generation X: How to Bring out the Best in Young Talent*, New York: Nolo Press.

Zemke, R., Raines, C. and Filipczak, B. (2000) *Generations at Work: Managing the Clash of Veterans, Boomers, Xers and Nexters in your Workplace*, New York: Amacom.

PART I

Conceptualizing age and generations

2

THE AGE CUBE OF WORK

Jesse Segers, Ilke Inceoglu and Lisa Finkelstein

In response to an increased need for organizational leaders to know how to best handle and capitalize on the demographic changes in our workforce (Alley and Crimmins 2007; Baltes and Finkelstein 2011), the study of workplace similarities and differences among the four main generational groups in Western economies (i.e. Veterans, 1925–1942; Baby Boomers, 1943–1960; Generation X, 1961–1981; and Generation Y, 1982 to present; see Strauss and Howe (1991), as well as age differences, has exploded. This is often observed in the media and practitioner-oriented publications, but in scholarly work as well (e.g. Parry and Urwin 2011; Twenge and Campbell 2008).

Parry and Urwin (2011: 79), in their academic review of the literature, pointed out, however, that the

> [e]mpirical evidence of the generational differences in work values is, at best, mixed. Many studies are unable to find the predicted differences in work values, and those that do often fail to distinguish between "generation" and "age" as possible drivers of such observed differences. In addition, the empirical literature is fraught with methodological limitations through the use of cross-sectional research designs in most studies, confusion about the definition of a generation as opposed to a cohort, and a lack of consideration for differences in national context, gender, and ethnicity.

Given the methodological problems found in evidence on generational differences in work values, Parry and Urwin (2011) question the value of the notion of generations for practitioners. They conclude their review with a call for more significant research to solve some of the issues in the existing literature. Therefore, this book focuses on new perspectives for researching generations at work. Yet it is clear from Parry and Urwin's perspective that generations cannot be considered without regard to age. Our chapter considers expanding the way we think about, conceptualize, and measure age, and where the concept of generations fits into a broader framework.

The measurement of age as a mere control variable in the work literature has shifted to one of increasing theoretical and practical interest. This change has brought about scrutiny over what age actually is, what it means, and how it is best conceptualized and measured (Finkelstein 2011), going beyond chronological age. Over the past few decades, the aging and work literature has shown some attention to alternative, subjective measures of age accompanying the traditional, objective, chronological age; some examples include relative age, psychological age, social age, and age and generational identification (see Barak 1987; Cleveland et al. 1997; Finkelstein et al. 2001; Kooij et al. 2008 for examples). The alternative measures consider variables that influence the perception of one's own or other people's age and may predict workplace outcomes in conjunction with or above and beyond chronological age.

In line with this shift, generation reflects a very broad conceptualization and imprecise measurement of subjective age in relation to time and place, and we suggest that a more fine grained, multidimensional, and more context sensitive measurement of age is often more appropriate for specific research questions. The broadness of the generational concept is reflected in the societal factors on a macro scale that are taken into consideration to predict how large groups of people within an age cohort experience the world (Green et al. 2012). Stated differently, we think that generations may prove to be a useful concept in some research contexts with adequate theoretical justification, but organizational scientists can and should be mindful in choosing the most appropriate conceptualization and measurement of age for their purposes. Consequently, this chapter is offered as part of a book on generations in the workplace as an alternative perspective that suggests generations are but one of several ways to frame age issues in the workplace, and perhaps not always the most appropriate choice.

In this chapter, we present an expanded framework for conceptualizing subjective age called the Age Cube of Work. We will talk about the evolution of this idea, stemming originally from work by researchers at the Sloan Center for Aging and Work on the Prism of Age (Pitt-Catsouphes et al. 2010b), developing into work by Finkelstein and colleagues termed the Matrix of Age (Finkelstein et al. in progress), and further expanded into our idea for the Age Cube. This concept is still in its early stages, and we see it serving not as a directive and prescriptive model for choosing the one best way to formulate and measure age in any particular research study, but as a guiding structure for researchers to explore the best options for specific research questions.

The prism of age

Researchers at the Sloan Center for Aging and Work have made great conceptual strides to provide some structure to alternatives to chronological age with their creation of the Prism of Age model (Pitt-Catsouphes et al. 2010a, 2010b). Building upon the work of gerontologists, they articulate that subjective age is composed of a multitude of dimensions, "each of which may have different relevant experiences at the workplace" (Pitt-Catsouphes et al. 2010b: 84). Therefore they use the analogy of a prism, as the various "lenses" allow us to see different perspectives on age. Indeed, though we have a chronological age determined solely by the number of years we have lived, our more subjective ages may vary quite extremely. Consequently, any two people of the same chronological age can be different from each other when other perspectives are considered (Cleveland and Shore 1992; Settersten and Mayer 1997) and if they are not considered, important individual differences that are related to other perceptions of age may be overlooked.

The original Prism of Age model (Pitt-Catsouphes et al. 2010a) puts forth the following nine dimensions as lenses in the prism that will comprise subjective age: generational (using the typical USA-derived generations); physical–cognitive (a combination of physical and cognitive capacities to function in the work environment); socio-emotional (reflecting developmental needs and pursuits, such as generativity); relative (age compared to others in a particular environment); normative (a perception of being ahead or behind of some age-appropriate expectations in society); life events (the number of major life events one has or is currently experiencing); occupational (what career stage one is at); organizational (tenure); and social (the age others perceive an individual to be). Each of these dimensions could operate independently and contribute to one's subjective age at any point in time; the weight or salience of any particular dimension at any point in time to any one person is thought to be driven in part by the context.

As one illustrative example, consider two 45-year-old co-workers, Jane and Kim. Although they are of identical chronological age and do an identical job, Jane has been with the organization for 15 years while Kim arrived last year (organizational age); Jane is a newlywed while Kim has been married for 20 years, has four children, and a live-in elderly parent (life events age); Jane is extremely physically fit, while Kim suffers from the early stages of a degenerative condition (physical–cognitive age). Not only are Jane and Kim quite different, the age that they see themselves (and who is "older") quite likely depends on the nature of the context in which the comparison is being made. In some cases, they each would likely feel more affinity with (and "equal" to) another co-worker of perhaps a vastly different chronological age who matches them on a different dimension.

The Sloan Center of Aging and Work (2010, 2011) points out that this multitude of lenses on age is becoming more and more important at the workplace as there is no neat mapping between, for example, objective age, tenure, career stage, and life-stage as perhaps there once was when people were more likely to enter one organization and have one career, and follow life-trajectories (e.g. age of getting married and having children) that were dictated by social norms. For example, Pitt-Catsouphes and Matz-Costa (2009) demonstrated in a sample of 2,200 employees that early career ranged from age 17–61 years, mid-career from 23–62 years, and late career from 28–81 years. In other words, the age span within different career stages has become much larger. Hence, the Sloan Center has also begun using their framework in presentations and training with various employers and employees, as the effectiveness of different programs at the workplace is likely to depend on which age dimension one focuses. They point out that the life-stage of a person might, for example, influence what they want in their career, and could influence the type of programs that are needed in organizations – from dependent care programs for employees with younger families to older employees with aging parents. Just think about the expectations that Jane or Kim might have towards their employer, and one can imagine that they are likely to be quite different, and their supervisor may have different expectations towards them in terms of trainability and future career paths.

While organizations operate within the context of laws and regulations that, for example, provide disabled employees with the same opportunities at work as non-disabled employees (e.g. the Equality Act in the UK and the American Disabilities Act in the US), supervisor expectations regarding trainability and future career paths may be influenced by their perception of factors such as physical–cognitive age. The concept of subjective age that includes factors such as physical–cognitive age may therefore help to explain variance in real phenomena observed in the workplace, such as training and career support given to specific employees and not to others. Shore et al. (2003), for example, demonstrated that employees that are (perceived) to be older or feel older relative to their manager suffer negative consequences in terms of development opportunities. Obviously, this is unfortunate, as Kooij et al. (2013b) used theories of life-span development and self-regulation to find that the relation between well-being and development human resource (HR) practices (e.g. training) weakens with age, while the opposite is true for maintenance HR practices (e.g. performance appraisal). In addition, the relationship between development HR practices and employee performance strengthens when workers age, and job enriching HR practices elicit higher job performance among aging workers. Hence, they concluded that "HR managers should ensure that aging workers have challenging jobs that make full use of their training, knowledge and skills" (Kooij et al. 2013b: 32). Their results support the suggestion of the Sloan Center of Aging and Work that, depending on the life-stage, different programs or policies could be needed in organizations.

Although Montepare (2009: 33) makes clear that "subjective age is interesting in its own right as it represents an opportunity to explore new ways in which individuals define themselves and experience their lives," from an academic perspective it is equally interesting to wonder if subjective age is a better predictor than chronological age at work for certain criterion variables, or offers prediction of additional variance beyond chronological age, particularly because several scholars (Kanfer and Ackerman 2004; Ng and Feldman 2008; Settersen and Mayer 1997; Sterns and Doverspike 1989; Zacher et al. 2010) have suggested that chronological age "may only serve as a proxy for age-related processes that influence work motivation more directly" (Kooij et al. 2013a: 89). Cleveland et al. (1997), for example, demonstrated that after controlling for chronological age, a subjective age measure uniquely contributed to self-ratings on employee's health, retirement intentions, and managers ratings of the employee's promotability.

Some work has begun to include measures of some of the dimensions in workplace relevant research. For example, Pitt-Catsouphes et al. (2010a) found that occupational age and physical–cognitive age interacted with different variables (learning and development and flexibility, respectively) in predicting increased job satisfaction in a sample of over 18,000 employees in a wide variety of industries. McCausland and King (2011) found, in a national survey database of over 2,700 employed adults, a curvilinear (U-shaped) relationship between chronological age and supervisor support, and between occupational age and supervisor support, but that organizational age did not show a relationship. An inverted U appeared in relation to challenging experiences on the same variables. Another example is Kooij et al. (2013a) who found that the negative relation between chronological age and growth motivations and the positive relation between chronological age and security motivations was mediated by subjective general health (i.e. subjective physical–cognitive age).

The Matrix of Age

Finkelstein et al. (2001) and Finkelstein et al. (in progress) recognized that some of the dimensions in the Prism of Age appear to be more substantive dimensions while others are actually more points of comparison or reference. In other words, some dimensions are derived from a particular experience or condition of the target person, such as their health or their employment history, whereas others explain more a point of view, such as a comparison to others, or to an expectation, or one's own or others' perceptions. Taken further, this acknowledgment of a separate type of dimensions allows the substantive dimensions to be crossed with the perspective dimensions, producing finer distinctions. Thus, they re-conceptualized the Prism of Age into the Matrix of Age.

In the Matrix of Age, seven dimensions (chronological, generational, physical–cognitive, socio-emotional, occupational, organizational, and life events age) appear down the first, vertical column, and five dimensions (absolute, relative, normative, social, and meta-perception) appear across the first horizontal row. Thus, explained in this order, each of the substantive content dimensions can be considered either in an absolute sense, relative to others in a given context, as compared to the expected age norms of a given context, in terms of how others view a target, and in terms of how the target believes others view him/her. This latter addition of a meta-perception stems from work by Finkelstein et al. (in progress) and Ryan et al. (2011), who argue that people's perceptions of how their age group is seen by others can play just as important if not more important a role in inter-age interactions than their belief about the characteristics of others' age groups.

To illustrate, let's take one substantive form of age – occupational – and describe it from each of the perspective dimensions (columns) of the matrix. Recall that occupational age is a way of viewing one's career stage. Although there was a time when careers tended to develop and proceed in a uniform way, where people began one career and proceeded in it throughout their lives until retirement, there is now much more variance in the pattern and number of careers one experiences and the trajectories that they take (Hall 1996). So, if we look at occupational age in an absolute sense, it would be the career stage that a person has currently reached. Perhaps this is defined as "mid-career" using a broad-brush operationalization of career stage, or from a more fine-grained, developmental perspective, something like the "Age 30 Transition" period in early adulthood of Levinson (1986) where the person reflects on his/her past (career) successes and plans for future (career) success, as well as starts planning to settle down with a family. If we look at it in a relative sense, it is the stage one is at in comparison to others *in some meaningful context* (more on this to come). For example, it might be what career stage one is at in comparison to his/her friends, or in comparison to the individuals on his/her office floor. From a normative perspective, it would be the career stage people would be typically expected to be at *in their society (or other meaningful context) at their chronological age.* Although as we noted, careers do not always follow a traditional timetable, the awareness of those cultural expectations still exists and may drive judgments of what is appropriate (e.g. Lawrence 1988; Shore et al. 2003). One may be ten years into a particular career, and that may seem mid-career in an absolute sense, but if one is 63 years old, only ten years into a career would be normatively surprising in expected traditional, linear career paths. The social–occupational age would reflect others' perceptions of the occupational age of a target individual. These perceptions could be accurate or not, and could drive how those others relate to the target in situations where occupational age is of consequence. Finally, the meta-perception of occupational age reflects the target's own belief about what others believe is their level of career achievement. For example, one may be under the impression (correctly or not) that others of consequence believe he/she is further along in their career than is the case.

Measurement development and validation work on the various elements of the Matrix of Age is currently ongoing (Finkelstein et al. in progress). The expansion of the prism to the matrix has conceptually refined the model to allow for a more nuanced approach to studying subjective age at work.

The Age Cube of Work

In the present chapter, we argue that the Matrix of Age can and should be expanded further to add a third dimension – that of context, which is particularly relevant in the discussion of the concept "generation." Context had not been ignored in the conceptualizations we have described thus far, but it had not been explored fully or in any detail. A similar pattern is observed in the gerontological literature where calls "to probe deeper into the distinguishing situational factors" are made (Montepare 2009: 45). Context was acknowledged to be important in determining the weighting of dimensions in the prism. Further, in the matrix, context is recognized to play an important role in the points of reference. For example, someone considering the notion of generational relative age would be asking, is the target person in an earlier, the same, or a later generation *relative to the people in the target's context*? But what *is* the target's context? Any one context can be examined in a micro or macro fashion, and this distinction is usually not explicit in the definition of generations. Thus the value of the age cube is that we take the previous work a step further and explicate a third, contextual dimension to the matrix – and now we have the Age Cube (see Figure 2.1). The Age Cube combines substantive forms of age (e.g. chronological, generational) with context variables (e.g. job, industry) and type of comparison (e.g. relative, social). The resulting combinations lend themselves to diagnostic questions that examine the age constructs in the cube by considering moderating factors.

To illustrate how the Age Cube of Work would further refine the example provided above in the matrix, we can look at just one dimension we discussed – normative occupational age – and further elaborate on its nature with the cube. Recall above we discussed normative occupational age, as a concept in the Matrix of Age, as the career stage people would be typically expected to be at *in their society (or other meaningful context) at their chronological age*. The Age Cube of Work requires researchers to justify the context more specifically. At what contextual level are those norms derived? Is it as compared to what is expected of others in a particular job? Or does the industry make more sense of the research question at hand? Perhaps expectations in a certain organization are that people are at a more advanced career level by a certain age. Does the culture where age is being considered dictate different expectations than what might be found in others? It is expected that ignoring these types of questions and formulating research questions solely using chronological age as a predictor of various individual outcomes (attitudes, job or career satisfaction, affect on the job) or organizational outcomes (turnover, productivity) can result in reduced variance predicted, or age effects that may be important to the organization being masked by limited measurement of facets of age.

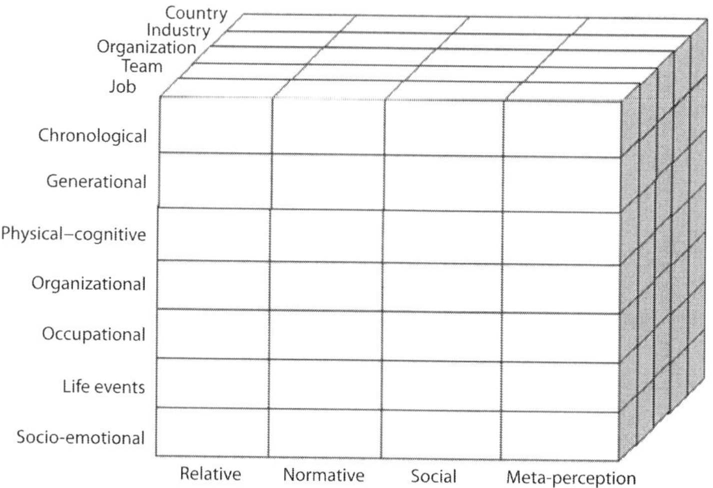

FIGURE 2.1 The Age Cube of Work

Looking at the current literature, it seems that the importance of context has been taken into account at least at four different levels: job, team, organization, and country. In prototype matching (Perry 1994; Perry and Finkelstein 1999), for example, context is considered at the job level, as employees are compared to age-related traits (e.g. energetic and open minded) of prototypical jobholders by, for example, managers and recruiters in order to decide if there is a good fit between the employee and the job. Therefore prototype matching can be defined in the Age Cube as the physical–cognitive social age at the job level, as it combines how others in the workplace gauge a person's age to be (i.e. social age) in terms of the physiological characteristics needed for the job. The requirements of a job should be based on a thoroughly conducted job analysis, focusing on competencies and skills required for a job role, but prototype matching is an approach often observed in organizations that take it as a proxy for a job analysis. In addition, Kanfer and Ackerman (2004) suggest that another aspect of physical–cognitive absolute age plays a role at the job level. Fluid intelligence (i.e. working memory, abstract reasoning, processing of novel information) has been shown to decline and crystalized intelligence (i.e. general knowledge, extent of vocabulary, verbal comprehension) to increase with chronological age. Therefore, Kanfer and Ackerman (2004) suggest that, in jobs that require a lot of fluid intelligence, the performance peak will be earlier in chronological age terms compared to jobs that require more crystalized intelligence. A similar rationale is made for physically demanding jobs (e.g. health care work), but the results are non-conclusive, which is probably due to the high variability in the decline of physical competencies with age. The latter depends heavily on people's lifestyle (exercise, healthy food, etc.) (Ilmarinen 2006).

On the team level, some research has been conducted in terms of chronological, relative age. The risk of being treated negatively, for example, is higher if a person is the only older member in a team compared to a team full of older employees (Wegge et al. 2008). Teams with members of equal age can experience more conflict due to higher competition and jealousy (Pelled et al. 1999). Wegge et al. (2008) concluded in their study that age diversity in teams is only positively related to performance for complex decision-making tasks, and not, or even negatively, for routine decision-making tasks.

The concept of career timetables (Lawrence 1984, 1988), on the other hand, is an example of normative chronological age at the organizational level. Career timetables are age-related norms within an organization that employees use to specify which hierarchical level to reach by what chronological age in that organization.

Other age-related norms in the literature are related to country level, such as late versus early retirement countries. Inceoglu et al. (2009) suggested, for example, that the motivation to be promoted declines later in terms of chronological absolute age in late retirement countries compared to early retirement countries. Another example where the importance of national context is demonstrated is the study of Egri and Ralston (2004), who developed different generational cohorts for the US and China, based upon absolute age at different political and historical events in the countries, and found significant differences in terms of values between US and Chinese generations. The influence of country-level norms is also demonstrated in several studies that have compared the gap between subjective and objective age, where the discrepancy was each time larger in the US compared to Finland (Uotinen 1998), Japan (Ota et al. 2000), or Germany (Westerhof et al. 2003; Westerhof and Barrett 2005). These differences are attributed to differences in the social and cultural systems between the countries, and show that in the US "the incentive to maintain a youthful identity may be especially strong" (Westerhof et al. 2003: 67).

We propose that in addition to job, team, organization, and country, *industry* as a context variable should be taken into account as well, as relative or social age and age norms in terms of physical–cognitive, organizational, or occupational age are likely to be different in a fast-changing industry such as information technology versus a more stable industry as the government. We are aware of only one study that has empirically examined the impact of industry age norms. Goldberg et al. (2004) found agreement regarding the age type of several different industries among a sample of MBA alumni, and further demonstrated that younger men tended to receive more promotions in older age-typed industries, whereas the opposite trend was found for younger women. This study suggests an additional potential complexity added by gender regarding matching vs. mismatching the expectations of a context. The Age Cube highlights the importance of context by separating it out as a separate dimension compared to the Prism of Age and the Age Matrix. We have selected job, team, organization, industry, and country as five key contextual variables that previous research into subjective and chronological age has examined and that organizations are interested in from an applied perspective.

Taken together, the Age Cube specifies a substantive form of age (dimension 1: e.g. chronological, generational), the type of comparison (dimension 2: e.g. relative, normative), and a specific context (dimension 3: e.g. job, organization). More specifically, the first dimension of the Age Cube is a substantive form of age and is similar to the vertical column of the Age Matrix: year of birth, generation in which one is born, one's physical–cognitive capabilities, tenure, career stage, amount of life events, and the adult development stage. The second dimension of the Age Cube is the type of comparison that is made, and is similar to the horizontal row of the Age Matrix, except that "Absolute" is no longer part of it: relative (compared to others), normative (compared to expectations), social (how others look at it), and meta-perception (how you think others look at it). "Absolute" was no longer included as it implies that no comparison is made, as something is absolute regardless of context, which is the third dimension of the Age Cube: job, organization, industry, and country. Table 2.1 gives an overview of the three dimensions and underlying constructs that make up the Age Cube.

TABLE 2.1 Definitions of dimensions and constructs in the Age Cube

Dimension of cube	*Categories*	*Definition*
Substantive form of age	Chronological	Chronological age as determined by birth date
	Generational	"Generation as a cohort of persons passing through time who come to share a common habitus and lifestyle… [and] has a strategic temporal location to a set of resources as a consequence of historical accident and the exclusionary practices of social closure" (Turner 1998: 302)
	Physio-cognitive	The person's capacities (physical, intellectual/ cognitive) in relation to tasks and demands of the work environment (Pitt-Catsouphes et al. 2010b)
	Organizational	Tenure in an organization
	Occupational	Time in a specific occupation
	Life events	The number of major life events one has experienced (e.g. death, divorce, rehousing, Bhagat 1983)
	Socio-emotional	Developmental phases in relation to life stages (e.g. Carstensen 1998; Erikson 1959)
Context	Job	A job
	Team	A team
	Organization	An organization
	Industry	An industry sector
	Country	A country
Type of comparison	Relative	Comparison relative to others in a given context (e.g. job)
	Normative	Comparison to norms/expectations in a given context ("ought")
	Social	How others view a target
	Meta-perception	Perception of how a target believes others view him/her (Finkelstein et al. in progress; Ryan et al. 2011)

Theoretically, by combining these three dimensions of the Age Cube, one can approach the concept of subjective age in at least 140 ways (7 × 4 × 5), which leads to at least 140 diagnostic questions one can ask oneself. For the purposes of introducing this framework, we have explicitly chosen completeness over parsimony. It becomes clear that not all of these combinations will be practical or meaningful to consider, but many provide the basis for formulating specific research questions in relation to subjective age by making explicit what variables are most relevant to consider for a specific purpose. For example, consider the combination of chronological age with a relative comparison in relation to a job: "Are you in terms of year of birth younger, the same, or older compared to others who do that job?". Or generational age in terms of meta-perception in relation to the organization: "How do you think others perceive you in terms of generation: earlier, the same or of a later generation compared to others in that organization?". Or examining physical–cognitive age by drawing relative comparisons in relation to an industry sector: "Are you in terms of physical–cognitive capabilities younger, the same, or older compared to others in that industry?" (See Table 2.2 for an overview of all the combinations and the resulting questions.) Some of the dimensions are likely to be related (for example, occupational and organizational age, and life events and chronological age), but they do not measure the same aspects of age and distinguishing between them helps to explore specific questions related to subjective age in the work environment.

The following example further illustrates the importance of context for age constructs: Jon is of Generation X and is on the board of directors within a small private bank in Belgium. He is generationally relatively young to have a job on the board of directors compared to others who have such a job, and especially compared to the "team" as they are all Baby Boomers, but he is chronologically relatively old to have a job in that organization as the most common generation is Y. Finally, he is generationally relatively normal to work in that industry in Belgium as the most common generation is X. As the example shows, one's generational relative age might be young or old depending on the context one uses. The Age Cube therefore provides a structure to examine a wide range of questions on different conceptualizations of age by considering the moderating influence of context and specifying the type of comparison. The Age Cube can help to guide future research, but also provides a structure that can be applied to existing research for systematic review or meta-analysis. For example, Avery et al. (2007) examined the relationship between perceived age similarity, satisfaction with coworker, and employee engagement. In this study age similarity consisted of a relative comparison of one's chronological age to others in an organizational context – made up of three dimensions from the Age Cube – and was investigated in relation to well-being.

TABLE 2.2 The 140 possible combinations of age constructs according to the Age Cube

The substantive form of age	*Type of comparison*	*Context*	*What you want to know*
Chronological	Relative	Job	Are you in terms of year of birth younger, the same or older compared to others who do that job?
Generational	Relative	Job	Are you in terms of generation younger, the same, or older compared to others who do that job?
Physical–cognitive	Relative	Job	Are you in terms of physical–cognitive capabilities younger, the same, or older compared to others who do that job?
Organizational	Relative	Job	Are you in terms of tenure younger, the same, or older compared to others who do that job?
Occupational	Relative	Job	Are you in terms of your career stage earlier, the same, or later compared to others who do that job?
Life events	Relative	Job	Have you experienced less, the same, or more life events compared to others who do that job?
Socio-emotional	Relative	Job	Are you in terms of adult development stage ahead, the same, or behind compared to others who do that job?
Chronological	Normative	Job	Are you in terms of year of birth ahead, on target, or behind the expectations for that job?
Generational	Normative	Job	Are you in terms of generation ahead, on target, or behind the expectations for that job?
Physical–cognitive	Normative	Job	Are you in terms of physical–cognitive capabilities ahead, on target, or behind the expectations for that job?
Organizational	Normative	Job	Are you in terms of tenure ahead, on target, or behind the expectations for that job?
Occupational	Normative	Job	Are you in terms of your career stage ahead, on target, or behind the expectations for that job?
Life events	Normative	Job	Have you experienced less, the same, or more life events according to the expectations for that job?
Socio-emotional	Normative	Job	Are you in terms of adult development stage ahead, on target, or behind compared to the expectations for that job?
Chronological	Social	Job	The perception of others about you in terms of year of birth: younger, the same, or older compared to others who do that job?

The substantive form of age	*Type of comparison*	*Context*	*What you want to know*
Generational	Social	Job	The perception of others about you in terms of generation: younger, the same, or older compared to others who do that job?
Physical–cognitive	Social	Job	The perception of others about you in terms of physical–cognitive capabilities: younger, the same, or older compared to others who do that job?
Organizational	Social	Job	The perception of others about you in terms of tenure: younger, the same, or older compared to others who do that job?
Occupational	Social	Job	The perception of others about you in terms of career stage: earlier, the same, or later compared to others who do that job?
Life events	Social	Job	The perception of others about you in terms of life events: have you experienced less, the same, or more life events compared to others who do that job?
Socio-emotional	Social	Job	The perception of others about you in terms of adult development stage: ahead, the same, or behind compared to others who do that job?
Chronological	Meta-perception	Job	How you think others perceive you in terms of year of birth: younger, the same, or older compared to others who do that job?
Generational	Meta-perception	Job	How you think others perceive you in terms of generation: younger, the same, or older compared to others who do that job?
Physical–cognitive	Meta-perception	Job	How you think others perceive you in terms of physical–cognitive capabilities: younger, the same, or older compared to others who do that job?
Organizational	Meta-perception	Job	How you think others perceive you in terms of tenure: younger, the same, or older compared to others who do that job?
Occupational	Meta-perception	Job	How you think others perceive you in terms of career stage: earlier, the same, or later compared to others who do that job?

Continued

TABLE 2.2 *Continued*

The substantive form of age	*Type of comparison*	*Context*	*What you want to know*
Life events	Meta-perception	Job	How you think others perceive you in terms of life events: have you experienced less, the same, or more life events compared to others who do that job?
Socio-emotional	Meta-perception	Job	How you think others perceive you in terms of adult development stage: ahead, the same, or behind compared to others who do that job?
Chronological	Relative	Team	Are you in terms of year of birth younger, the same or older compared to others in that team?
Generational	Relative	Team	Are you in terms of generation younger, the same, or older compared to others in that team?
Physical–cognitive	Relative	Team	Are you in terms of physical–cognitive capabilities younger, the same, or older compared to others in that team?
Organizational	Relative	Team	Are you in terms of tenure younger, the same, or older compared to others in that team?
Occupational	Relative	Team	Are you in terms of your career stage earlier, the same, or later compared to others in that team?
Life events	Relative	Team	Have you experienced less, the same, or more life events compared to others in that team?
Socio-emotional	Relative	Team	Are you in terms of adult development stage ahead, the same, or behind compared to others in that team?
Chronological	Normative	Team	Are you in terms of year of birth ahead, on target, or behind the expectations in that team?
Generational	Normative	Team	Are you in terms of generation ahead, on target, or behind the expectations in that team?
Physical–cognitive	Normative	Team	Are you in terms of physical–cognitive capabilities ahead, on target, or behind the expectations in that team?
Organizational	Normative	Team	Are you in terms of tenure ahead, on target, or behind the expectations in that team?
Occupational	Normative	Team	Are you in terms of your career stage ahead, on target, or behind the expectations in that team?
Life events	Normative	Team	Have you experienced less, the same, or more life events according to the expectations in that team?

The substantive form of age	*Type of comparison*	*Context*	*What you want to know*
Socio-emotional	Normative	Team	Are you in terms of adult development stage ahead, on target, or behind compared to the expectations in that team?
Chronological	Social	Team	The perception of others about you in terms of year of birth: younger, the same, or older compared to others in that team?
Generational	Social	Team	The perception of others about you in terms of generation: younger, the same, or older compared to others in that team?
Physical–cognitive	Social	Team	The perception of others about you in terms of physical–cognitive capabilities: younger, the same, or older compared to others in that team?
Organizational	Social	Team	The perception of others about you in terms of tenure: younger, the same, or older compared to others in that team?
Occupational	Social	Team	The perception of others about you in terms of career stage: earlier, the same, or later compared to others in that team?
Life events	Social	Team	The perception of others about you in terms of life events: have you experienced less, the same, or more life events compared to others in that team?
Socio-emotional	Social	Team	The perception of others about you in terms of adult development stage: ahead, the same, or behind compared to others in that team?
Chronological	Meta-perception	Team	How you think others perceive you in terms of year of birth: younger, the same, or older compared to others in that team?
Generational	Meta-perception	Team	How you think others perceive you in terms of generation: younger, the same, or older compared to others in that team?
Physical–cognitive	Meta-perception	Team	How you think others perceive you in terms of physical–cognitive capabilities: younger, the same, or older compared to others in that team?
Organizational	Meta-perception	Team	How you think others perceive you in terms of tenure: younger, the same, or older compared to others in that team?

Continued

TABLE 2.2 *Continued*

The substantive form of age	*Type of comparison*	*Context*	*What you want to know*
Occupational	Meta-perception	Team	How you think others perceive you in terms of career stage: earlier, the same or later compared to others in that team?
Life events	Meta-perception	Team	How you think others perceive you in terms of life events: have you experienced less, the same or more life events compared to others in that team?
Socio-emotional	Meta-perception	Team	How you think others perceive you in terms of adult development stage: ahead, the same, or behind compared to others in that team?
Chronological	Relative	Organization	Are you in terms of year of birth younger, the same, or older compared to others in that organization?
Generational	Relative	Organization	Are you in terms of generation younger, the same, or older compared to others in that organization?
Physical–cognitive	Relative	Organization	Are you in terms of physical–cognitive capabilities younger, the same, or older compared to others in that organization?
Organizational	Relative	Organization	Are you in terms of tenure younger, the same, or older compared to others in that organization?
Occupational	Relative	Organization	Are you in terms of your career stage earlier, the same, or later compared to others in that organization?
Life events	Relative	Organization	Have you experienced less, the same, or more life events compared to others in that organization?
Socio-emotional	Relative	Organization	Are you in terms of adult development stage ahead, the same, or behind compared to others in that organization?
Chronological	Normative	Organization	Are you in terms of year of birth ahead, on target, or behind the expectations in that organization?
Generational	Normative	Organization	Are you in terms of generation ahead, on target, or behind the expectations in that organization?
Physical–cognitive	Normative	Organization	Are you in terms of physical–cognitive capabilities ahead, on target, or behind the expectations in that organization?
Organizational	Normative	Organization	Are you in terms of tenure ahead, on target, or behind the expectations in that organization?
Occupational	Normative	Organization	Are you in terms of your career stage ahead, on target, or behind the expectations in that organization?

The substantive form of age	*Type of comparison*	*Context*	*What you want to know*
Life events	Normative	Organization	Have you experienced less, the same, or more life events according to the expectations in that organization?
Socio-emotional	Normative	Organization	Are you in terms of adult development stage ahead, on target, or behind compared to the expectations in that organization?
Chronological	Social	Organization	The perception of others about you in terms of year of birth: younger, the same, or older compared to others in that organization?
Generational	Social	Organization	The perception of others about you in terms of generation: younger, the same, or older compared to others in that organization?
Physical–cognitive	Social	Organization	The perception of others about you in terms of physical–cognitive capabilities: younger, the same, or older compared to others in that organization?
Organizational	Social	Organization	The perception of others about you in terms of tenure: younger, the same, or older compared to others in that organization?
Occupational	Social	Organization	The perception of others about you in terms of career stage: earlier, the same, or later compared to others in that organization?
Life events	Social	Organization	The perception of others about you in terms of life events: have you experienced less, the same, or more life events compared to others in that organization?
Socio-emotional	Social	Organization	The perception of others about you in terms of adult development stage: ahead, the same, or behind compared to others in that organization?
Chronological	Meta-perception	Organization	How you think others perceive you in terms of year of birth: younger, the same, or older compared to others in that organization?
Generational	Meta-perception	Organization	How you think others perceive you in terms of generation: younger, the same, or older compared to others in that organization?

Continued

TABLE 2.2 *Continued*

The substantive form of age	*Type of comparison*	*Context*	*What you want to know*
Physical–cognitive	Meta-perception	Organization	How you think others perceive you in terms of physical–cognitive capabilities: younger, the same, or older compared to others in that organization?
Organizational	Meta-perception	Organization	How you think others perceive you in terms of tenure: younger, the same, or older compared to others in that organization?
Occupational	Meta-perception	Organization	How you think others perceive you in terms of career stage: earlier, the same, or later compared to others in that organization?
Life events	Meta-perception	Organization	How you think others perceive you in terms of life events: have you experienced less, the same, or more life events compared to others in that organization?
Socio-emotional	Meta-perception	Organization	How you think others perceive you in terms of adult development stage: ahead, the same, or behind compared to others in that organization?
Chronological	Relative	Industry	Are you in terms of year of birth younger, the same, or older compared to others in that industry?
Generational	Relative	Industry	Are you in terms of generation younger, the same, or older compared to others in that industry?
Physical–cognitive	Relative	Industry	Are you in terms of physical–cognitive capabilities younger, the same, or older compared to others in that industry?
Organizational	Relative	Industry	Are you in terms of tenure younger, the same, or older compared to others in that industry?
Occupational	Relative	Industry	Are you in terms of your career stage earlier, the same, or later compared to others in that industry?
Life events	Relative	Industry	Have you experienced less, the same, or more life events compared to others in that industry?
Socio-emotional	Relative	Industry	Are you in terms of adult development stage ahead, the same, or behind compared to others in that industry?
Chronological	Normative	Industry	Are you in terms of year of birth ahead, on target, or behind the expectations in that industry?
Generational	Normative	Industry	Are you in terms of generation ahead, on target, or behind the expectations in that industry?

The substantive form of age	*Type of comparison*	*Context*	*What you want to know*
Physical–cognitive	Normative	Industry	Are you in terms of physical–cognitive capabilities ahead, on target, or behind the expectations in that industry?
Organizational	Normative	Industry	Are you in terms of tenure ahead, on target, or behind the expectations in that industry?
Occupational	Normative	Industry	Are you in terms of your career stage ahead, on target, or behind the expectations in that industry?
Life events	Normative	Industry	Have you experienced less, the same, or more life events according to the expectations in that industry?
Socio-emotional	Normative	Industry	Are you in terms of adult development stage ahead, on target, or behind compared to the expectations in that industry?
Chronological	Social	Industry	The perception of others about you in terms of year of birth: younger, the same, or older compared to others in that industry?
Generational	Social	Industry	The perception of others about you in terms of generation: younger, the same, or older compared to others in that industry?
Physical–cognitive	Social	Industry	The perception of others about you in terms of physical–cognitive capabilities: younger, the same, or older compared to others in that industry?
Organizational	Social	Industry	The perception of others about you in terms of tenure: younger, the same, or older compared to others in that industry?
Occupational	Social	Industry	The perception of others about you in terms of career stage: earlier, the same, or later compared to others in that industry?
Life events	Social	Industry	The perception of others about you in terms of life events: have you experienced less, the same, or more life events compared to others in that industry?
Socio-emotional	Social	Industry	The perception of others about you in terms of adult development stage: ahead, the same, or behind compared to others in that industry?

Continued

TABLE 2.2 *Continued*

The substantive form of age	*Type of comparison*	*Context*	*What you want to know*
Chronological	Meta-perception	Industry	How you think others perceive you in terms of year of birth: younger, the same, or older compared to others in that industry?
Generational	Meta-perception	Industry	How you think others perceive you in terms of generation: younger, the same, or older compared to others in that industry?
Physical–cognitive	Meta-perception	Industry	How you think others perceive you in terms of physical–cognitive capabilities: younger, the same, or older compared to others in that industry?
Organizational	Meta-perception	Industry	How you think others perceive you in terms of tenure: younger, the same, or older compared to others in that industry?
Occupational	Meta-perception	Industry	How you think others perceive you in terms of career stage: earlier, the same, or later compared to others in that industry?
Life events	Meta-perception	Industry	How you think others perceive you in terms of life events: have you experienced less, the same, or more life events compared to others in that industry?
Socio-emotional	Meta-perception	Industry	How you think others perceive you in terms of adult development stage: ahead, the same, or behind compared to others in that industry?
Generational	Relative	Country	Are you in terms of generation younger, the same, or older compared to others in that country?
Physical–cognitive	Relative	Country	Are you in terms of physical–cognitive capabilities younger, the same, or older compared to others in that country?
Organizational	Relative	Country	Are you in terms of tenure younger, the same, or older compared to others in that country?
Occupational	Relative	Country	Are you in terms of your career stage earlier, the same, or later compared to others in that country?
Life events	Relative	Country	Have you experienced less, the same, or more life events compared to others in that country?
Socio-emotional	Relative	Country	Are you in terms of adult development stage ahead, the same, or behind compared to others in that country?

The substantive form of age	*Type of comparison*	*Context*	*What you want to know*
Chronological	Normative	Country	Are you in terms of year of birth ahead, on target, or behind the expectations in that country?
Generational	Normative	Country	Are you in terms of generation ahead, on target, or behind the expectations in that country?
Physical–cognitive	Normative	Country	Are you in terms of physical–cognitive capabilities ahead, on target, or behind the expectations in that country?
Organizational	Normative	Country	Are you in terms of tenure ahead, on target, or behind the expectations in that country?
Occupational	Normative	Country	Are you in terms of your career stage ahead, on target, or behind the expectations in that country?
Life events	Normative	Country	Have you experienced less, the same, or more life events according to the expectations in that country?
Socio-emotional	Normative	Country	Are you in terms of adult development stage ahead, on target, or behind compared to the expectations in that country?
Chronological	Social	Country	The perception of others about you in terms of year of birth: younger, the same, or older compared to others in that country?
Generational	Social	Country	The perception of others about you in terms of generation: younger, the same, or older compared to others in that country?
Physical–cognitive	Social	Country	The perception of others about you in terms of physical–cognitive capabilities: younger, the same, or older compared to others in that country?
Organizational	Social	Country	The perception of others about you in terms of tenure: younger, the same, or older compared to others in that country?
Occupational	Social	Country	The perception of others about you in terms of career stage: earlier, the same, or later compared to others in that country?
Life events	Social	Country	The perception of others about you in terms of life events: have you experienced less, the same, or more life events compared to others in that country?

The study by Shore et al. (2003) focused on work attitudes and decisions as a function of manager age and employee age. Here chronological age was related to relative comparisons within an occupational context and used to predict work criteria. Shore et al. (2003: 532) emphasized "the importance of conceptualizing the age construct as reflecting both the person (i.e. employee chronological and subjective age) and context variables (manager chronological and subjective age) in the work setting." Lawrence (1988: 309) observes that "evaluating and comparing employee ages is an everyday pastime in organizations, insignificant in its appearance, yet significant in its results." Her study examined relationships between age distributions, age norms, and employee behavior. One of her findings shows that normative age groups differ across managerial career levels. Normative age was measured by asking respondents' perceptions of the typical age of individuals in that level and the age range of individuals in that level. According to the Age Cube this conceptualization would represent a normative comparison of occupational or chronological age in the context of a specific organization. The Age Cube can help to formulate linkages for predicting specific outcomes with subjective age over and above chronological age. For example, occupational age may be a better predictor of participating in further training and career development than chronological age. This relationship would be influenced by the type of comparisons people make (e.g. relative to others) and the context they work in (e.g. country, industry).

Limitations and implications

The Age Cube of Work has, of course, its limitations. Clearly, other levels of contexts (e.g. department, divisions, regions in country, etc.) are possible or more detailed subdivisions of some categories are possible (e.g. splitting up life events into historic, physical, normative, and interpersonal events; see Montepare 2009) and might make up different Age Cubes. Empirical research is, however, needed to determine which levels and types of context are helpful in explaining (additional) variance in the criterion of interest.

In addition, some of the existing combinations in the Age Cube might not make any practical sense or only be useful for very specific groups. For example, drawing relative comparisons of life events in a given industry sector might have little practical relevance in the world of work, although one can imagine that the number and type of life events of people working in illegal industries such as drugs and people trafficking, prostitution, etc. might be higher than for those people working in the marketing industry. Asking the question: "How do you think others perceive you (meta-perception) in terms of organizational tenure (organizational age): younger, the same, or older compared to others in that country (country)?" might only make (temporary) sense for expatriates or immigrants.

Moreover, even if some of the combinations in the Age Cube do make conceptual sense, one can wonder if and when people use them in their daily (working) lives, and hence if they predict any human behavior or other organizationally relevant criteria. Although Montepare (2009) came to the conclusion that the existing measurement research on subjective age suggests that it is a multifaceted construct, individuals may not make the distinction between 140 age conceptualizations at work, especially as some parts of the dimensions are likely to correlate with each other (e.g. a relative and a normative comparison). Stated differently, what is the divergent validity of the different constructs?

So why should researchers and practitioners who are reading this book and interested in generational definitions consider the Age Cube in their work? We offer it as is as a general guideline and starting point – rather than making a call of which blocks in the cube to "black out," we offer them all to researchers to make their own decisions to its usefulness and to expand or contract as they see fit. As mentioned earlier, we selected completeness over parsimony as a point of departure. In addition, proponents of the generational perspective to understanding differences in the workplace argue that it is not just age per se, but the time period in which one was born, each with its historical markers and zeitgeists, that contribute to differences in employee attitudes, values, and behaviors (i.e. Twenge and Campbell 2008). Critics of the generational perspective cite lack of clear evidence that the existing generational cutoffs have, meaning and lack of theoretical foundation regarding the process by which these generational differences are formed (i.e. Costanza et al. 2012). Using the guidance of the Age Cube, a researcher could perhaps conceptualize why generations might be meaningful in some contexts, where other aspects of one's age might take on more meaning in other contexts.

Further, researchers could potentially empirically rule out the role of other aspects of age as drivers of age differences at work. More complex and nuanced investigations could consider the other aspects of age and age in context that moderate the potential effects of generational and other substantive age construct differences at work. For example, maybe generational membership is proposed to impact communication patterns, but perhaps those effects would only manifest in an organizational context when generation is different from the norm. Or, maybe researchers do not find that individuals communicate more openly with those from the same age group, and assume no age effects, but did not consider the life events age of participants, which in some contexts may be a salient feature and might have shown clear relationships to communication choices. Existing work on generational differences and on age differences that considers only these aspects of age and explains less variance in work-related outcomes due to generation or age could be missing the potential explanatory power that dimensions of the Age Cube could have provided. To use a recent example from the work of one of the chapter authors, Finkelstein et al. (2012) investigated dyadic age differences between mentors and protégés and their effect on relationship perceptions and outcomes and failed to find the expected effects that theory would suggest. If this could have been examined while considering the Age Cube dimensions – perhaps to look at life events or organizational age differences – it is possible the role of age in how these relationships unfolded would be more clearly elucidated.

The Age Cube conceptualizes subjective age by combining three independent dimensions: substantive forms of age (of which generation is just one), type of comparison made, and context in which this happens, which leads to 140 age concepts. Its ultimate purpose is to provide a clear structure by using these age concepts to progress future research and better predict outcomes such as subjective well-being, and optimize working practices, such as career guidance, health and safety policies, training, etc. We hope this will serve as food for thought as researchers more carefully plan their conceptualization and measurement of subjective age to best fit their theories.

References

Alley, D. and Crimmins, E. (2007) 'The demography of aging and work', in K. Shultz and G. Adams (eds) *Aging and Work in the 21st Century*, Mahwah, NJ: Erlbaum.

Avery, D.R., McKay, P.F. and Wilson, D.C. (2007) 'Engaging the aging workforce: the relationship between perceived age similarity, satisfaction with coworkers, and employee engagement', *Journal of Applied Psychology*, 92: 1542–1556.

Baltes, B.B. and Finkelstein, L.M. (2011) 'Contemporary empirical advancements in the study of aging in the workplace', *Journal of Organizational Behavior*, 32: 151–154.

Barak, B. (1987) 'Cognitive age: a new multidimensional approach to measuring age identity', *The International Journal of Aging and Human Development*, 25: 109–127.

Bhagat, R.S. (1983) 'Effects of stressful life events on individual performance effectiveness and work adjustment processes within organizational settings: a research model', *Academy of Management Review*, 8: 660–671.

Carstensen, L.L. (1998) 'A life-span approach to social motivation', in J. Heckhausen and C.S. Dweck (eds) *Motivation and Self-regulation Across Life Span*, New York: Cambridge University Press, pp. 341–364.

Cleveland, J.N. and Shore, L. (1992) 'Self-and supervisory perspectives on age and work attitudes and performance', *Journal of Applied Psychology*, 77: 469–484.

Cleveland, J.N., Shore, L.M. and Murphy, K.R. (1997) 'Person- and context-oriented perceptual age measures: additional evidence of distinctiveness and usefulness', *Journal of Organizational Behavior*, 18: 239–251.

Costanza, D., Badger, J.M., Fraser, R.L., Severt, J.B. and Gade, P.A. (2012) 'Generational differences in work-related attitudes: a meta-analysis', *Journal of Business and Psychology*, 27: 375–394.

Egri, C. and Ralston, D. (2004) 'Generation cohorts and personal values: a comparison of China and the United States', *Organization Science*, 15: 210–220.

Erikson, E.H. (1959) *Identity and the Life Cycle*, New York: International Universities Press.

Finkelstein, L.M. (2011) *Muddy Measurement in the Study of Age Differences and Age Bias at Work*, presentation at the 15th Conference of the European Association of Work and Organizational Psychology, Maastricht, The Netherlands, May.

Finkelstein, L.M., Gonnerman, M.E. and Foxgrover, S.K. (2001) 'The stability of generation identification over time and across contexts', *Experimental Aging Research*, 27: 377–397.

Finkelstein, L.M., Allen, T.D., Ritchie, T.D., Lynch, J.E. and Montei, M.S. (2012) 'A dyadic examination of the role of relationship characteristics and age on relationship satisfaction in a formal mentoring programme', *European Journal of Work and Organizational Psychology*, 21: 803–827.

Finkelstein, L.M., Ryan, K.M. and King, E.B. (2013) 'What do the young (old) people think of me? The content and accuracy of age-based stereotypes and meta-stereotypes', *European Journal of Work and Organizational Psychology*, 22: 633–657.

Finkelstein, L., Heneghan, C., Jenkins, J., McCausland, T. and Siemieniec, G. (in progress) 'The matrix of age', unpublished research, Northern Illinois University.

Goldberg, C.B., Finkelstein, L.F., Perry, E.L. and Konrad, A.M. (2004) 'Job and industry fit: the effects of age and gender matches on career outcomes', *Journal of Organizational Behavior*, 25: 807–829.

Green, A., Eigel, L.M., James, J.B., Hartmann, D. and Malter, K. (2012) 'Multiple generations in the workplace: understanding the research, influence of stereotypes and organizational applications', in J.W. Hedge and W.C. Borman (eds) *Oxford Handbook of Work and Aging*, Oxford: Oxford University Press.

Hall, D.T. (1996) 'Protean careers of the 21st century', *Academy of Management Executive*, 10: 8–16.

Ilmarinen, J. (2006) 'The ageing workforce: challenges for occupational health', *Occupational Medicine*, 56: 362–364.

Inceoglu, I., Segers, J., Bartram, D. and Vloeberghs, D. (2009) 'Age differences in work motivation in a sample of five Northern European countries', *Zeitschrift für Personalpsychologie*, 8(2): 59–70.

Kanfer, R. and Ackerman, P.L. (2004) 'Aging, adult development and work motivation', *Academy of Management Review*, 29: 440–458.

Kooij, T.A.M., De Lange, A.H., Jansen, P.G.W. and Dikkers, J.S.E. (2008) 'Older workers? Motivation to continue to work: five meanings of age. A conceptual review', *Journal of Managerial Psychology*, 23: 364–394.

Kooij, T.A.M., De Lange, A.H., Jansen, P.G.W. and Dikkers, J.S.E. (2013a) 'Beyond chronological age: examining time and health as age-related mediators in relations to work motives', *Work and Stress*, 27(1): 88–105.

Kooij, T.A.M., Guest, D., Clinton, M., Knight, T. and Dikkers, J.S.E. (2013b) 'How the impact of HR practices changes with age: the happy and productive aging worker', *Human Resource Management Journal*, 23(1): 18–35.

Lawrence, B.S. (1984) 'Age grading: the implicit organizational timetable', *Journal of Occupational Behaviour*, 5: 23–35.

Lawrence, B.S. (1988) 'New wrinkles in the theory of age: demography, norms, and performance ratings', *Academy of Management Journal*, 31: 309–337.

Levinson, D.J. (1986) 'A conception of adult development', *American Psychologist*, 41: 3–13.

McCausland, T.C. and King, E.B. (2011) *Examining Age in the Workplace: Operational Definitions and the Impact on Older Women*, paper presented at the EAWOP Small Group Meeting 'Age Cohorts in the Workplace: Understanding and Building Strength Through Differences', Rovereto, Italy, November.

Montepare, J.M. (2009) 'Subjective age: toward a guiding lifespan framework', *International Journal of Behavioral Development*, 33(1): 42–46.

Ng, T.W.H. and Feldman, D.C. (2008) 'The relationship of age to ten dimensions of job performance', *Journal of Applied Psychology*, 93: 392–423.

Ota, H., Harwood, J., Wiliams, A. and Takai, J. (2000) 'A cross-cultural analysis of age identity in Japan and the United States', *Journal of Multilingual and Multicultural Development*, 21: 33–41.

Parry, E. and Urwin, P. (2011) 'Generational differences in work values: a review of theory and evidence', *International Journal of Management Reviews*, 13: 79–96.

Pelled, L.H., Eisenhardt, K.M. and Xin, K.R. (1999) 'An analysis of work group diversity, conflict, and performance', *Administrative Science Quarterly*, 44: 1–28.

Perry, E.L. (1994) 'A prototype matching approach to understanding the role of applicant gender and age in the evaluation of job applicants', *Journal of Applied Social Psychology*, 24: 1433–1473.

Perry, E.L. and Finkelstein, L.M. (1999) 'Toward a broader view of age discrimination in employment related decisions: a joint consideration of organizational factors and cognitive processes', *Human Resource Management Review*, 9: 21–49.

Pitt-Catsouphes, M. and Matz-Costa, C. (2009) *Engaging the 21st Century Multi-generational Workforce: Findings from the Age and Generations Study*, issue brief no. 20, Chestnut Hill, MA: Sloan Center on Aging and Work at Boston College. Viewed on 17 January 2013 from http://www.bc.edu/content/dam/files/research_sites/agingandwork/pdf/publications/IB20_Engagement.pdf.

Pitt-Catsouphes, M., Besen, E. and Matz-Costa, C. (2010a) *Age Management: Approaches to Age Diversity in the Workplace*, paper presented at the Annual Meeting of the Academy of Management, Montreal, Canada, August.

Pitt-Catsouphes, M., Matz-Costa, C. and Brown, M. (2010b) 'The prism of age: managing age diversity in the twenty-first century workplace', in E. Parry and S. Tyson (eds) *Managing an Age Diverse Workforce*, London: Palgrave Macmillan, pp. 80–94.

Ryan, K.M., King, E.B. and Finkelstein, L.M. (2011) *Younger Workers' Meta-stereotypes in Relations to Impression Management Behaviors*, paper presented at the 21st Annual Meeting of the Society for Industrial and Organizational Psychology, Chicago, IL, April.

Settersten, R.A. and Mayer, K.U. (1997) 'The measurement of age, age structuring, and the life course', *Annual Review of Sociology*, 23: 233–261.

Shore, L.M., Cleveland, J.N. and Goldberg, C.B. (2003) 'Work attitudes and decisions as a function of manager age and employee age', *Journal of Applied Psychology*, 88(3): 529–537.

Sloan Center of Aging and Work (2010) *Talent Management and the Prism of Age: Executive Case Reports*. Viewed on 17 January 2013 from http://www.bc.edu/content/bc/research/agingandwork/archive_pubs/case_TM.html.

Sloan Center of Aging and Work (2011) *As Old as you Feel*. Viewed on 17 January 2013 from http://www.bc.edu/research/agingandwork/archive_news/2011/2011-02-17.html.

Sterns, H.L. and Doverspike, D. (1989). 'Aging and the retraining and learning process in organizations', in J. Goldstein, and R. Katzel (eds) *Training and Development in Work Organizations*, San Francisco, CA: Jossey-Bass, pp. 299–332.

Strauss, W. and Howe, N. (1991) *Generations: The History of America's Future 1584–2069*, New York: William Morrow.

Turner, B. (1998) 'Ageing and generational conflicts: a reply to Sarah Irwin', *British Journal of Sociology*, 49(2): 299–304.

Twenge, J.M. and Campbell, S.M. (2008) 'Generational differences in psychological traits and their impact on the workplace', *Journal of Managerial Psychology*, 23: 862–877.

Uotinen, V. (1998) 'Age identification: a comparison between Finnish and North-American cultures', *International Journal of Aging and Human Development*, 46: 109–124.

Wegge, J., Roth, C., Neubach, B., Schmidt, K.-H. and Kanfer, R. (2008) 'Age and gender diversity as determinants of performance and health in a public organization: the role of task complexity and group size', *Journal of Applied Psychology*, 93: 1301–1313.

Westerhof, G.J. and Barrett, A.E. (2005) 'Age identity and subjective well-being: a comparison of the United States and Germany', *Journal of Gerontology: Series*, 60(3): S129–S136.

Westerhof, G.J., Barrett, A.E. and Steverink, N. (2003) 'Forever young? A comparison of age identities in the United States and Germany', *Research on Aging*, 25(4): 366–383.

Zacher, H., Heusner, S., Schmitz, M., Zwierzanska, M.M. and Frese, M. (2010) 'Focus on opportunities as a mediator of the relationships between age, job complexity, and work performance', *Journal of Vocational Behavior*, 76: 374–386.

3

WHY DO GENERATIONAL DIFFERENCES IN PSYCHOLOGICAL CONTRACTS EXIST?

Xander D. Lub, P. Matthijs Bal, Robert J. Blomme and René Schalk

> Focusing on cohorts and other salient demographic entities helps us bring into focus the importance of generations, generational change, and the relative permanence of social structural arrangements. This is not to suggest that change within persons is impossible, but only that generational or cohort change is another important mechanism by which transformations of organizations occur.
>
> (Pfeffer 1985: 80)

In recent years, there has been increasing interest in generational dynamics in contemporary organizations (Parry and Urwin 2011). This interest seems to reflect a growing realization of the impact that changes in organizations and society at large have on the employment relationship and the experience of the individual employee concerning the relationship with the employer. Over the past few decades, a number of dramatic social, economic and political shifts have taken place which have created a new work reality. For instance, life expectancy in most societies has increased, and the ageing of a demographically large 'Baby Boom' generation is placing a strain on social security and pension plans (Dencker *et al.* 2008). Moreover, globalization and technological advances have forced organizations to become more competitive (Kalleberg 2009). Organizations' attempts to achieve increased competitiveness have led to a range of corporate restructuring efforts, which in turn have led to a growth in less secure employment contracts and transformations in the nature of the employment relationship (Osterman 1999). This has had, and continues to have, far-reaching effects on all of society. New generational cohorts, having grown up in a different societal reality, are likely to expect and experience different employment relationships than those who grew up in earlier decades in a setting where full-time employment and lifelong tenure with one organization was the standard (Anderson and Schalk 1998).

A better understanding of the employment relationship and its particular meaning to different generational cohorts therefore seems a relevant topic of study. Although generational differences in workplace attitudes and behaviours have been studied in relation to many aspects of human resource management (HRM), including recruitment, training and development, career development, rewards, working arrangements and management style (Parry and Urwin 2011), very little attention has yet been given to generational differences in the way the employment relationship is experienced.

In this chapter, we seek to determine how experiences of different generational cohorts may affect the perception of their employment relationship. A key theory for understanding the employment relationship is psychological contract theory (Rousseau 1995). This theory enhances our understanding of human behaviour within an organizational context and assists us in understanding how generational differences may impact people in the workplace. Many studies executed so far have highlighted the changing nature of psychological contracts as a result of societal changes, and some even consider the theory of psychological contracts to be a product of organizational responses to changes in the societal environment (cf. Anderson and Schalk 1998; Hiltrop 1996). Moreover, a number of papers within the psychological contract literature address the role of the environment–individual nexus and how this influences the psychological contract (e.g. through concepts such as the social contract: Rousseau 1995, 2012; development of identity: Rousseau 1998; Dabos and Rousseau 2004; and the role of mental schemas: Rousseau 2001, 2003).

In this chapter, psychological contract theory will form the basis of our discussion, and based on our conceptual model (see Figure 3.1) we will argue how generational experiences affect the different aspects of the psychological contract. We will present six propositions pertaining to our conceptual model – the numbers listed in the model below refer to the numbering of the propositions to be found in the remainder of this chapter.

First, we will discuss what constitutes a generation, and we shall address definitional issues. In particular, we will discuss the role of formative experiences in the development of generational values, and we will propose how these formative experiences relate to generational values. Second, we shall discuss the importance of the psychological contract as a key determinant of perceptions of the employment relationship; we shall highlight the different mechanisms in the psychological contract and in particular address ways in which the psychological contract is formed. Third, in line with the literature on psychological contract development, we argue how and why generational experiences and identities may shape the psychological contract, resulting in work attitudes and behaviours such as commitment and turnover intention. In this section, we will propose that generational values and beliefs affect perceptions of employers' and employees' obligations as well as work outcomes. Fourth, we shall highlight the importance of the organizational context as a specific environment in which generational identities develop. We will also propose that organizations mediate the relationship between formative experiences, generational values and ultimately the psychological contract and work outcomes. Finally, we will end with concluding notes and present avenues for future research.

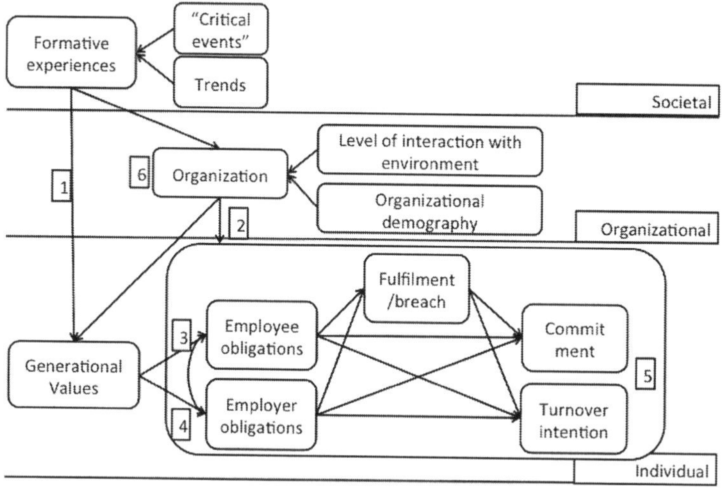

FIGURE 3.1 Conceptual model of the influence of societal and organizational factors on the psychological contract

Note: numbers in model refer to propositions in this chapter.

A definition of generations

As a concept, 'generation' has a long history. The word 'generation' stems from the ancient Greek *genos* (γένος) or the verb *genesthai*, which means 'coming into existence', 'to become' and also 'birth'. An extensive definition is provided by the Dutch sociologist Becker (1992: 23), who sees generations as 'a clustering of birth cohorts that are marked by a specific historic location, common traits at an individual level (life courses, value orientations and behavioural patterns) and at a system level (size and composition, generational culture and generational organizations)'. This definition builds on Karl Mannheim's work, whose publications are widely accepted as the starting point for contemporary thinking on generations. Mannheim (1952) signifies three analytical elements that are important for the formation of generations: *Generationslagerung*, *Generationszusammenhang* and *Generationseinheit*. First, *Generationslagerung* or 'generational position' concerns a group of individuals who were born and raised in the same period. As such, they take a historical position in the succession of generations. Second, *Generationszusammenhang* or 'generational context' refers to the connections among individuals created by the shared experiencing of a common destiny and major societal events. Finally, Mannheim reflects on *Generationseinheit* or generational unit, a term that according to him refers to organizations or informal co-operations that crystallize and reflect the style of the generation involved. So, for example, according to Eisner (2005), Generation Y was born between 1980 and 1995 (generational position) and grew up in a time of expanding possibilities offered by the Internet and social media. This has drastically changed the way this generation communicates. It has also altered the way it perceives power and hierarchy as well as the way in which it connects with others – 24/7 – without being in the same physical spot, or even without actually meeting in real life. Organizations such as Facebook or Electronic Arts could be defined as typical of this generation: they are characterized by relatively flat hierarchies, open structures, new business models, high levels of teamwork and co-creation with the users of the product. Therefore, they can be considered to reflect the style of Generation Y as a generational unit.

Most contemporary management research typically only addresses the generational location in Mannheim's approach in that 'birth cohort' is the starting point for empirical study and shared experience is assumed (Deal 2002; Parry and Urwin 2011). Moreover, contemporary management research generally aims to predict behaviours and attitudes based on generations that are *currently* active in the workforce, limiting the measurability of the construct. This research approach sets it apart from sociological and philosophical areas of research. These areas tend to be reflective and retrospective in their approach, and they therefore allow the identification of important societal events and groups that signify the identity of a specific generation (Spitzer 1973).

The single focus on birth cohorts as adopted in most management studies leads to a number of key conceptual and methodological problems in the empirical study of generations. A major issue is the age-period-cohort confound which has been extensively discussed in the life stage and ageing literature (Parry and Urwin 2011; Schaie 1986). Age effects are currently mostly attributed to biological factors and assumed to be formed by a linear process of change over the course of life (Kooij *et al.* 2008). With respect to period effects, most present in the historical and sociological literature, it is generally assumed that individuals of all ages in the sphere of certain events are similarly impacted by these events and developments. Finally, with respect to cohort effects as used in the generational literature, it is assumed that individuals in a particular formative life stage are particularly susceptible to being affected by critical events and developments: events that shape values and beliefs for the remainder of their lives (Schaie 1986). Thus far, however, management research has lacked the multi-decade, longitudinal, time-lagged datasets needed to control for these interactions, leaving this issue unresolved for now.

For the purpose of our discussion, we will present our propositions starting with the assumption that age effects can be controlled for, and we focus on another aspect of the generational definition which is highly relevant in explaining our conceptual model and which could help to separate generational effects from age effects: the nature and role of formative events. For a more extensive discussion of conceptual and methodological issues, we refer to the introductory chapter of this book. In the next section, we will discuss different opinions on what constitutes a formative experience, address how they are formed and consider the issue of permanence of these experiences.

First, there is the issue of what constitutes a 'formative event'. Although most management studies on generations suggest it is distinct historical events that shape a generational identity through collective memories (Schuman and Rodgers 2004; Schuman and Scott 1989), others broaden this definition to include trends of a demographical, economic, political or socio-cultural nature in a specific era, or even a set of specific resources available to a specific generation (Inglehart 1997; Turner 1998). For instance, the assassination of John F. Kennedy can be perceived as a single event, whereas the Vietnam War lasted for 20 years. In other words, most definitions are based on the notion that single large societal events will trigger generational differences. Others argue that these formative events function as 'icons', but should rather be considered representative of larger developments and trends in a specific period that shape a generational cohort (Alwin and McCammon 2003). In this chapter, we assume that significant events include single distinct events as well as societal trends and that both can be considered formative experiences. For example, Generation Y's formative period is suggested to include broader trends such as a renewed focus on children and family (Eisner 2005), demographic developments that enhance opportunity in the labour market, and most importantly a key role for technological developments, as well as distinct events such as 9/11 and Columbine (Eisner 2005; Tulgan 2003).

The notion of formative events is important because it provides a theoretical fundament that differentiates it from the age-diversity literature (which assumes a gradual change in a person over his or her lifetime due to a range of age-related factors; cf. Kooij *et al.* 2008). The concept of 'formative events' suggests that in adolescence or young adulthood people experience particularly significant societal events and consequently form a shared memory of those events which will affect their future attitudes, preferences and behaviour, also referred to as 'generational imprinting' (Parry and Urwin 2011). Mannheim (1952) compares the effect of formative experiences to the concept of *Gestalt* in the sense that events later in life are interpreted in the light of global impressions or mental schemas shaped during a formative phase of life. This formative phase is considered to occur in late adolescence and early adulthood, roughly between the ages of 16–25 years (Mannheim 1952).

According to developmental psychologists, core attitudes, beliefs and values crystallize during a period of great mental 'plasticity' in this formative phase (Krosnick and Alwin 1989). During this period of early socialization, socializing influences have the most profound impact, and values, attitudes and worldviews acquired during this time become fixed within individuals and resistant to change (Alwin and Krosnick 1991). Erikson also refers to this life stage as a period for identity formation in which a person 'needs to reconcile between "the person one has come to be" and "the person society expects one to become"' (Erikson 1964, cited in Wright 1982: 73). The concept of a formative phase in late adolescence and early adulthood is further corroborated by recent findings in neuropsychology. With the use of functional MRI scanning, several studies of the brain have found that during adolescence (defined as the period between puberty and the attainment of a stable independent role in society; cf. Steinberg and Morris 2001, the social brain used for interpreting other's actions is developed (Blakemore 2008, 2010, 2012). Blakemore found that experiences in this life stage shape synaptic activities in the brain. Through a process called 'synaptic pruning', the brain reorganizes synaptic connections in response to the environment in order to run more efficiently with the help of so-called pre-programmed responses (Blakemore 2010). These findings are in line with Erikson's (1964) concept of crystallized identities and social realities as well as schema theory (introduced later in this chapter).

Schuman and Scott (1989) and Schuman and Rodgers (2004), studying a large national sample in the US, found that different cohorts remembered different critical events and particularly remembered events that took place during their formative phase. They also found that their respondents often gave personal motivations to support their choice for specific events, suggesting a level of saliency and mental processing that would support Mannheim's hypothesis of 'formative' experiences. Several other authors, however, have suggested that the meaning and importance of these events may vary among individuals within a cohort in relation to personal proximity to the event or the level of education, race and gender (Griffin 2004; Schuman and Rodgers 2004), which may affect the extent to which different studies have been able to determine whether these events had different effects on subsequent behaviours between generations (Dencker *et al.* 2008). Therefore, we propose the following:

> **Proposition 1:** Distinct generational cohorts arise based on proximity to significant social events and trends during a formative phase in their lives.

So far, we have argued that generational groups emerge based on collective memories of critical events during a formative phase in life. In addition, we have argued that these events and societal developments have shaped a person's values. The question then arises if these events and resulting life values also affect relevant workplace beliefs, attitudes and ultimately behaviours – and the psychological contract in particular.

Psychological contract

The psychological contract refers to the employees' beliefs regarding mutual obligations, promises and expectations between the employee and the organization (Rousseau 1995). These beliefs develop from societal influences (e.g. social contract, norms), pre-employment factors (e.g. motives, values) as well as on-the-job experiences (e.g. socialization practices) (Dabos and Rousseau 2004). Psychological contracts are characterized as 'schemas shaped by multi-level factors' (Rousseau 2001: 525). The topic of schemas is discussed in the next section. These schemas affect the creation of meaning around promises and commitments that employees and employers make to each other, perceptions of the extent of their obligations and the degree of reciprocity and mutuality that the parties to the contract demonstrate (Dabos and Rousseau 2004).

Since the psychological contract consists of *perceived* obligations, the individual is conceived as an active constructor of reality (Robinson 1996). How the psychological contract is conceived is therefore not simply a response to inducements offered by the other party, but based on perceptions of mutual obligations. These perceptions are typically affected by pre-existing schemas (Rousseau 2001). We propose that individual employees bring to the organization a set of values and beliefs that shape perceived employer obligations and become part of the psychological contract (McFarlane *et al.* 1994). For example, Baby Boomers, who started their careers at a time of affluence and in a society with strong labour laws, may perceive greater job security obligations than members of Generation X, who started their careers in environments with weak labour laws and during a period of economic crisis. Hence, we propose that psychological contracts as they are perceived by employees are influenced by formative events. Therefore, we propose the following:

> **Proposition 2:** Psychological contracts differ as a result of different formative experiences and beliefs that individuals bring to the employment relationship.

Schemas are defined as cognitive structures that represent organized knowledge about a person or situation (Fiske and Taylor 1984) and that develop gradually from past experiences (Stein 1992). Schemas typically affect the perception of incoming information, the retrieval of stored information and inferences based on that information (Fiske and Taylor 1984). When these schemas are applied to a work setting, Rousseau (2001) suggests that they typically consist of elements that are widely shared by members in a particular society combined with idiosyncratic elements connected to individual experiences in work settings. Once formed, subsequent information is interpreted in the light of pre-existing schemas (Stein 1992). As such, schemas serve as cognitive bases for defining situations, and they increase receptivity and sensitivity to certain cues for behaviour (Stryker and Burke 2000). Attraction to, identification with and dedication toward an organization that coincides with an individual's personal values are a natural reaction of individuals given that such activities reinforce and preserve the continuity of one's self-concept and mental schemas (Dutton *et al.* 1994). Similarly, in psychological contract theory, the beliefs that construct the obligations between employer and employee are often shaped by pre-employment factors such as values and motives in a broader societal context (Rousseau 2001).

The above would suggest that different generational cohorts, having experienced different societal circumstances during their formative years, would have formed schemas about work and would connect these to what they expect from an organization. This position is supported by Inglehart's (1997) theory of intergenerational values change. This theory is based on two hypotheses. First, there is the socialization hypothesis, which suggests that basic values held by adults reflect the socio-economic conditions of their childhood and adolescence. The second hypothesis, the 'scarcity' hypothesis, proposes that the greatest value is placed on those socio-economic aspects that were in short supply during a generation's childhood and adolescence (Egri and Ralston 2004; Inglehart 1997). Although limited evidence is available for generational differences in perceived psychological contract obligations, a longitudinal study by De Hauw and De Vos (2010) among Generation Y indicates that differences among generations in terms of their psychological contracts remain stable over time. This would suggest that formative experiences have some degree of permanence, which is in line with our remarks on formative experiences mentioned earlier in this chapter. We therefore propose that generational identities, albeit sometimes implicit, are shaped through these formative events and changes in society as a generational cohort passes through adolescence and young adulthood. Moreover, these societal events and circumstances shape the perceptions these generations have of their employer's psychological contract obligations. For example, Generation X grew up experiencing economic crisis and reduced job security as well as increasing divorce rates among their parents, which may explain their increased focus on work–life balance (Lub *et al.* 2012). We therefore propose that each generation will perceive their employers' psychological contract obligations differently.

> **Proposition 3:** Different generations will have different perceptions of employers' psychological contract obligations.

Based on social exchange theory (Blau 1964) and equity theory (Adams 1965), in the context of the employee–employer exchange, the employer who fulfils his obligations to employees creates an obligation on the part of the employee. According to the norm of reciprocity, the reverse should then also apply: if employees fulfil their obligations to their employer, an obligation is generated on the part of the employer (Rousseau 1995). Moreover, according to Blau (1964), employees strive for balance in the exchanges between them and the organization. Consequently, the expected reciprocity in the exchange relationship causes employees to attempt to restore balance if an imbalance in exchanges is perceived.

In exchange relationships, however, certain obligations such as job security or developmental opportunities may be ongoing. Blau (1964) argued that employees will try to avoid feeling indebted to their employer and will take steps to create a positive imbalance through fulfilling employee obligations as a way of avoiding indebtedness and making sure that future benefits are realized. For example, Baby Boomers are often suggested to operate under a schema that loyalty and hard work is rewarded by promotion (Kupperschmidt 2000). Generation Y, raised with a more performance-oriented focus, may rather expect promotion in return for finished projects regardless of loyalty or efforts invested. This would suggest that different generational cohorts, having experienced different societal circumstances during their formative years, would also have formed schemas about what they, as employees, owe an organization in return. Hence, we expect that employees from different generations have different perceptions regarding their own obligations. Therefore we propose the following:

> **Proposition 4:** Different generations will have different perceptions of employees' psychological contract obligations.

The psychological contract has been used as a relevant construct to explain important employee behaviours such as commitment, turnover and organizational citizenship behaviours (De Vos *et al.* 2003; Lub *et al.* 2011). According to psychological contract theory, employees will reciprocate the fulfilment of obligations by demonstrating positive work behaviours and attitudes (Rousseau 1995). Moreover, several studies have found the psychological contract and its relations with work outcomes vary for different age groups (see for a meta-analysis Bal *et al.* 2008). Since age and generational differences are often confounded in most studies, this could alternatively imply that generational differences would exist in the way the psychological contract affects work outcomes such as commitment, turnover intention and organizational citizenship behaviour. Given the different experiences during formative periods that have led to different mental schemas about the employment relationship, it could be assumed that different generations then reciprocate the fulfilment of employer obligations with different levels of commitment and turnover intention.

Although very few studies have looked at the psychological contract from a generational perspective, a small number of (cross-sectional) studies have in fact found evidence that psychological contracts do indeed relate differently to work outcomes for different generations (Hess and Jepsen 2009; Lub *et al.* 2011, 2012). For example, a stronger negative relationship was found between transactional fulfilment and turnover intention for Generation Xers than Generation Yers (Hess and Jepsen 2009). Hence, we suggest that fulfilment of psychological contract obligations impacts different generations differently in relation to affective commitment and turnover intention. Therefore, we propose the following:

> **Proposition 5:** Different generations will respond differently to (non-)fulfilment of psychological contract obligations by their organizations.

The organizational context

A final issue concerns the role that organizations play in creating formative experiences for different generational cohorts. A first answer can be found in the field of value research, which suggests a hierarchical structure in which values at the societal level influence values at group or organizational levels, which in turn influence values at an individual level (Roe and Ester 1999).

This suggests that societies influence organizations, which in turn affect individuals (see Figure 3.1). Similarly, since the mid-1960s the macro perspective in organization studies has operated with a set of assumptions called the 'open-systems' approach' (Pondy and Mitroff 1979). In this approach, organizations are perceived as interacting in broader systems and as being affected by changes in the broader societal environment (Pfeffer 1997; Schein 1996). This does not only happen at a macro level with organizations responding to environmental changes, but also at the micro level of individual, interpersonal and intergroup behaviour. Moreover, the attraction–selection–attrition theory (ASA) states that it is specifically the attributes of people that fundamentally determine organizational behaviour, rather than traits of the organization itself (Schneider *et al.* 1995). The combination of attraction (people being attracted to organizations that fit their interests and beliefs), selection (organizations selecting people that share common attributes) and attrition (people leaving environments that do not fit them) could result in organizational demographics that are typical of specific generational cohorts sharing common values, but it could also mean that organizational cultures suppress certain generational identities. If organizations largely consist of one cohort, or if influential members within the organization belong to a specific generational cohort, it is likely that in its structure, culture and ways of communicating, the organization reflects the values and attitudes of the dominant generation (Daft and Weick 1984). For example, a typical hierarchical Baby Boom organization such as General Motors has rather different organizational demographics, structure and culture than a typical Generation Y company such as Facebook.

To summarize, organizations can influence (generational) values in several ways: by reflecting broader societal developments in their actions towards members of the organizations, by generating formative experiences in an organizational context, and finally by functioning as *Generationseinheiten* that magnify generational values through organizational demographics or cultures representative of a specific generational cohort (cf. Facebook or Electronic Arts representing Generation Y). Therefore, we propose that organizations can moderate the effect of formative events and trends on generational values as well as their perception of the psychological contract; generational values are both shaped directly by formative trends and events in the larger environment and in (sub-units of) the organizational context.

> **Proposition 6:** Organizational contexts moderate the effects of formative trends and events on generational values and perceptions of the psychological contract.

Conclusion and discussion

In line with the topic of this book, this chapter offers a new perspective on generational diversity. In particular, it offers an approach to improve our understanding of ways in which collective generational memories may impact the psychological contract of different generations of employees.

Our research model represents a necessary first step in assessing if and how different generations influence critical workplace attitudes and behaviours. In short, we propose that generational values are developed through a wide range of experiences and circumstances during a formative phase in life. Furthermore, we propose that these values affect all aspects of the psychological contract. Finally, in line with Mannheim's concept of *Generationseinheit*, we propose that the organizational context is affected by the same societal events and trends as individuals are, but also that it may provide a specific environment that could enhance or suppress generational identities, mostly as a result of organizational demographics.

The considerations mentioned above have a number of theoretical implications. First, we agree with most scholars that future research on generations needs to extend its operationalization of the concept beyond birth cohorts. It should include operationalizations of formative experiences and the way they affect the attitude or behaviour under study. Moreover, given that generational identities may develop more strongly in environments (such as organizations) that reinforce them, exploring the impact of the environment could be a worthy pursuit. An interesting perspective on the relation between generational identity and the organization is offered by Dencker *et al.* (2008). This topic could be studied in a quantitative sense by introducing a multi-level design that, for example, compares organizations with different organizational demographics, or by adopting a case-study approach in which organizations are selected that could possibly function as generational units (e.g. Facebook). More interestingly, it could also prove insightful to introduce more qualitative, perhaps even ethnographic, research to better understand how formative events specifically lead to generational identities, beliefs and attitudes, in particular in organizational settings. A recent study by Lyons *et al.* (2012) that retrospectively explored careers of different generations using interviews provides a good initial example of the rich insights that qualitative data could provide.

Furthermore, a number of authors have suggested that generational differences should be studied in conjunction with other diversity variables such as gender, education and cultural diversity (Deal *et al.* 2010; Parry and Urwin 2011). We support this position and would like to stress that the confounding effects with age (a proxy for a range of underlying effects: Kooij *et al.* 2008) should not be underestimated. However, we would like to add that these demographic variables, beyond their direct effect, also probably interact with the generational cohort variable. For example, access to education and resulting levels of education are different between generations, as are gender distributions in the workforce and cultural diversity; as such, they form a generational context that will impact a generational identity.

We specifically recommend further study of generational differences in the psychological contract. The psychological contract is a construct particularly suited for studying the changing employment relationship and the roles played therein by individuals, yet very little research has addressed this gap in our knowledge. Areas of research could include generational diversity in the content of the psychological contract (Lub *et al.* 2011) as well as the perception of fulfilment of the psychological contract (Lub *et al.* 2012). Furthermore, breach and violation of the psychological contract is an intensively studied topic within the psychological contract literature, but very little is known about the levels of breach or responses to breach by different generations. Finally, a particularly interesting area could be that of ideological currency in the psychological contract, or 'an exchange of values and norms at the employee-organization nexus' (Thompson and Bunderson 2003: 574). Ideological contracts are suggested to act as 'moral hot buttons'; organizations that violate these value exchanges by, for example, acting incongruently with employees' value systems may have to expect employees' negative responses (Thompson and Bunderson 2003). This may be especially relevant from a generational perspective, where organizations would have to take into account different cohorts' value systems.

Studying the psychological contract from a generational perspective can be of value to HRM/organizational behaviour academics and practitioners as they seek to understand how broader societal contexts impact individuals engaging in and developing employment relationships with organizations. Understanding critical events and societal developments at the time of growing up as well as determining their formative impact may help provide a broader understanding of how different generations of employees can have different perceptions of work and psychological contracts. This may provide new perspectives with which the potentially increasing generational diversity in the workforce can be managed in the light of changes in society at large.

References

Adams, J.S. (1965) 'Inequity in social exchange', in L. Berkowitz (ed.) *Advances in Experimental Social Psychology*, New York: Academic Press, pp. 267–299.

Alwin, D.F. and Krosnick, J.A. (1991) 'Aging, cohorts and the stability of socio-political orientations over the life span', *American Journal of Sociology*, 97(1): 169–195.

Alwin, D.F. and McCammon, R.J. (2003) 'Generations, cohort, and social change', in J.T. Mortimer and M.J. Shannahan (eds) *Handbook of the Life Course*, New York: Kluwer Academic/Plenum Publishers, pp. 23–50.

Anderson, N. and Schalk, R. (1998) 'The psychological contract in retrospect and prospect', *Journal of Organizational Behaviour*, 19: 637–647.

Bal, P.M., De Lange, A.H., Jansen, P.G.W. and van der Velde, M.E.G. (2008) 'Psychological contract breach and job attitudes: a meta-analysis of age as a moderator', *Journal of Vocational Behavior*, 72: 143–158.

Becker, H.A. (1992) *Generaties en hun kansen* [*Generations and Their Opportunities*], Amsterdam: Meulenhof.

Blakemore, S.J. (2008) 'The social brain in adolescence', *Nature Reviews: Neuroscience*, 9: 267–277.

Blakemore, S.J. (2010) 'The developing social brain: implications for education', *Neuron*, 69(6): 744–747.

Blakemore, S.J. (2012) 'Imaging brain development: the adolescent brain', *NeuroImage*, 61(2): 397–406.

Blau, P.M. (1964) *Exchange and Power in Social Life*, New York: Wiley.

Dabos, G.E. and Rousseau, D.M. (2004) 'Mutuality and reciprocity in the psychological contracts of employees and employers', *The Journal of Applied Psychology*, 89(1): 52–72.

Daft, R.L. and Weick, K.E. (1984) 'Towards a model of organizations as interpretation systems', *Academy of Management Review*, 9(2): 284–295.

Deal, J. (2002) 'Generational differences: we all want the same basic thing at any age', *Leadership Excellence*, 23(4): 363–382.

Deal, J.J., Altman, D.G. and Rogelberg, S.G. (2010) 'Millennials at work: what we know and what we need to do (if anything)', *Journal of Business and Psychology*, 25(2): 191–199.

De Hauw, S. and De Vos, A. (2010) 'Millennials' career perspective and psychological contract expectations: does the recession lead to lowered expectations?', *Journal of Business and Psychology*, 25(2): 293–302.

Dencker, J., Joshi, A. and Martocchio, J. (2008) 'Towards a theoretical framework: linking generational memories to workplace attitudes and behaviors', *Human Resource Management Review*, 18(3): 180–187.

De Vos, A., Buyens, D. and Schalk, R. (2003) 'Psychological contract development during organizational socialization: adaptation to reality and the role of reciprocity', *Journal of Organizational Behavior*, 24(5): 537–559.

Dutton, J.E., Dukerich, J.M. and Harquail, C.V. (1994) 'Organizational images and member identification', *Administrative Science Quarterly*, 39: 239–263.

Egri, C.P. and Ralston, D.A. (2004) 'Generation cohorts and personal values: a comparison of China and the United States', *Organization Science*, 15(2): 210–220.

Eisner, S.P. (2005) 'Managing Generation Y', *SAM Advanced Management Journal*, 8(2): 4–15.

Erikson, E. (1964) *Insight and Responsibility*, New York: Norton.

Fiske, S.T. and Taylor, S.E. (1984) *Social Cognition*, Reading, MA: Addison-Wesley.

Griffin, L.J. (2004) '"Generations and collective memory" revisited: race, religion, and memory of civil rights', *American Sociological Review*, 69(4): 544–557.

Hess, N. and Jepsen, D.M. (2009) 'Career stage and generational differences in psychological contracts', *Career Development International*, 14(3): 261–283.

Hiltrop, J.M. (1996) 'Managing the psychological contract', *Employee Relations*, 18(1): 36–49.

Inglehart, R. (1997) *Modernization and Postmodernization: Cultural, Economic, and Political Change in 43 Societies*, Princeton, NJ: Princeton University Press.

Kalleberg, A.L. (2009) 'Precarious work, insecure workers: employment relations in transition', *American Sociological Review*, 74(1): 1–22.

Kooij, D., De Lange, A., Jansen, P. and Dikkers, J. (2008) 'Older workers' motivation to continue to work: five meanings of age: a conceptual review', *Journal of Managerial Psychology*, 23(4): 364–394.

Krosnick, J.A. and Alwin, D.F. (1989) 'Aging and susceptibility to attitude change', *Journal of Personality and Social Psychology*, 57(3): 416–425.

Kupperschmidt, B.R. (2000) 'Multigeneration employees: strategies for effective management', *The Health Care Manager*, 19(1): 65–76.

Lub, X.D., Bal, P.M. and Blomme, R. (2011) 'Psychological contract and organizational citizenship behaviour: a new deal for new generations?', *Advances in Hospitality and Leisure*, 7: 109–130.

Lub, X.D., Nije Bijvank, M., Bal, P.M., Blomme, R. and Schalk, R. (2012) 'Different or alike: exploring the psychological contract and commitment of different generations of hospitality workers', *International Journal of Contemporary Hospitality Management*, 24(4): 553–573.

Lyons, S.T., Schweitzer, L., Ng, E.S.W. and Kuron, L.K.J. (2012) 'Comparing apples to apples: a qualitative investigation of career mobility patterns across four generations', *Career Development International*, 17(4): 333–357.

Mannheim, K. (1952) 'The problem of generations', in P. Kecskemeti (ed.) *Essays on the Sociology of Knowledge*, London: Routledge, pp. 378–404.

McFarlane, L., Shore, L. and Tetrick, L.F. (1994) 'The psychological contract as an explanatory framework in the employment relationship', *Trends in Organizational Behaviour*, 1: 91–109.

Osterman, P. (1999) *Securing Prosperity: How the American Labor Market Has Changed and What To Do about It*, Princeton, NJ: Princeton University Press.

Parry, E. and Urwin, P. (2011) 'Generational differences in work values: a review of theory and evidence', *International Journal of Management Reviews*, 13: 79–96.

Pfeffer, J. (1985) 'Organizational demography: implications for management', *California Management Review*, 28(1): 67–81.

Pfeffer, J. (1997) *New Directions for Organization Theory: Problems and Prospects*, New York: Oxford University Press.

Pondy, L.R. and Mitroff, I.I. (1979) 'Beyond open system models of organization', *Research in Organizational Behavior*, 1: 3–39.

Robinson, S.L. (1996) 'Trust and breach of the psychological contract', *Administrative Science Quarterly*, 41: 574–599.

Roe, R.A. and Ester, P. (1999) 'Values and work: empirical findings and theoretical perspective', *Applied Psychology: An International Review*, 48(1): 1–21.

Rousseau, D.M. (1995) *Psychological Contracts in Organisations: Understanding the Written and Unwritten Agreements*, London: Sage.

Rousseau, D.M. (1998) 'Why workers still identify with organizations', *Journal of Organizational Behavior*, 19(3): 217–233.

Rousseau, D.M. (2001) 'Schema, promises and mutuality: the building blocks of the psychological contract', *Journal of Occupational and Organisational Psychology*, 74: 511–542.

Rousseau, D.M. (2003) 'Extending the psychology of the psychological contract: a reply to "putting psychology back into psychological contracts"', *Journal of Management Inquiry*, 12(3): 229–238.

Rousseau, D.M. (2012) 'Free will in social and psychological contracts', *Society and Business Review*, 7(1): 8–13.

Schaie, K.W. (1986) 'Beyond calendar definitions of age, time, and cohort: the general developmental model revisited', *Developmental Review*, 6(3): 252–277.

Schein, E.H. (1996) 'Three cultures of management: the key to organizational learning', *Sloan Management Review*, Fall: 7–20.

Schneider, B., Goldstein, H.W. and Smith, D.B. (1995) 'The ASA framework: an update', *Personnel Psychology*, 48(4): 747–773.

Schuman, H. and Rodgers, W.L. (2004) 'Cohorts, chronology, and collective memories', *Public Opinion Quarterly*, 68(2): 217–254.

Schuman, H. and Scott, J. (1989) 'Generations and collective memories', *American Sociological Review*, 54(3): 359–381.

Spitzer, A.B. (1973) 'The historical problem of generations', *The American Historical Review*, 78(5): 1353–1385.

Stein, D.J. (1992) 'Schemas in the cognitive and clinical sciences', *Journal of Psychotherapy Integration*, 2: 45–63.

Steinberg, L. and Morris, A.S. (2001) 'Adolescent development', *Annual Review of Psychology*, 52: 83–110.

Stryker, S. and Burke, P.J. (2000) 'The past, present, and future of an identity theory', *Social Psychology Quarterly*, 63(4): 284–297.

Thompson, J.A. and Bunderson, J.S. (2003) 'Violations of principle: ideological currency in the psychological contract', *The Academy of Management Review*, 28(4): 571–586.

Tulgan, B. (2003) 'Generational shift: what we saw at the workplace revolution', *RainmakerThinking*, 17 September 2003, viewed from https://greenleaf.org/winning-workplaces/workplace-resources/research-studies/open-communications/generational-shift-what-we-saw-at-the-workplace-revolution-2/.

Turner, B. (1998) 'Ageing and generational conflicts: a reply to Sarah Irwin', *British Journal of Sociology*, 49: 299–304.

Wright, J.E. (1982) *Erikson: Identity and Religion*, New York: The Seabury Press.

4

WORK–HOME VALUES

The interplay between historical trends and generational work–home values

Jenny M.H. Sok, Xander D. Lub and Robert J. Blomme

Introduction

In the political, public and academic arenas, work–home balance has long been the subject of a vivid debate (Geurts and Demerouti 2003). Over the years, socio-economic factors including job security, the rapid growth in the number of dual-earner families and an increase in the number of women entering the job market have made it harder to combine work with home obligations and demands (Duxbury and Higgins 2001; Geurts and Demerouti 2003). In this chapter, we will argue that the increasing difficulty in maintaining a good work–home balance can be explained by different perspectives on work–home balance as held by the three generations operating in today's workforce. First, we claim that these generations have different interests with regard to their work–home balance. We build on the notion that every generation receives a distinctive imprint from the social trends that occurred during its youth (Mannheim 1952). The profound societal changes of the past decades with regard to the work–home interface can therefore be expected to have resulted in the formation of different work–home values and behaviours in different generations. Consequently, we argue that the three current (and the next) generations require different approaches from policymakers and employers. Following the literature on work–home balance (for an overview, see for example Guest 2002), we claim that the generational perspective on work–home balance has been somewhat neglected (Beutell and Wittig-Berman 2008). However, we believe that precisely this perspective can offer an interesting addition to the present literature on work–home balance.

We shall first consider the fact that work–home balance has become a matter of some concern in today's world. We shall discuss the theories used in the field of work–home balance and the formation of work–home values. We shall then examine the interplay between historical trends and the work–home values held by Baby Boomers, Generation X and Generation Y. We shall conclude with a discussion and implications for research and practice. An overview of the concepts and definitions we use in this chapter is given in Table 4.1.

TABLE 4.1 Concepts and definitions used in this chapter

Concept	*Definition*	*Source*
Generation	An identifiable group (cohorts) that shares birth years, (social) location and significant life events at critical development stages	Kupperschmidt 2000
Baby Boom generation	The generation born between 1945 and 1964	Eisner 2005
Generation X	The generation born between 1965 and 1980	Eisner 2005
Generation Y	The generation born between 1981 and 1995	Eisner 2005
Values	An individual's basic convictions that a specific mode of conduct or end-state of existence is personally or socially preferable	Rokeach 1973
Work values	The importance that individuals place on their work outcomes	Elizur and Sagie 1999
Work–home values	The importance that individuals place on work and home outcomes at the same time	Sok *et al.* this chapter
Work–home balance	The maintenance of a balance between responsibilities inside and outside the work environment	De Cieri *et al.* 2005
Work–home conflict	Occurs when simultaneous pressures from the work and home or family domains are mutually incompatible in some respect, such that meeting the demands of one role makes it difficult to meet the demands of the other role	Greenhaus and Singh 2003
Work–home arrangements	Arrangements that may enable workers to manage work and domestic obligations more successfully	Dikkers *et al.* 2007
Traditional	More gender-role-segregated	Barnett 2005
Gender egalitarian	Less gender-role-segregated	Barnett 2005
Identity centrality	The importance or psychological attachment that individuals place on their role identities	Settles 2004

Work–home balance

Most scholars agree that work and home life constitute the two most important domains of people's adult lives. In the past 60 years, both domains have undergone profound changes, which have nowhere been more evident than in the western industrial societies of Europe and the US (Barnett 2005). As a result of these changes, balancing work and home life has become more difficult for many employees and private individuals, and a primary concern to employers and policymakers.

Both in Europe and in the US, several interconnected developments in the work domain and the home domain have taken place. Authors seem to agree that work demands have grown excessively. Globalization, in combination with increasing competitive pressures on businesses, has resulted in increased work effort and extended hours, leading to more exhaustion, stress-related problems and work–home conflict (Allan *et al.* 1999; Burchielli *et al.* 2008; Guest 2002). This process is sometimes referred to as 'work intensity' (Guest 2002: 257). In addition, the ageing population is gradually leading to a shrinking labour pool and a higher proportion of older employees in the workplace (Magd 2003). Furthermore, since employees are increasingly expected to move self-sufficiently within the labour market instead of holding a job for life, they feel forced to constantly work on their employability (Forrier *et al.* 2009). This development causes, among other things, job insecurity (Sturges *et al.* 2005). One of the most significant changes, however, is the growing labour force participation of women that has been witnessed since the 1950s and 1960s (Bianchi and Raley 2005). This has brought about a dramatic shift in the allocation of time and energy devoted to work and home roles.

It is generally assumed that the developments in the work environment increasingly dominate people's home life (cf. Guest 2002). The growing need of earning two (or three) incomes to support a family is one cause of increased stress and pressures (Christensen 2005). Many people also have to take care of older relatives (Spillman and Pezin 2000). Furthermore, the rise in the number of dual earner families causes difficulty in dealing with the tensions resulting from competing demands (Barnett 2005). In addition, families are becoming more diverse, as a result of increasing divorce rates (Christensen 2005). Single parents and co-parenting ex-couples have more difficulty in combining work and home tasks (Spillman and Pezin 2000).

Concluding, we can say that authors and scholars generally hold the view that societies and organizations do not seem to fulfil the work–home needs of their increasingly diverse and varied workforce (Christensen 2005).

Life roles and work–home values

Perrewé and Hochwarter (2001) argue that considering values and value attainment is critical to understanding work–home balance. Until now, management and psychological (work–home) research has not devoted much attention to individual differences in employees' personal values, work values or home values (Kossek 2005). In addition, research into such values has taken place in isolated streams (Elizur and Sagie 1999).

Still, several scholars have looked into life roles, and some of them have made the connection with values. Here, we wish to discuss two general views on life roles and values. First, Super's *life–career rainbow* (1980) shows that, at different points in their lives, individuals play several roles simultaneously. Super explains that these roles impact each other, and that success and failure can spill over to other life roles. In addition, Schwartz *et al.* (2012) present a *theory of basic individual values*, in which 19 basic values are placed on a continuum based on compatible and conflicting motivations. These values are considered to influence choices and behaviours in all life roles.

In an attempt to work towards a more holistic view regarding values, Elizur and Sagie developed a 'multifaceted definition of personal values, incorporating both life and work values' (1999: 73). In their research, the *spillover* hypothesis in particular proved to be successful in explaining the relationships between work and non-work values. Staines (1980) was among the first to recognize that emotions and behaviours related to the work environment can spill over to the home environment (or the other way around), therewith transcending the physical and temporal boundaries of both domains. Furthermore, Perrewé and Hochwarter (2001) contend that an individual can experience conflict between work and home demands because of value incongruence, either between the individual and a family member, or between the individual and the organization. Carlson and Kacmar's (2000) research outcomes point in the same direction. They found that the importance individuals attach to different life roles is related to the level of work–home conflict.

The approaches described here suggest that work–home balance largely depends on the interplay between work values, home values and the more general personal or life values held by individuals. However, the notion of the integration of work values and home values merits further discussion. In order to develop a truly integrated approach, we have to determine that people do indeed integrate work values and home values in a combined set of work–home values. Moreover, we have to investigate *how* people integrate these different sets of values in their lives in order to create work–home balance (Figure 4.1). To this end, we need to develop a better understanding of the processes underlying the integration of different sets of values. Clark's (2000) *border theory* could be a good starting point for this. This approach focuses on the interplay between the work domain and the home domain. Clark argues that the borders between work and home domains are becoming more and more fluid. In her view, people are daily border-crossers between the world of work and the home world. 'People shape these worlds, mould the borders between them, and determine the border-crosser's relationship to that world and its members' (Clark 2000: 748). This emphasis on how individuals shape their activities in both environments and create meaning could, perhaps, be a good starting point for developing a novel view on how 'work–home values' are formed within the individual. However, this would require more research. Settles' (2004) *identity centrality* approach could, from a psychological point of view, also prove to be fruitful here, since it focuses on how people deal with combining different central value systems.

Concluding, we propose that work–home values be investigated for their usefulness as a linking mechanism between work values and home values. We suggest that work–home values are formed and shaped simultaneously via personal values, work-related values and home-related values. When the integration is successful, work–home balance is achieved. To illustrate this, we refer to Burchielli *et al.* (2008), who explain that the internalization of organizational values, for instance, can have a personal cost in terms of time pressures, stress and exhaustion.

In the next section, we will explore how the process of developing work–home values is different for the three generations that are currently active in the labour market.

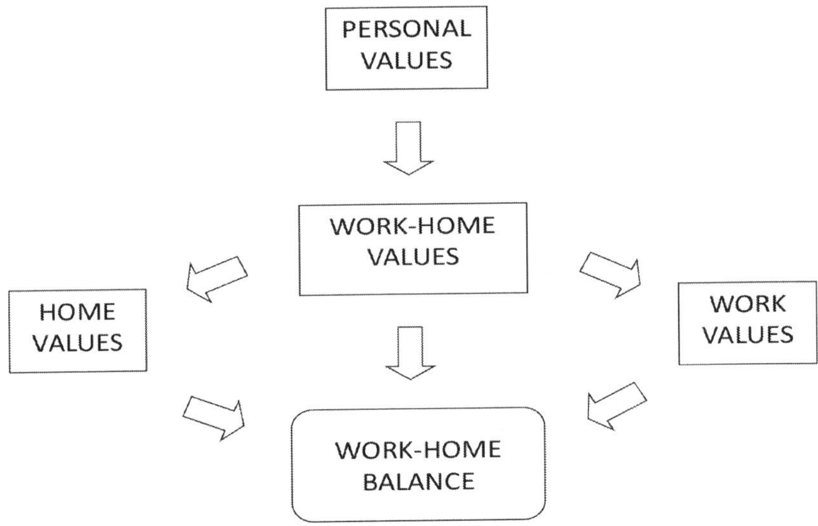

FIGURE 4.1 A model of values and work–home balance

The three generations and their work–home values

Although research in the field of work or home values has been growing, there is still a dearth of research on possible generational differences in this field. Scholars, however, argue that during adolescence and young adulthood, individual self-concept and identity take shape and become consolidated (Inglehart 1997). Therefore, career aspirations and family plans are likely to be influenced by the work and family life that children and young adults experience and observe in the world around them and in the home domain (Riggio and Desrochers 2005). Consequently, individuals within generations often share similar life courses. We argue, therefore, that individuals within generations develop similarities in work–home values. This view is supported by Riggio and Desrochers, who explain that identity formation is crucial during childhood and early adolescence, 'including the development of gender roles and personal ideas toward work and personal relationships, with parents in particular serving as role models of what it means to be an adult' (2005: 177). We also propose that differences can be found between generations with regard to work–home values and, consequently, expectations toward an employer with regard to work–home arrangements. It would therefore be important to enlarge our framing of the issue by studying work–home values of generations.

Factors influencing work–home values

First, we have to identify the factors that might have created shifts in work–home values. Two theoretical approaches can be helpful in understanding which developments have affected demands and resources in the work–home sphere. First, let us consider the *conservation of resources theory* (Hobfoll and Shirom 2001). Hobfoll and Shirom argue that stress can occur when individuals experience a loss of resources (self-esteem, energy) in the work or home domain, which might result in a spillover of negative emotions and stress into the other domain. In addition, the *resources–demands model* (Voydanoff 2005) can help us to understand how the perception of work–home balance derives from assessing the relative demands and resources associated with work roles and home roles.

Both theories, when applied to the development of generational values, are congruent with Inglehart's (1997) *theory of intergenerational values change*. This theory is based on two hypotheses. The first, the 'socialization hypothesis', suggests that the basic values held by adults reflect the socio-economic conditions of their childhood and adolescence. The second hypothesis, the 'scarcity hypothesis', proposes that the greatest value is placed on those socio-economic aspects that were in short supply during a generation's childhood years and adolescence. Although Inglehart (1997) focuses merely on economic resources, several other authors have indicated that the same processes might also apply to other resources. For example, researchers who have investigated national trends, world trends or changes over the past 50 years have identified developments that are thought to have influenced generations' values. Scott's (2000) research, for instance, identified economic factors such as unemployment to be important for the formation of work values and home values. In addition, the author mentions increased pressure in the workplace and family breakdown as important factors. She also observed several 'value clashes between generations' (Scott 2000: 355) with regard to these trends. Several researchers have identified other significant changes in the work domain as well as in the home domain. They can be summarized as demographic factors, such as family stability, education, female labour market participation and income (cf. Christensen 2005; Kossek 2005); economic factors, such as prosperity, employment, type of work and the possibility to live on one income (e.g. Bianchi and Raley 2005); and finally factors in the work environment, the home environment and the work–home sphere, such as technological advances, views on gender division of labour, work demands and work–home boundaries (cf. Barnett 2005; Jackson 2005). The value-forming trends are summarized in Table 4.2.

TABLE 4.2 Historical trends since World War II by generation (Baby Boom, X, Y)

Baby Boom (1945–1964)	*Generation X (1965–1980)*	*Generation Y (1981–1995)*
Demographic trends		
Stable families	Growing divorce rates	Growing divorce rates
Traditional families	More diverse families	More diverse families
Low-educated mothers	More higher-educated mothers	More higher-educated mothers
Low female labour market participation	Growing female labour market participation (temporary)	High female labour market participation (permanent)
Low household incomes	Growing household incomes, recessions	Growing household incomes, insecurity
Economic trends		
Scarcity, rebuilding	Growth, unemployment	Prosperous, insecurity
Agricultural	Industrial	Knowledge work
Possible to live on one income	Difficult to live on one income	Two-income necessity
Work–home trends		
Traditional	More gender-egalitarian	Gender egalitarian
Single-earner families	More dual-earner families	More dual-earner families
Hard work, less pressure	Harder work, more pressure	Harder work, more pressure
Strong work–home boundaries	Blurring work–home boundaries	Blurring work–home boundaries

The work–home values of the Baby Boom generation, Generation X and Generation Y

In this section, we will explore the demographic, economic and work–home developments that have shaped the three cohorts and we will extrapolate these developments to the work–home values that these generational cohorts may hold.[1] Our historical overview (Table 4.2) shows that the three generations discussed in this chapter (Baby Boomers, X, Y) grew up and spent their formative life stages (age 16–25) under different circumstances. We expect them, therefore, to have developed different values with regard to the work domain and the home domain. In discussing the three generations, we follow the most commonly used generational taxonomy (Eisner 2005; Lub *et al.* 2012).

The Baby Boom generation

In many western countries, the end of World War II brought about a baby boom. This boom is usually considered to have lasted from 1945–1964, but in European countries that had suffered war damage the boom began and ended a few years later. After 1957, in both the US and in most European countries, birth rates started to decline. Baby Boomers grew up in the difficult phase after World War II. However, economic circumstances, incomes and educational attainment started to improve slowly during this era (Whitehead 2008). These developments were slightly slower in Europe because of the post-war reconstruction. In all western countries, a gradual shift took place from agriculture to industry and services (Whitehead 2008).

One of the most dramatic demographic trends in the 1950s and 1960s was the entrance of women in paid labour (Bianchi and Raley 2005). Initially, working mothers were seen as 'unfeminine', and men who were active parents and shared the housework with their wives were 'mama's boys' (Barnett 2005). Nevertheless, more gender-egalitarian views and habits became widely adopted in the 1960s and 1970s, but Baby Boomers still predominantly experienced a two-parent, traditional context, with families living on one income: the father's (Cherlin 1992). In their formative years, however, the gender-specialized division of labour in western countries became less universal (Bianchi and Raley 2005), probably mainly as a result of the democratization processes accompanied with growing individualization and women's independence. Their mothers' educational and occupational opportunities expanded. Still, the main role of their fathers lay outside the home, and the main role of their mothers lay inside the home.

The Baby Boomers grew up in relatively large and stable families. During the baby boom period, family life was characterized by early and nearly universal marriage, low divorce rates and high fertility (Cherlin 1992). During their formative years, in the second half of the twentieth century, the general marital pattern started to change and divorce rates went up (Bianchi and Raley 2005). As a result, families gradually started to become more diverse.

Values of the Baby Boom generation

With regard to work values, the work orientation of Baby Boomers is likely to be quite high. They can also be expected to hold more traditional values with regard to the division of work outside and inside the home, compared with the other generations. The era in which the Baby Boom generation grew up can be characterized by two main developments. The first is the rebuilding process after World War II, which caused economies to start growing slowly. The second concerns the traditional work division structure based on gender, which started to show its first cracks. This must be seen against the backdrop of democratization processes that started to evolve, combined with new economic developments. Beutell and Wittig-Berman (2008: 509) indeed found that, also as a result of economic circumstances while growing up, Baby Boomers 'live to work' (as opposed to Xers, who 'work to live', and Yers, who seem to value home and leisure life more). In addition, the Baby Boomers predominantly grew up in families with a traditional gender division in terms of work. The main role of the men was outside the home, and the role of the women inside the home; female labour market participation was low. Families were still quite stable. Indeed, work seems to be quite central in the lives of the Baby Boomers, especially in the lives of the male members, and they seem to experience lower levels of work–home conflict compared to both Xers and Yers (Beutell and Wittig-Berman 2008).

Generation X

The identity development of Generation X, born between 1965 and 1980, took shape between the 1980s and 2000s. Although members of this generation generally grew up in an era of economic growth, many Xers experienced a series of serious economic recessions in the 1980s, during their formative years (Twenge *et al.* 2010). The 1990s saw the longest period of economic growth and stability after World War II. When some of the Xers were still in their formative phase, economies in general grew steadily, despite most economies showing significant recessions in the 1980s and 1990s.

Generation X grew up in smaller and more diverse families compared to the Baby Boomers, as birth rates declined, divorce rates grew and the number of single parents went up. Increasingly, families had one or two higher-educated parents. Women in particular more often engaged in higher education. In addition, children of Generation Xers were more and more raised in families with working mothers. Gender-egalitarian views were widely adopted (Bianchi and Raley 2005) and many of their mothers were part of the labour force. Both their parents increasingly combined roles, taking care of children and other family members and holding more demanding jobs, part-time jobs, contracts of limited duration or flexible work schedules (Bianchi and Raley 2005). The 1980s and 1990s saw the introduction of some (state-provided) care-giving facilities in western Europe and, to a lesser extent, in the US (Bianchi and Raley 2005) to improve work–home balance, but work and home remained increasingly hard to combine.

Values of Generation X

Xers are likely to be less work-centric than the Baby Boomers. In addition, this generation is also more likely than the Baby Boomers to value work–home balance. The formative years of Generation X were characterized by prosperity, with periods of severe economic insecurity. Work life started to give more pressure and, for families, it became increasingly difficult to live on one income, which forced mothers to enter the labour market as well. Research carried out by Twenge *et al.* (2010) in fact confirms the lower work-centrality of Generation X. According to Beutell and Wittig-Berman (2008), Xers are less loyal to organizations. Instead of seeking job security, they place more value on developing their own careers (Kupperschmidt 2000).

Generation X experienced their mothers moving into the working world and expanding their life roles. Some empirical evidence for this can be found in the literature (Beutell and Wittig-Berman 2008; Twenge *et al.* 2010). Eisner (2005) reported Xers in particular having difficulty dealing with disappearing boundaries between work and private life. In addition, the growing divorce rates of their parents will probably make Xers place more value on their home life. Xers are therefore more likely to experience negative spillover from work to home and a loss of resources, resulting in stress.

Generation Y

Generation Y, born between 1981 and 1995, generally grew up in prosperity. The rise in household income was largely the result of an increase in personal income, mostly due to higher educational levels. Moreover, the increase in the number of women entering the labour force had led to a rising percentage of dual-earner households. Since the start of the most recent financial crisis (2007 in the US and 2008 in Europe[2]), however, this generation has been experiencing considerable economic insecurity.

Compared with the Baby Boomers and Xers, Generation Y increasingly grew up in more gender-egalitarian eras. Many of them have mothers who are highly educated and are active in the labour market. Yers are currently experiencing a situation in which people have to work harder than ever, due to work intensification, and in which people are engaged in various and changing labour patterns because of growing job insecurity (Kossek 2005). They will be less able to survive on one income, and differences in income within societies will continue to grow (Whitehead 2008).

Yers grew up in smaller and more diverse families, compared to the Baby Boomers and Xers: dual-earner families, divorced parents, single-parent homes, part-time working parents and parents working two (or more) jobs (Whitehead 2008). This is a result of growing divorce rates and the increase in the number of people who married late or who never married (Bianchi and Raley 2005). Moreover, the burden of caring for dependants is likely to increase, because of the growth in the number of single-parent families and the ageing population (Kossek 2005).

During the past few decades, due to the growing use of technology and growing flexibility in the work life, the boundaries between work and private life have become 'blurred' (Kossek 2005). Although from the 1970s onwards attention to the difficult interplay between labour market demands and family care-giving tasks has increased (Bianchi and Raley 2005), combining work and home life continues to be very problematic.

Values of Generation Y

One would expect Yers to place less value on work than the Baby Boomers, and to hold more gender-egalitarian views. Generation Y on the one hand grew up in prosperity but, on the other hand, also experienced growing economic insecurity. Research carried out by Beutell and Wittig-Berman (2008) indeed revealed that Yers are less likely to allocate energy to work tasks. Findings from a study held by Twenge *et al.* (2010) indicated that, in contrast to older generations, they also prefer jobs that provide more vacation time. Twenge *et al.* (2010), not surprisingly, also found Yers to be quite self-confident, to have high expectations of their employers and to be more likely to leave the organization if their expectations are not met.

Yers grew up in times in which many mothers held permanent jobs outside the home. Research indeed shows that girls and boys with employed mothers report less traditional gender-role attitudes than children of non-employed mothers (cf. Barnett 2005). Beutell and Wittig-Berman (2008), for example, found that Yers embrace family values more than Xers. Yers, however, are currently entering their childbearing years and it remains to be seen what, ultimately, their work–home values will be. The same holds for their expectations with regard to work–home arrangements and their attitude toward their employers. Finally, because of today's continuous technical advances, Yers can be expected to be faced with more blurred boundaries than the Baby Boom generation and the Xers were (Clark 2000; Jackson 2005). Still, they may have less difficulty in dealing with this phenomenon than the Xers.

Concluding this section, we can say that the values that people place on their work life and their home life have shifted quite substantially between the three generations. The Baby Boom generation places more value on work, with the men still putting greater emphasis on the work role and the women putting greater emphasis on the home role. The boundaries between both spheres are still solid, but permeable. Work–home balance, however, is starting to become a problem. In Generation X, men and women have grown closer together, placing value on the work role as well as the home life role and valuing the boundaries between both spheres. As a result, they are more heavily affected by negative spillover processes and experience a greater loss of resources than the Baby Boomers. Generation Y seems to value both roles, trying increasingly hard to prevent the work role from interfering with their much-valued home role.

Discussion and implications for practice and future research

Western industrial societies are in search of a healthy integration of the work domain and the home domain (Christensen 2005; Van der Lippe and Bäck-Wicklund 2011). We feel that, in order to accomplish a sustainable workforce, the work–home values of the Baby Boomers, Generation X and Generation Y must be taken into consideration.

Of course, in different areas around the world people grow up differently with regard to socio-cultural and socio-demographic circumstances, and these differences will always have to be taken into account. Still, in this chapter we argued that different generations (Baby Boomers, Xers, Yers) have developed different value systems in response to general changes in their life experiences during childhood and early adolescence (Inglehart 1997). Therefore, they can be expected to not only have formed different *work* values and *home* values, but also to show differences in the integration of both sets of values into *work–home* values. Existing research indeed suggests that, again, Baby Boomers generally seem to be more work-oriented, Xers to be more work–home-balance-oriented, and Yers, in comparison, to be more home-oriented (Beutell and Wittig-Berman 2008). Research outcomes like these show that important similarities exist in value systems within generations. These value systems can be seen as a 'natural view of the world' (Scott 2000: 356) within generations that separates them from other generations.

With regard to work–home research, we therefore suggest the following. First, we have to gain a deeper insight into how the work–home values of workers from different generations have taken shape and what precisely they are today. Which combination and level of integration of values is successful when we consider work–home balance? We suggest that the border theory (Clark 2000) could be a good starting point, because it places emphasis on how people shape their work and their home environments. The identity centrality approach (Settles 2004) could also be of use here, since it focuses on how people deal with different central value systems for different life roles. Second, more research is needed into the needs of different generations with regard to work–home arrangements. Questions to be answered concern ways in which generations differ with regard to specific work–home arrangements expected to be provided by employers. Future research could also address the question of how generations differ with regard to reactions to employers' efforts to accomplish work–home balance. Finally, we could investigate which factors influence the reactions of the different generations.

Conclusions

This chapter discussed our claim that a better understanding of generational perspectives contributes to the existing knowledge about the increase in problems in balancing the work and home domains. For example, although Baby Boomers will gradually be leaving the labour market, many of them will be around for another 15–20 years. Eventually, they will be replaced by Xers and Yers. The first Generation Y employees entered the labour force about ten years ago. Often, they will encounter managers from a different generation, with different (work–home) values, attitudes and behaviours. Therefore, organizations need to realize that employees from different generations often have different work–home values and needs. In order to attract and retain talent, organizations have to find ways to reconcile the two most important institutions in the lives of their employees: work and home life. When employers become more acquainted with the work–home values and expectations held by employees from different generations, they will be able to respond to them more adequately and improve current working conditions and work–home arrangements (Van der Lippe and Bäck-Wicklund 2011).

Notes

1 Unless indicated otherwise, the information in this section is derived from the US Census Bureau and Eurostat.
2 Based on data from the Centre for Economic Policy Research; see www.cepr.org.

References

Allan, C., O'Donnell, M. and Peetz, D. (1999) 'More tasks, less secure, working harder: three dimensions of labour utilisation', *Journal of Industrial Relations*, 41: 519–535.

Barnett, R.C. (2005) 'Dual-earner couples: good/bad for her and/or him?', in D. Halpern and S. Murphy (eds) *From Work–Family Balance to Work–Family Interaction: Changing the Metaphor*, Mahwah, NJ: Lawrence Erlbaum, pp. 151–172.

Beutell, N. and Wittig-Berman, U. (2008) 'Work–family conflict and work–family synergy for Generation X, Baby Boomers, and Matures: generational differences, predictors, and satisfaction outcomes', *Journal of Managerial Psychology*, 23(5): 507–523.

Bianchi, S.M. and Raley, S.B. (2005) 'Time allocations in families', in S. Bianchi, L. Casper and T. Berkowitz King (eds) *Work, Family, Health, and Well-being*, Mahwah, NJ: Lawrence Erlbaum, pp. 19–40.

Burchielli, R., Bartram, T. and Thanacoody, R. (2008) 'Work–family balance or greedy organizations?', *Industrial Relations*, 63: 108–133.

Carlson, D.S. and Kacmar, K.M. (2000) 'Work–family conflict in the organization: do life role values make a difference?', *Journal of Management*, 26(5): 1031–1054.

Cherlin, A. (1992) *Marriage, Divorce, Remarriage*, Cambridge, MA: Harvard University Press.

Christensen, K.E. (2005) 'Foreword', in S. Bianchi, L. Casper and R. Berkowitz King (eds) *Work, Family, Health, and Well-being*, Mahwah, NJ: Lawrence Erlbaum, pp. x–xi.

Clark, S.C. (2000) 'Work/family border theory: a new theory of work/family balance', *Human Relations*, 53: 747–770.

De Cieri, H., Holmes, B., Abbott, J. and Pettit, T. (2005) 'Achievements and challenges for work/life balance strategies in Australian organizations', *The International Journal of Human Resource Management*, 16: 90–103.

Dikkers, J.S.E., Geurts, S.A.E., Dulk, L.D., Peper, B., Taris, W. and Kompier, M.A.J. (2007) 'Dimensions of work–home culture and their relations with the use of work–home arrangements and work–home interaction', *Work & Stress*, 21: 155–172.

Duxbury, L. and Higgins, C. (2001) *Work–Life Balance in the New Millennium: Where are We? Where Do We Need to Go?*, discussion paper W12, Ottawa: Canadian Policy Research Networks.

Eisner, S.P. (2005) 'Managing Generation Y', *SAM Advanced Management Journal*, 704: 4–15.

Elizur, D. and Sagie, A. (1999) 'Facets of personal values: a structural analysis of life and work values', *Applied Psychology: An International Review*, 48(1): 73–87.

Forrier, A., Sels, L. and Stynen, D. (2009) 'Career mobility at the intersection between agent and structure: a conceptual model', *Journal of Occupational and Organizational Psychology*, 82(4): 739–759.

Geurts, S.A.E. and Demerouti, E. (2003) 'Work/non-work interface: a review of theories and findings', in M.J. Schabracq, J.A.M. Winnubst and C.L. Cooper (eds) *The Handbook of Work and Health Psychology*, Chichester: Wiley, pp. 279–312.

Greenhaus, J. and Singh, R. (2003) *Work–Family linkages: A Sloan Work and Family Encyclopaedia Entry*, Chestnut Hill, MA: Boston College.

Guest, D.E. (2002) 'Perspectives on the study of work–life balance', *Social Science Information*, 41: 255–279.

Hobfoll, S.E. and Shirom, A. (2001) 'Conservation of resources theory: applications to stress and management in the workplace', *Public Administration and Public Policy*, 87: 57–80.

Inglehart, R. (1997) *Modernization and Postmodernization: Cultural, Economic, and Political Change in 43 Societies*, Princeton, NJ: Princeton University Press.

Jackson, M. (2005) 'The limits of connectivity: technology and 21st century life', in D. Halpern, and S. Murphy (eds) *From Work–Family Balance to Work–Family Interaction: Changing the Metaphor*, Mahwah, NJ: Lawrence Erlbaum, pp. 135–150.

Kossek, E.E. (2005) 'Workplace policies and practices to support work and families', in S. Bianchi, L. Casper and R. Berkowitz King (eds) *Work, Family, Health, and Well-being*, Mahwah, NJ: Lawrence Erlbaum, pp. 95–114.

Kupperschmidt, B.R. (2000) 'Multigenerational employees: strategies for effective management', *Health Care Manager*, 19(1): 65–76.

Lub, X., Bijvank, M.N., Bal, P.M., Blomme, R. and Schalk, R. (2012) 'Different or alike? Exploring the psychological contract and commitment of different generations of hospitality workers', *International Journal of Contemporary Hospitality Management*, 24(4): 553–573.

Magd, H. (2003) 'Management attitudes and perceptions of older employees in hospitality management', *International Journal of Contemporary Hospitality Management*, 15(7): 393–401.

Mannheim, K. (1952) 'The problem of generations', in P. Kecskemeti (ed.), *Essays on the Sociology of Knowledge*, London: Routledge, pp. 378–404.

Perrewé, P.L. and Hochwarter, W.A. (2001) 'Can we really have it all? The attainment of work and family values', *Current Directions in Psychological Science*, 10(1): 29–33.

Riggio, H.R. and Desrochers, S. (2005) 'The influence of maternal employment on the work and family expectations of offspring', in D. Halpern and S. Murphy (eds) *From Work–Family Balance to Work–Family Interaction: Changing the Metaphor*, Mahwah, NJ: Lawrence Erlbaum, pp. 177–196.

Rokeach, M. (1973) *The Nature of Human Values*, New York: Free Press.

Schwartz, S.H., Cieciuch, J., Vecchione, M., Davidov, E., Fischer, R., Beierlein, C., Ramos, A., Verkasalo, M., Lönnqvist, J. E., Demirutku, K., Dirilen-Gumus, O. and Konty, M. (2012) 'Personality processes and individual differences: refining the theory of basic individual values', *Journal of Personality and Social Psychology*, 103(4): 663–688.

Scott, J. (2000) 'Is it a different world to when you were growing up? Generational effects on social representations and child-rearing values', *The British Journal of Sociology*, 51(2): 355–376.

Settles, I.H. (2004) 'When multiple identities interfere: the role of identity centrality', *Personality and Social Psychology Bulletin*, 30(4): 487–500.

Spillman, B.C. and Pezin, L.E. (2000) 'Potential and active family caregivers: changing networks and the "sandwich generation"', *Milbank Quarterly*, 78: 347–374.

Staines, G.L. (1980) 'Spillover versus compensation: a review of the literature on the relationship between work and nonwork', *Human Relations*, 33: 111–129.

Sturges, J., Conway, N., Guest, D. and Liefooghe, A. (2005) 'Managing the career deal: the psychological contract as a framework for understanding career management, organizational commitment and work behavior', *Journal of Organizational Behavior*, 26: 821–838.

Super, D.E. (1980) 'A life-span, life-space approach to career development', *Journal of Vocational Behavior*, 16(3): 282–298.

Twenge, J.M., Campbell, S.M., Hoffman, B.J. and Lance, C.E. (2010) 'Generational differences in work values: leisure and extrinsic values increasing, social and intrinsic values decreasing', *Journal of Management*, 36(5): 1117–1142.

Van der Lippe, T. and Bäck-Wicklund, M. (2011) 'Quality of life and work in a changing Europe', in M. Bäck-Wiklund, T. Van der Lippe, T.L. Den Dulk and A. Doorne-Huiskes (eds) *Quality of Life and Work in a Changing Europe: A Theoretical Framework*, London: Palgrave Macmillan, pp. 1–16.

Voydanoff, P. (2005) 'Toward a conceptualization of perceived work–family fit and balance: a demands and resources approach', *Journal of Marriage and Family*, 67(4): 822–836.

Whitehead, D.L. (2008) 'Historical trends in work-family: the evolution of earning and caring', in K. Korabik, D.S. Lero and D.L. Whitehead (eds) *Handbook of Work–Family Integration: Research, Theory and Best Practices*, London: Academic Press, pp. 13–36.

PART II

Methodological approaches to investigating generational diversity

5

IS IT KIDS TODAY OR JUST THE FACT THAT THEY'RE KIDS?

Disentangling generational differences from age differences

Stacy M. Campbell and Jean M. Twenge

"Kids! They are disobedient, disrespectful oafs! Noisy, crazy, sloppy, lazy, loafers!" While it is certainly plausible that these lines are being muttered by a manager in today's workforce as he reviews his young subordinates' work, these are some of the lyrics from the Broadway musical, *Bye Bye Birdie*, written by Lee Adams in 1959. So more than 50 years ago, before the Internet, smart phones, and Facebook, before anyone could blame kids' laziness on technology or participation trophies, adults were puzzled by the actions of "kids today" and wondered why these kids were so different from themselves as children. The question is: are today's young people different because they grew up during a different time and experienced different events, people, objects that shaped their generation, or are they not actually different – in other words, is this just how kids always act, regardless of generation?

The recent cover of *Time Magazine* identifying Millennials as "The Me Me Me Generation" suggests that this younger generation is seen as different from the generations before them – Generation X, Baby Boomers, and the Silent Generation. Compared to previous generations that have been described as "hard-working," Millennials are, Joel Stein writes, "lazy, entitled, selfish, and shallow" (Stein 2013: 28). Born between 1980 and 1999, Millennials (also called Generation Y and Generation Me) are 80 million strong, and represent the biggest age grouping in American history and the current wave of employees entering today's workforce. On an international level, especially in the growing economies of Brazil, Russia, India, and China (BRIC countries), Millennials already represent the same or a greater percentage of the workforce than other generations (Rasch and Kowske 2013). In the US, amid slow economic recovery and high unemployment, Millennials are also the generation with the highest likelihood of having unmet expectations regarding their careers (Lyons et al. 2012). These young employees have high expectations regarding progression in their companies, expect to be able to talk directly with the CEO, and want their managers and co-workers to listen to what they have to say. It has been reported that generations express different levels of satisfaction, commitment, and trust towards organizations (Cogin 2012; Putnam 2000). But is it the age of these young employees that makes them believe they are not given respect from older co-workers and supervisors? Have 20-somethings always been so overconfident yet lazy?

Generational researchers argue that while birth year is used as a proxy to group them into generational cohorts, age is not the key factor these cohorts have in common (Chen and Choi 2008; Mannheim 1952; Twenge et al. 2010). Generational cohorts include individuals born around the same time who share distinctive social or historical life events (e.g. Mannheim 1952). That is, generations are influenced by broad forces such as parents, peers, media, economic and social events, and popular culture. These forces create common value systems distinguishing one generation from the next (Twenge et al. 2010) and subsequently influence attitudes and behaviors. A criticism of generational research, however, is that most of the existing literature relies on non-empirical sources such as anecdotal accounts and the few systematic studies that have been done (Cennamo and Gardner 2008; Wong et al. 2008) use cross-sectional data. Cross-sectional designs rely primarily on measurements taken at one point in time, and thus these studies fail to address the big challenge of generational research. That is, how to distinguish between differences due to age or actual generational differences? An alternative is to use a time-lag method in which samples of individuals of different generations are measured at one age across different cohorts at different times.

The goal of this chapter is to highlight the challenge of teasing apart developmental and age effects from generational effects and discuss time-lag design as a useful method for overcoming this challenge. The chapter starts with a comparison between age and generation as research variables and discusses the criticism that much generational research fails to disentangle these two variables, thereby calling into question the validity of the findings. To address this challenge and respond to criticism, the chapter outlines a time-lag study design that helps to overcome this challenge by looking at individuals over time at a specific age. The chapter concludes with some recommendations of where to obtain such datasets and areas for future research.

Age versus generation

To start, let us look at the definitional differences between age and generation. Chronological age is the year when an individual was born or how long the individual has been alive. Often the birthdate and corresponding age of an individual is used as a proxy measure for age-related individual human development. In addition to an increase in age, there are physical changes, as well as social, emotional, and cognitive changes that correspond to age. However, chronological age is not the only way to define age. Researchers have looked at alternative ways to define age such as functional age, when an individual is judged on the basis of his or her functional capabilities, or relative age, when an individual is compared to other organisms (Cleveland and Lim 2007; Kooij et al. 2010; Sterns and Doverspike 1989). In the workplace, career stage is another important variable related to age (Super 1969; see also Chapter 2 of this book for a detailed analysis of the different conceptualizations of age). But regardless of how it is defined, age represents a fixed point in time.

The term generation has been defined as "an identifiable group that shares birth years, age, location and significant life events at critical developmental stages" (Kupperschmidt 2000: 66). In addition to being in the same generational age band (typically a 15–20 year span), individuals belonging to a generation are influenced by broad forces (i.e. religion, education, technology, parents, peers, media, economic, and social events) during critical developmental years that shape their value systems and distinguish them from other individuals who grew up at different times (Meglino and Ravlin 1998; Scott 2000). So while age effects are developmental in nature and are caused by psychosocial or biological ageing, cohort or generational effects arise as a result of the impact of the environment or shared experiences over time (Rhodes 1983). Furthermore, differences in work-related attitudes or behaviors due to age effects should decrease over time with younger adults becoming more like the older adults as they go through developmental stages, while differences due to generational effects could be relatively stable after the formative years of adolescence. But while they are different variables, age versus generational effects are hard to distinguish in data collected at one time (Mason and Wolfinger 2001), making methodological difficulties inherent when conducting generational research.

The idea of grouping people into generations is not without controversy. As some have argued (Cogin 2012; Twenge et al. 2010), generational groupings ignore the variance within generations. In addition, birth year cutoffs are chosen somewhat arbitrarily. For example, Millennials are often defined as those born between 1980 and 2000. Is someone born in 1980 a Generation Xer or a Millennial? If she is a Millennial, is she really that different from a Generation Xer born in 1979, at least based on birth year? Probably not. And how similar is someone born in 1980 to someone born in 2000 based on birth year and cultural experience? Not very. As many generational changes are linear, it might be better to simply consider how many years apart two individuals are in birth year. In addition, some argue that it is impossible to generalize about a generation, because not everyone in the group will fit the average. This is true. However, such statements are true of any study that examines differences among groups – for example, sex differences or cross-cultural differences. Experiments comparing experimental and control groups also rely on mean-level differences. So if we are going to discard generational differences because they do not apply to everyone, we would be have to discard virtually all scientific studies. Thus, despite the debate, researchers have shown that generational cohorts provide another useful way to group individuals and have established the legitimacy of generational differences as an important social categorization variable (Cogin 2012).

Generational research

The traditional generational labels and birth year cutoffs are: the Silent Generation or the Veterans, born 1925–1945; Baby Boomers, 1946–1964; Generation X, 1965–1979; and Generation Me/Generation Y/Millennials born 1980–2000. With these four generations in today's workplace, organizations are now faced with the challenges of integrating different generations as well as the complexity of creating environments to attract and satisfy workers of each generation. The need to understand generations has sparked numerous publications and books aimed at explaining the differences between younger and older workers. But despite the fact that generational research has become a hot topic, both in the popular press and academia, the empirical research on generational differences is still a new undertaking.

Much of the existing literature on generational differences relies on non-empirical sources such as anecdotal accounts based on different generations' life experience or qualitative interviews of selected samples (e.g. Chester 2002; Lancaster and Stillman 2003; Tulgan 2003; Zemke et al. 1999). The academic studies on generations, which usually do report empirical data, often suffer from another challenge: most are cross-sectional (collecting data at one time), so any differences could be due to age or to generation (e.g. Cennamo and Gardner 2008; Chen and Choi 2008; Lamm and Meeks 2009; Sessa et al. 2007; Smola and Sutton 2002). While these studies are useful as they capture the attitudes of different generations at one point in time, they cannot disentangle the effects of age and generation. For example, these findings cannot say whether today's young workers are any different than young workers were ten or 20 years ago, and thus whether programmes for recruiting and retaining young workers should be changed or kept the same. If the differences in a cross-sectional study are due to age, generational problems should also solve themselves as the young workers grow older, or older managers can understand younger workers simply by remembering being a young worker themselves. In addition, studies can produce varied results depending on the specific cross-section of the population they sample. For example, samples drawn from a Western culture such as the United States would likely yield different results for certain attitudes and behaviors versus an Eastern culture such as China due to cultural differences. Recruitment methods and incentives given to individuals to complete surveys may also influence results beyond any generational differences that may exist. Such factors make it difficult to draw firm conclusions. As a result there have been some concerns about the validity of the evidence on which this idea of "generational diversity" is based (Lyons et al. 2007; Parry and Urwin 2011). To confidently identify generational differences in important workplace variables and move this research area forward, over-time designs are necessary.

Disentangling generation and age – time-lag design

The ideal design for a study of generational differences is a cohort-sequential design (Schaie 1965), which combines longitudinal and cross-sectional approaches. The data collection for such a design begins at a young age and follows each generation longitudinally over many years so that all cohorts at all ages are measured. Given that it is time-consuming and expensive, very few studies have used this design. Sequential cohort design also suffers from threats to internal validity due to the selective dropout of participants due to fatigue, death, or other changes that may occur over time.

An alternative is to use a time-lag method in which individuals of different generations are measured at one age at different times (for example, college students between the 1960s and the present) to determine if there are differences in a given characteristic (Schaie 1965). In other words, only one age is studied but across different cohorts at different times. This method can also be applied to multi-age samples if they are large enough to analyze the data separately by age group. Figure 5.1 provides a graphical view of the cross-sectional design and over-time designs possible when conducting research. Compared to the other designs, the time-lag design examines whether there are differences in a given characteristic for samples of equal age but drawn from different cohorts measured at different times (Schaie 1965). With age held constant, this design can isolate differences due to generation or time period (though it is important to note the time-lag method cannot separate the effects due to generation from those due to time period, which affect all generations equally).

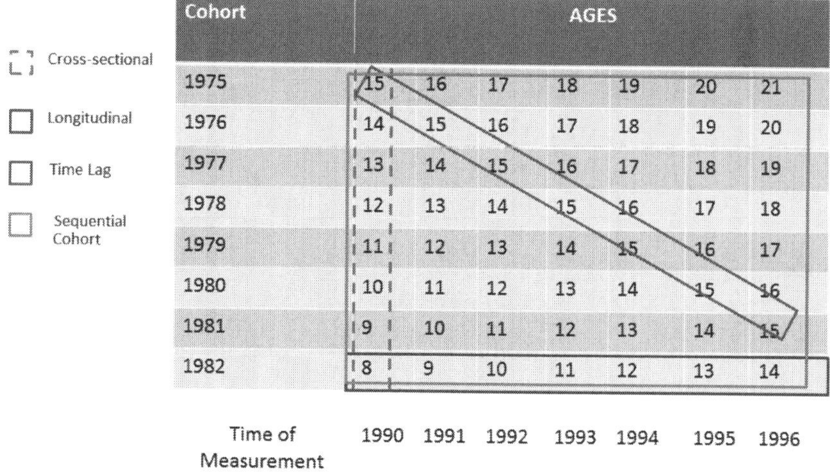

FIGURE 5.1 Cross-sectional and over-time designs

Source: adapted from Schaie (1965).

Using this time-lag method enables us to inform managers of whether young workers now differ from young workers in the past and whether leaders need to adapt their management strategies for a new generation. If the differences in the previous one-time, cross-sectional studies are due to age or career stage rather than generation, then managers can use the same techniques they have always used to recruit, retain, and supervise young workers. However, if there are true generational differences, then managers may need to deal with young workers differently than they dealt with workers in the past. For example, the same benefits may not be important to young workers or the performance feedback tools that were successful for young managers moving up in the company may not be as effective. Organizations need to understand if their younger workers today are different from the younger workers in the past so that they can adjust and modify policies and procedures as needed.

Findings using time-lag design

Time-lag studies are usually either large national surveys or cross-temporal meta-analyses. One of the earliest, the Seattle Longitudinal Study (SLS), was started by Schaie in 1965 as part of his dissertation. The SLS began with a focus on age differences and age changes in cognitive abilities among individuals in the Pacific Northwest. Since then the study has expanded to include personality traits, lifestyles, and family environment (Schaie et al. 2004). There were seven major testing cycles used for data collection for the SLS – 1956, 1963, 1970, 1977, 1984, 1991, and 1998. One of the major questions addressed in the SLS during each of these testing cycles concerned the pattern of generational differences and the magnitude of these differences. With an increase of sophisticated methodologies that have emerged over the years, the researchers have been able to ask this question with greater clarity and have demonstrated the relevance of substantial generational differences in five mental ability measures used throughout the study (Schaie 1974, 1984, 1996; Schaie et al. 2004).

As the interest in generational differences has increased, researchers have looked to existing research projects that have captured large amounts of data over years as a way to leverage the time-lag design approach. For example, "Monitoring the Future" (MtF; Johnston et al. 2006) is an on-going project that selects high schools from across the USA to represent a cross-section of the US population on variables such as region, race, gender, and socioeconomic status by participating in the study (see www.monitoringthefuture.org). Since 1976, the MtF project has surveyed a sample of US high school seniors every year on a wide array of questions – focusing on the behaviors, attitudes, and values of American secondary school students, college students, and young adults. Many of the items on these existing scales represent constructs that are relevant for the workplace. From this data, several studies have been conducted with a few recent ones focused on generational differences (Twenge et al. 2010, 2012; Twenge and Kasser 2013). Results indicated that there has been substantial growth in research on generational differences in individualism, personality traits, and work attitudes (for a further review, see Twenge 2006). There is also recent research on generational differences in work values (Twenge et al. 2010) that used a time-lag design using the MtF data. To understand how this time-lag design works, refer to Figure 5.2, which shows how data from this sample of US high school seniors, average age of 18, in 1976, 1991, and 2006 (n = 16,507) were used to represent three generations getting ready for college/entry into the workplace: Boomers (high school graduates of 1976–1980), Gen X (high school graduates of 1981–1999), and Gen Y/Gen Me/Millennials (high school graduates of 2000–2011). The items assessed five clusters of work values: intrinsic, extrinsic, leisure, social, and altruistic.

An important step to highlight in using this time-lag design is demonstrating measurement invariance. To make meaningful cross-generational comparisons, a crucial step is to show that the measurement scales used are invariant to group membership (Vandeneberg and Lance 2000) – if the same construct is being measured across some specified groups (in this case, generations). To do so one can use confirmatory factor analyses to determine if the loadings for those items on the scale are the same across groups. So in the study above, testing for measurement invariance was necessary to determine if participants in 1976 (Baby Boomers) read and interpret the items (related to the five work values) on the scale in the same way as participants using the scale in 1991 (Gen X), and then in 2006 (Gen Y). The results of the invariance analyses revealed that the work values were assessed equivalently across generations, providing support that any differences across generations were not due to changes in the measurement scale.

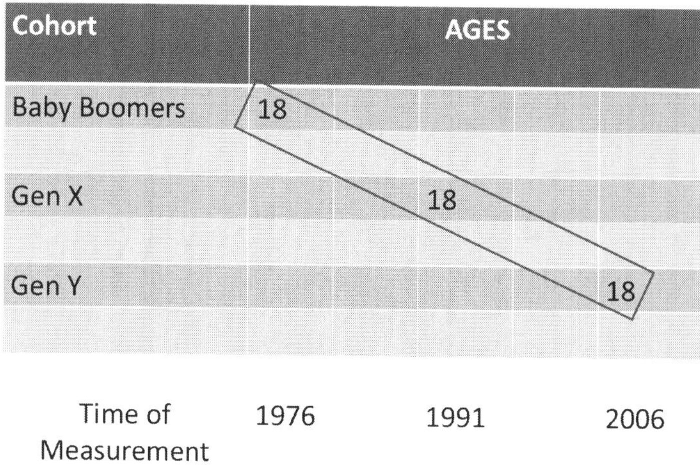

FIGURE 5.2 Time-lag design for Twenge et al. (2010)

Results showed an increase among the younger generations agreeing "work is just making a living" and those saying "they prefer a job with enough vacation time that allows them to work free of supervision." In addition, the younger generations were also less likely to say "they were willing to work overtime," and less likely to say "they expected work to be a central part of their lives." In addition, extrinsic values (e.g. status, money) increased for both Gen Me and Gen X compared to Boomers. These findings provide support for the notion that the younger generation wants more work–life balance but with the same compensation. However, contrary to popular press reports, Gen Me does not favor altruistic work values (e.g. helping, societal worth) more than previous generations. Another interesting finding was that social values (e.g. making friends) and intrinsic values (e.g. an interesting, results-oriented job) were rated lower by Gen Me than by Boomers.

Specifically for this chapter, we further examined whether Gen Me's attitudes had changed since 2006 (the cut-off date for data used in the 2010 study), given the severe recession that affected the country during that time. Many work values did not change much with the recession (e.g. extrinsic, intrinsic). Leisure values were slightly less important in 2011 compared to 2006, with more young people saying they were willing to work overtime and fewer saying they wanted a job with more vacation time, although these items did not return to the levels of the 1970s. Altruistic work values continued to show no difference from those expressed by Gen X or the Boomers. The largest change between 2006 and 2011 appeared in social rewards, with fewer saying they valued a job where they could make friends or be in contact with many people. Because this difference appears in a time-lag design with everyone the same age, it is not that when people are young and looking for jobs they prefer jobs that allow them to make friends and be social. When Baby Boomers and Gen X were young, seeking friends at work might have been more important. With the Millennials, however, the need to obtain social rewards from work is not as crucial. Perhaps these young people who can always be connected to friends outside of work via technology do not feel the need to make friends at work. Unfortunately, this may have negative consequences for the cohesion of teams in the workplace if more young people feel that their co-workers are not their friends.

Practical implications for managers/organizational decision-makers

By relying on time-lag data, managers can tailor their recruitment and retention strategies specifically for this generation instead of relying on the same strategies that worked ten or 20 years ago for previous cohorts of young workers. If differences in work attitudes are due to age (as results might indicate in cross-sectional studies) the strategies used to recruit young workers could stay exactly the same from year to year. With generation or time period differences, however, these strategies need to be changed. For example, the time-lag data suggest that work–life balance is especially important for Gen Y/Millennials. Thus recruiting and retention strategies should shift to accommodate more frequent requests for flex-time and vacation time. Previous generations of workers did not emphasize these values as much when they were young, so strategies and programs need to be modified based on findings using time-lag design studies so that the time, money, and effort focused on such programs is not wasted.

Future research

Future academic research should continue to work on disentangling the effects of age, career stage, cohort, and period, while also recognizing that generational analyses may be more appropriately applied to specific groups within cohorts, such as women and ethnic minorities, and within national cultures. The majority of the research has been focused on the Western cultures (US, UK, and Australia) while the workplace continues to become more multi-cultural. Given that the BRIC countries, combined, currently account for more than 40 percent of the world's population (Rasch and Kowske 2013), generational researchers will need to search for international datasets. While the MtF data are from the United States, there are an increasing number of datasets available in Europe and Asia. In the UK, researchers have used data from the National Child Development Survey and the British Cohort Study (which track the lives of cohorts born in 1958 and 1970, respectively) to investigate a range of outcomes (i.e. Elliott and Vaitilingam 2008).

Another place to look for data is in journal articles and dissertations, gathering data from past studies using cross-temporal meta-analysis (CTMA; Konrath et al. 2011; Twenge 2006). The technique gathers mean scores from previous research through a systematic search of the literature. If a measure of workplace attitudes has been used for at least 20 years among relatively similar samples, CTMA can reveal if scores on the measure have changed over time. An example of a cross-temporal meta-analysis that used a time-lag design involved gathering data from journal articles and dissertations that reported average scores on a measure of empathy in college student samples between 1979 and 2008 (Konrath et al. 2011). In each case, samples are the same age but surveyed at different points in time. Because age is held constant, any differences must be due to generation or time period. Because over-time surveys such as the MtF only ask a limited number of questions, CTMA has the potential to examine a much wider array of work-related (and other) variables using a time-lag design. Future research should exploit this method to examine generational differences in more variables of interest.

Conclusion

Overall, the research literature on generational differences in workplace attitudes is not as sparse as some have portrayed, nor is it extensive, especially given the limitations of one-time cross-sectional studies and the small number of over-time studies. More studies using data collected across time will help us discover a more complete picture of generational differences. As interest in generational differences continues to grow, it will be important for researchers to use a time-lag method to disentangle the differences due to generation from the differences due to age. With a cross-sectional design, it is difficult to know whether today's "kids" have certain attitudes, values, or beliefs because of the external factors (i.e. parents, school, politics, economy, social events, media) that shaped their generation or because that's just how "kids" of a certain age think or behave. Given the money and time that organizations continue to invest in trying to manage diverse generations, it is critical that interventions and programs are based on real generational differences rather than differences that may go away as the employees mature.

References

Cennamo, L. and Gardner, D. (2008) 'Generational differences in work values, outcomes and person-organization values fit', *Journal of Managerial Psychology*, 23: 891–906.

Chen, P.J. and Choi, Y. (2008) 'Generational differences in work values: a study of hospitality management', *International Journal of Contemporary Hospitality Management*, 20(6): 595–615.

Chester, E. (2002) *Employing Generation Why?* Katy, TX: Tucker House Books.

Cleveland, J.N. and Lim, A.S. (2007) 'Employee age and performance in organizations', in K.S. Shultz and G.A. Adams (eds) *Aging and Work in the 21st Century*, Mahwah, NJ: Lawrence Erlbaum, pp. 109–138.

Cogin, J.A. (2012) 'Are generational differences in work values fact or fiction? Multi-country evidence and implications', *International Journal of Human Resource Management*, 23(11): 2268–2294.

Elliot, J. and Vaitilingam, R. (2008) *Now We Are 50: Key Findings from the National Child Development Study*, London: The Centre for Longitudinal Studies.

Johnston, L.D., Bachman, J.G. and O'Malley, P.M. (2006) *Monitoring the Future: A Continuing Study of the Lifestyles and Values of Youth*, conducted by University of Michigan, Survey Research Center, computer file, 2nd ICPSR edn, Ann Arbor, MI: Inter-university Consortium for Political and Social Research.

Konrath, S.H., O'Brien, E.H. and Hsing, C. (2011) 'Changes in dispositional empathy in American college students over time: a meta-analysis', *Personality and Social Psychology Review*, 15(2): 180–198.

Kooij, D.T., De Lange, A.H., Jansen, P.G., Kanfer, R. and Dikkers, J.S. (2010) 'Age and work-related motives: results of a meta-analysis', *Journal of Organizational Behavior*, 10: 212–257.

Kupperschmidt, B.R. (2000) 'Multigeneration employees: strategies for effective management', *Health Care Manager*, 19: 65–76.

Lamm, E. and Meeks, M.D. (2009) 'Workplace fun: the moderating effects of generational differences', *Employee Relations*, 31(6): 613–631.

Lancaster, L.C. and Stillman, D. (2003) *When Generations Collide: Who They Are; Why They Clash; How to Solve the Generational Puzzle at Work*, New York: HarperCollins.

Lyons, S.T., Duxbury, L. and Higgins, C. (2007) 'An empirical assessment of generational differences in basic human values 1, 2', *Psychological Reports*, 101(2): 339–352.

Lyons, S.T., Schweitzer, L., Ng, E.S. and Kuron, L.K.J. (2012) 'Comparing apples to apples: a qualitative investigation of career mobility patterns across four generations', *Career Development International*, 17(4), 333–357.

Mannheim, K. (1952) 'The problem of generations', in K. Mannheim (ed.) *Essays on the Sociology of Knowledge*, New York: Oxford University Press, pp. 276–320.

Mason, W.M. and Wolfinger, N.H. (2001) 'Cohort analysis', in N.J. Smelzer and P.B. Baltes (eds) *International Encyclopedia of Social and Behavioral Sciences*, Amsterdam: Elsevier Sciences.

Meglino, B.M. and Ravlin, E.C. (1998) 'Individual values in organizations: concepts, controversies, and research', *Journal of Management*, 24: 351–389.

Parry, E. and Urwin, P. (2011) 'Generational differences in work values: a review of theory and evidence', *International Journal of Management Reviews*, 13(1): 79–96.

Putnam, R. D. (2000) *Bowling Alone: The Collapse and Revival of American Community*, New York: Simon & Schuster, pp. 24–26.

Rasch, R. and Kowske, B. (2013) 'Will Millennials save the world through work? International generational differences in the relative importance of corporate social responsibility and business ethics to turnover intentions', in E. Ng, S. Lyons, and L. Schweitzer (eds) *Managing the New Workforce: International Perspectives on the Millennial Generation*, Northampton, MA: Edward Elgar Publishing, pp. 222–241.

Rhodes, S.R. (1983) 'Age-related differences in work attitudes and behavior: a review and conceptual analysis', *Psychological Bulletin*, 93: 328–367.

Schaie, K.W. (1965) 'A general model for the study of developmental problems', *Psychological Bulletin*, 64: 92–107.

Schaie, K.W. (1974) 'Translations in gerontology – from lab to life: intellectual functioning', *American Psychologist*, 29: 802–807.

Schaie, K.W. (1984) 'Midlife influences upon intellectual functioning in old age', *International Journal of Behavioral Development*, 7: 463–478.

Schaie, K.W. (1996) *Intellectual Development in Adulthood: The Seattle Longitudinal Study*, New York: Cambridge University Press.

Schaie, K.W., Willis, S.L. and Caskie, G.I. (2004) 'The Seattle longitudinal study: relationship between personality and cognition', *Aging Neuropsychology and Cognition*, 11(2–3): 304–324.

Scott J. (2000) 'Is it a different world to when you were growing up: generational effects on social representations and child-rearing values', *British Journal of Sociology*, 51: 355–376.

Sessa, V.I., Kabacoff, R.I., Deal, J. and Brown, H. (2007) 'Generational differences in leader values and leadership behaviors', *The Psychologist-Manager Journal*, 10(1): 47–74.

Smola, K.W. and Sutton, C.D. (2002) 'Generational differences: revisiting generational work values for the new millennium', *Journal of Organizational Behavior*, 23: 363–382.

Stein, J. (2013) 'Millennials: the me me me generation', *Time Magazine*, 20 May.

Sterns, H.L. and Doverspike, D. (1989) 'Aging and the retraining and learning process in organizations', in I. Goldstein and R. Katzel (eds) *Training and Development in Work Organizations*, San Francisco, CA: Jossey-Bass, pp. 229–332.

Super, D.E. (1969) 'Vocational development theory: persons, positions, and processes', *The Counseling Psychologist*, 1(1): 2–9.

Tulgan, B. (2003) *Managing Generation X: How to Bring out the Best in Young Talent*, New York: John Wiley.

Twenge, J.M. (2006) *Generation Me: Why Today's Young Americans are more Confident, Assertive, Entitled—and more Miserable than ever Before*, New York: Free Press.

Twenge, J.M. and Kasser, T. (2013) 'Generational changes in materialism and work centrality, 1976–2007: associations with temporal changes in societal insecurity and materialistic role-modeling', *Personality and Social Psychology Bulletin*, 39(7): 883–897.

Twenge, J.M., Campbell, S.M., Hoffman, B.R. and Lance, C.E. (2010) 'Generational differences in work values: leisure and extrinsic values increasing, social and intrinsic values decreasing', *Journal of Management*, 36: 1117–1142.

Twenge, J.M., Campbell, W.K. and Freeman, E.C. (2012) 'Generational differences in young adults' life goals, concern for others, and civic orientation, 1966–2009', *Journal of Personality and Social Psychology*, 102: 1045–1062.

Vandenberg, R.J. and Lance, C.E. (2000) 'A review and synthesis of the measurement invariance literature: suggestions, practices, and recommendations for organizational research', *Organizational Research Methods*, 3: 4–70.

Wong, M., Gardiner, E., Lang, W. and Coulon, L. (2008) 'Generational differences in personality and motivation: do they exist and what are the implications for the workplace?', *Journal of Managerial Psychology*, 23(8), 878–890.

Zemke, R., Raines, C. and Filipczak, B. (1999) *Generations at Work: Managing the Clash of Veterans, Boomers, Xers, and Nexters in your Workplace*, New York: Amacom Press.

6

BACK TO BASICS

Is there a significant generational dimension and where does it 'cut'?

Peter Urwin, Franz Buscha and Emma Parry

Introduction

Within the management literature much attention has been paid to generational differences in workplace attitudes and behaviours (Filipczak 1994; Kupperschmidt 2000). Studies emphasize that the concept of a generation in relation to management practice is often very broadly defined (Parry and Urwin 2011). For example, Kupperschmidt (2000: 66) defines a generation as 'an identifiable group that shares birth years, age, location and significant life events at critical developmental stages'. Reviews of the academic management literature (see, for instance, Parry and Urwin 2011) confirm that most studies in countries such as the USA, UK and Australia follow the practitioner literature in assuming that there are four generations in the workforce: Veterans (born 1925–1942), Baby Boomers (1943–1960), Generation X (1961–1981) and Generation Y (born after 1982) (Strauss and Howe 1991).

Despite this apparent consistency across the academic and practitioner literatures, there are concerns over the validity of evidence on which this generational cohort concept is based (Lyons *et al.* 2007; Parry and Urwin 2009, 2011). While generational diversity has a reasonably strong theoretical basis in sociology (Edmunds and Turner 2002; Eyerman and Turner 1998; Mannheim 1952; Turner 1998), empirical evidence for the generational cohort concept is very limited. Empirical findings with regard to the existence of generational differences at work are mixed, with as many studies failing to find differences (Appelbaum *et al.* 2005; Jurkiewicz 2000; Jurkiewicz and Brown 1998; Mahoney 1976; Parker and Chusmir 1990) as those that do (Cennamo and Gardner 2008; Chen and Choi 2008; Lyons *et al.* 2007; Wong *et al.* 2008). This is probably a result of the methodological challenges inherent in the study of generations that the majority of existing studies do not overcome (see Twenge *et al.* 2010 for exception).

First, existing studies are problematic because of their cross-sectional research design in that they fail to distinguish between age, cohort and period effects (see, for instance, Mason and Wolfinger 2001). As Rhodes (1983) points out, age effects are caused by psychosocial or biological ageing. These are different to cohort effects, which arise due to the impact of environment or experiences of those born in a certain period, and would not be expected to alter as the cohort ages. As the authors underline in Parry and Urwin (2011), the majority of studies of generational diversity adopt a cross-sectional design and cannot therefore distinguish whether any findings are due to age, as opposed to generation/cohort effects.

Second, when one considers the theoretical basis for study of generations (Parry and Urwin 2011), the literatures that use Veterans, Baby Boomers, Generation X and Generation Y as generational categories would seem to be in line with the approach of Mannheim and others. That is, generations cannot be defined based purely on age of birth (as in the case of cohorts) and their formation is based on a more complex combination of birth cohort and a shared experience of historical and political events, collective culture (Mannheim 1952) and the competition for resources (Edmunds and Turner 2002; Eyerman and Turner 1998). Taking this view of generations, one can see that empirically a 'cohort' may be used as a proxy for a generational group, as a well chosen cohort may be likely to contain a predominance of members from a particular generation who have shared experiences. However, a cohort is a much simpler and more atheoretical grouping than a generation.

The approach to the issue of generations in most studies is to take pre-defined cohorts (of Veterans, Baby Boomers, Generation X and Y) as representing distinct generations. The a priori assumption would seem to be that there are four generations grouped according to birth year and implicit in this approach is the assumption that the job of proving proximity to historical events, social, cultural and economic phenomena has already been carried out. When we consider the empirical evidence, there is insufficient justification for the use of these birth-year cut-off points, as these four generational categories originate from the practitioner literatures based on anecdotal evidence.

Therefore, in studies that utilize existing cohort categorizations, any evidence that differing values, behaviours or attitudes are not apparent needs to be interpreted carefully. It can mean either that (i) these cohorts are not good proxies for the generations described or (ii) these are the correct categorizations and there are genuinely no differences between generations (generation is not a significant behavioural or attitudinal dimension). The suggestion is that a deductive approach to the question of whether generations exhibit significant differences in values, behaviours or attitudes is problematic, as there is no empirical or theoretical basis for the assumed generational categories. What we suggest is that an inductive approach is first needed to investigate where generational groups 'cut', if at all.

This chapter sets out the first stages of a research project that the authors have developed to begin the process of addressing this weakness in existing research by using historical datasets (repeated cross-sections and panel surveys) to distinguish between age differences, cohort (generational) effects and period effects. Ultimately, the question we are pursuing is, if generational differences exist, what are the generations? A key issue in the research at this early stage is the limited amount of appropriate data (i.e. that which contains responses to questions on values/behaviours; which can be tracked over decades, for individuals of different ages; in either panel datasets, or repeated cross-sections). As a result, the exact topics that form the focus of the following emerging analysis are necessarily 'opportunistic' and range from social capital to vegetarianism.

This may seem rather unfocused, but even covering such wide-ranging issues we are able to show how one approaches the question of generational diversity, without assuming from the start that there are four pre-defined generations. In the following analysis we show how survey data might be utilized in a way that allows us to identify generational categorizations and cut-off points, rather than taking these as given. Also, we should remember that the context for study of generational differences in the marketing literature and within workplace settings comes from a belief that generations are defined by shared experiences within the wider social, political and economic spheres (and that they then 'bring these' to the workplace and their consumption behaviours). A particular focus on employment and consumption may arise from our analysis, but in the initial stages we are interested in a wide range of social, political and cultural indicators, which may show us where generational differences cut – we can then see if/how these translate into differing workplace attitudes/behaviours.

Emerging findings

The analyses presented here draw on two datasets. Data from the British Household Panel Survey (BHPS) are analysed to consider an issue that often appears in the social capital literature, where membership of groups is often put forward as a form of 'linking' social capital (see, for instance, Di Pietro *et al.* 2008). The BHPS began in 1991 and follows the same representative panel of individuals. The first wave consisted of 5,500 households, and collected information on 10,300 individuals. The BHPS provides a starting point for our analysis because it focuses attention on the main methodological challenges we face. Over a period of 18 years we have responses from the same panel of individuals who were asked about their membership of a variety of associations and clubs, grouped into the following categories: Political Party, Trade Union, Environmental Group, Parents Association, Tenants or Residents Group, Religious Group, Voluntary Service Group, Other Community Group, Sports Club, Social Group, Women's Group and Other Group.[1]

We also present examples of an analysis carried out using National Food Survey (NFS) data, which is a repeated cross-section running from 1974 to 1997. The NFS is the longest-running continuous survey of household food consumption and expenditure in the world. The NFS contains approximately 8,000 households each year and members who did the most food shopping were interviewed on household composition and food purchasing. They were also asked to keep a diary for seven days, recording food coming into the household, including quantities and expenditure, and some detail of the household meals. We make use of the vegetarian question, which indicates whether the interviewee (i) eats meat and/or fish or (ii) eats no meat or fish.

As suggested earlier, the motivation for using these two particular datasets is opportunistic – they provide responses to questions on values/behaviours, which can be tracked over decades, for individuals of different ages. In addition, in the BHPS we have a panel dataset and our analysis of the NFS is made up of repeated cross-sections. Findings from both datasets are presented as an example of how both panel and repeated cross-sections can be used to possibly identify generational patterns, with the NFS acting as the focus for more detailed investigation of where the generations 'cut' simply because we have a greater number of years over which to observe behaviours.

Descriptive tables: a simplistic approach

Figure 6.1 presents a descriptive analysis of a set of questions within the BHPS. We create a standardized additive score, which can range from *zero* (for individuals who are not a member of any of the groups described previously) to *one* (if an individual is a member of all the groups listed). Each cell of Figure 6.1 represents the average of this standardized score for all individuals in a particular age group within a particular year of the BHPS. That is, the horizontal axis is simply calendar time/sample year and therefore each column contains data on all individuals from a particular wave of the BHPS. Each row of data represents respondents' age at the point in time when they answered the question within a particular wave of the survey. The average values range between 0.2 (low levels of average membership) and 0.7 (high average levels of membership).[2]

For example, considering the cell in the top left-hand corner of the diagram, we can see that the average standardized level of group membership is 0.4025 for those who were aged 16 in the 1991 wave of the BHPS. Because this is a panel dataset we can follow the responses of this small cohort through time, as they age – this is simply the main diagonal from top left where we observe this cohort aged 16 in 1991; then aged 17 in 1992; then 18 in 1993 and so on until our final observation of their responses when they reach 34 in 2008. Any shaded patterns of responses that move diagonally from top left to bottom right are therefore identifying potential differences between cohorts which could suggest lines of delineation between generational categories.

The darker shaded area on the left of Figure 6.1 includes those cells where our standardized measure of membership rises substantially above 0.5 and the darker the shading, the higher the rate recorded. In contrast, the darker shaded area on the top right includes cells that have values of group membership that are below 0.4 and somewhere in-between are the lighter-shaded cells that range between 0.4 and just above 0.5. It is noticeable that we have two possible dark-shaded 'hotspots' in Figure 6.1, delineated by a large swathe of middling values (lighter shading). We seem to have some consistency of responses within, and patterns of difference between, cohorts as they age.

Age	BHPS YEAR																	
	1991	1992	1993	1994	1995	1996	1997	1998	1999	2000	2001	2002	2003	2004	2005	2006	2007	2008
16	0.403	0.417	0.398	0.390	0.363	0.363	0.370	0.350	0.330	0.333	0.335	0.323	0.310	0.313	0.315	0.323	0.330	0.330
17	0.402	0.411	0.402	0.403	0.390	0.373	0.357	0.337	0.317	0.318	0.320	0.312	0.303	0.303	0.303	0.310	0.317	0.317
18	0.413	0.414	0.413	0.422	0.425	0.398	0.367	0.350	0.333	0.310	0.287	0.290	0.293	0.290	0.287	0.290	0.293	0.293
19	0.427	0.438	0.452	0.461	0.462	0.427	0.387	0.370	0.353	0.322	0.290	0.295	0.300	0.300	0.300	0.293	0.287	0.287
20	0.463	0.472	0.474	0.477	0.470	0.457	0.433	0.407	0.380	0.353	0.327	0.317	0.307	0.310	0.313	0.295	0.277	0.277
21	0.458	0.476	0.483	0.480	0.465	0.455	0.440	0.418	0.397	0.385	0.373	0.343	0.313	0.318	0.323	0.315	0.307	0.307
22	0.477	0.492	0.484	0.490	0.473	0.462	0.437	0.427	0.417	0.400	0.383	0.360	0.337	0.327	0.317	0.317	0.317	0.317
23	0.462	0.477	0.488	0.497	0.492	0.440	0.397	0.412	0.427	0.403	0.380	0.372	0.363	0.345	0.327	0.328	0.330	0.330
24	0.475	0.491	0.496	0.522	0.522	0.465	0.397	0.410	0.423	0.402	0.380	0.380	0.380	0.370	0.360	0.333	0.307	0.307
25	0.487	0.487	0.501	0.512	0.525	0.455	0.393	0.412	0.430	0.415	0.400	0.387	0.373	0.380	0.387	0.355	0.323	0.323
26	0.515	0.519	0.521	0.529	0.530	0.492	0.437	0.438	0.440	0.422	0.403	0.397	0.390	0.398	0.407	0.378	0.350	0.350
27	0.532	0.531	0.533	0.521	0.517	0.480	0.443	0.445	0.447	0.430	0.413	0.410	0.407	0.402	0.397	0.390	0.383	0.383
28	0.547	0.552	0.550	0.546	0.537	0.518	0.487	0.472	0.457	0.437	0.417	0.422	0.427	0.425	0.423	0.413	0.403	0.403
29	0.555	0.552	0.558	0.547	0.547	0.517	0.493	0.477	0.460	0.448	0.437	0.435	0.433	0.423	0.413	0.412	0.410	0.410
30	0.572	0.568	0.562	0.554	0.552	0.525	0.493	0.485	0.477	0.460	0.443	0.438	0.433	0.435	0.437	0.422	0.407	0.407
31	0.577	0.574	0.568	0.557	0.550	0.527	0.497	0.488	0.480	0.463	0.447	0.443	0.440	0.433	0.427	0.413	0.400	0.400
32	0.573	0.582	0.584	0.579	0.568	0.537	0.497	0.495	0.493	0.478	0.463	0.457	0.450	0.448	0.447	0.430	0.413	0.413
33	0.590	0.597	0.602	0.607	0.605	0.548	0.490	0.497	0.503	0.487	0.470	0.470	0.470	0.460	0.450	0.440	0.430	0.430
34	0.608	0.607	0.622	0.614	0.620	0.552	0.497	0.502	0.507	0.488	0.470	0.473	0.477	0.465	0.453	0.443	0.433	0.433
35	0.615	0.609	0.613	0.612	0.620	0.568	0.517	0.508	0.500	0.488	0.477	0.480	0.483	0.472	0.460	0.448	0.437	0.437
36	0.617	0.607	0.614	0.603	0.612	0.583	0.563	0.532	0.500	0.500	0.500	0.490	0.480	0.470	0.460	0.448	0.437	0.437
37	0.618	0.612	0.608	0.611	0.617	0.608	0.583	0.548	0.513	0.513	0.513	0.508	0.503	0.492	0.480	0.465	0.450	0.450
38	0.627	0.623	0.619	0.614	0.613	0.603	0.583	0.567	0.550	0.532	0.513	0.515	0.517	0.502	0.487	0.475	0.463	0.463
39	0.618	0.621	0.622	0.618	0.613	0.610	0.593	0.577	0.560	0.535	0.510	0.508	0.507	0.505	0.503	0.487	0.470	0.470
40	0.605	0.607	0.616	0.613	0.615	0.600	0.590	0.568	0.547	0.535	0.523	0.513	0.503	0.513	0.523	0.507	0.490	0.490
41	0.607	0.610	0.613	0.618	0.618	0.595	0.580	0.567	0.553	0.540	0.527	0.515	0.503	0.512	0.520	0.505	0.490	0.490
42	0.612	0.616	0.616	0.626	0.627	0.588	0.557	0.555	0.553	0.537	0.520	0.522	0.523	0.517	0.510	0.515	0.520	0.520
43	0.625	0.629	0.629	0.629	0.625	0.592	0.567	0.572	0.577	0.560	0.543	0.532	0.520	0.515	0.510	0.503	0.497	0.497
44	0.632	0.638	0.640	0.633	0.625	0.608	0.600	0.588	0.577	0.558	0.540	0.520	0.500	0.503	0.507	0.507	0.507	0.507
45	0.635	0.639	0.648	0.639	0.635	0.622	0.620	0.602	0.583	0.563	0.543	0.535	0.527	0.523	0.520	0.507	0.493	0.493
46	0.620	0.627	0.626	0.629	0.623	0.612	0.597	0.597	0.597	0.562	0.527	0.527	0.527	0.513	0.500	0.498	0.497	0.497
47	0.618	0.617	0.608	0.618	0.620	0.608	0.580	0.582	0.583	0.550	0.517	0.523	0.530	0.528	0.527	0.512	0.497	0.497
48	0.622	0.622	0.608	0.611	0.605	0.598	0.573	0.573	0.573	0.557	0.540	0.532	0.523	0.532	0.540	0.530	0.520	0.520
49	0.635	0.633	0.629	0.621	0.617	0.598	0.580	0.568	0.557	0.552	0.547	0.533	0.520	0.530	0.540	0.538	0.537	0.537
50	0.635	0.632	0.642	0.622	0.620	0.595	0.590	0.578	0.567	0.563	0.560	0.553	0.547	0.547	0.547	0.540	0.533	0.533
51	0.615	0.616	0.620	0.617	0.617	0.595	0.587	0.580	0.573	0.555	0.537	0.533	0.530	0.527	0.523	0.513	0.503	0.503
52	0.610	0.604	0.612	0.611	0.620	0.605	0.590	0.582	0.573	0.552	0.530	0.525	0.520	0.533	0.547	0.522	0.497	0.497
53	0.607	0.611	0.607	0.616	0.613	0.610	0.590	0.565	0.540	0.528	0.517	0.505	0.493	0.510	0.527	0.512	0.497	0.497
54	0.608	0.611	0.630	0.620	0.622	0.598	0.587	0.562	0.537	0.528	0.520	0.502	0.483	0.508	0.533	0.523	0.513	0.513
55	0.590	0.613	0.626	0.638	0.627	0.610	0.583	0.572	0.560	0.533	0.507	0.503	0.500	0.497	0.493	0.505	0.517	0.517
56	0.577	0.597	0.614	0.626	0.620	0.588	0.553	0.565	0.577	0.548	0.520	0.510	0.500	0.493	0.487	0.495	0.503	0.503
57	0.570	0.594	0.596	0.622	0.612	0.605	0.570	0.575	0.580	0.557	0.533	0.525	0.517	0.498	0.480	0.475	0.470	0.470
58	0.577	0.583	0.591	0.598	0.598	0.585	0.567	0.553	0.540	0.535	0.530	0.515	0.500	0.505	0.510	0.488	0.467	0.467
59	0.575	0.577	0.582	0.589	0.593	0.590	0.580	0.572	0.563	0.543	0.523	0.522	0.520	0.522	0.523	0.497	0.470	0.470
60	0.565	0.556	0.567	0.572	0.590	0.558	0.540	0.552	0.563	0.520	0.477	0.490	0.503	0.505	0.507	0.507	0.507	0.507
61	0.547	0.541	0.550	0.567	0.585	0.562	0.530	0.552	0.573	0.542	0.510	0.515	0.520	0.517	0.513	0.510	0.507	0.507
62	0.520	0.523	0.544	0.566	0.583	0.553	0.520	0.540	0.560	0.537	0.513	0.500	0.487	0.498	0.510	0.507	0.503	0.503
63	0.527	0.528	0.546	0.559	0.573	0.558	0.527	0.542	0.557	0.545	0.533	0.517	0.500	0.520	0.540	0.512	0.483	0.483
64	0.522	0.523	0.537	0.546	0.555	0.532	0.500	0.527	0.553	0.537	0.520	0.510	0.500	0.510	0.520	0.505	0.490	0.490
65	0.523	0.528	0.543	0.543	0.547	0.522	0.490	0.512	0.533	0.523	0.513	0.513	0.513	0.530	0.547	0.527	0.507	0.507
66	0.492	0.514	0.532	0.543	0.535	0.520	0.503	0.507	0.510	0.512	0.513	0.508	0.503	0.517	0.530	0.513	0.497	0.497
67	0.478	0.497	0.528	0.534	0.535	0.528	0.530	0.515	0.500	0.502	0.503	0.508	0.513	0.520	0.527	0.515	0.503	0.503
68	0.472	0.487	0.506	0.526	0.530	0.528	0.523	0.517	0.510	0.503	0.497	0.507	0.517	0.522	0.527	0.510	0.493	0.493
69	0.500	0.497	0.512	0.516	0.528	0.517	0.503	0.508	0.513	0.505	0.497	0.505	0.513	0.528	0.543	0.523	0.503	0.503
70	0.513	0.522	0.524	0.538	0.537	0.523	0.490	0.495	0.500	0.500	0.500	0.493	0.487	0.518	0.550	0.522	0.493	0.493
71	0.517	0.522	0.542	0.541	0.545	0.513	0.490	0.493	0.497	0.492	0.487	0.472	0.457	0.492	0.527	0.515	0.503	0.503
72	0.510	0.519	0.538	0.553	0.562	0.535	0.503	0.495	0.487	0.483	0.480	0.472	0.463	0.487	0.510	0.503	0.497	0.497
73	0.497	0.501	0.522	0.538	0.552	0.523	0.490	0.488	0.487	0.472	0.457	0.450	0.443	0.477	0.510	0.512	0.513	0.513
74	0.503	0.498	0.514	0.521	0.538	0.513	0.493	0.490	0.487	0.478	0.470	0.463	0.457	0.487	0.517	0.515	0.513	0.513
75	0.490	0.487	0.510	0.507	0.520	0.490	0.475	0.483	0.490	0.480	0.470	0.455	0.440	0.483	0.525	0.530	0.535	0.535

FIGURE 6.1 Generational mapping of intensity of group membership

If we use this pattern to delineate a cohort of individuals in the BHPS sample whose oldest members turned 16/17 around 1993/1994 and whose youngest members we observe turning 16 in 2008, we would seem to have some evidence of lower levels of group membership that persist in many of this cohort age – the problem is that only a few individuals in this low-membership cohort can be observed up to the age of 30 or 31. At the other extreme, we have a potential cohort of high-membership individuals whose youngest members reach the ages of between 28 and 30 in 1991. Unfortunately it is hard to determine a clear delineation for the oldest members in this cohort, as we only observe large numbers of them from age 30 onwards.

The most detailed evidence of any clear cohort or generational effect regarding membership intensity is therefore for the (light-shaded) cohort located somewhere in-between these high- and low-membership cohorts. However, even here we have problems in defining a cut-off point for the older members of the cohort, as we only observe the youngest members of the cohort at age 16 (i.e. in 1991 and 1992) and need to speculate on the age boundary that distinguishes them from the high-membership cohort. Despite these extensive challenges, even from such a descriptive starting point we may suggest tentative evidence that the following three cohorts exhibit distinctive behaviours that hint at generational categories:

> **Low-membership group:** born after 1976/1977 (that is, the oldest members turned 16 or 17 around 1993/1994).
>
> **Middling-membership group:** born between 1964/1965 (oldest members reach the ages of between 26 and 28 in 1991) and 1975/1976 (youngest members turn 16 in 1991/1992).
>
> **High-membership group:** born before 1964/1965.

It is interesting to note that these categories are not too far away from the categorizations used for Gen Y, Gen X and Boomers, respectively, but this is far from a robust analysis. In order to proceed with this avenue of investigation, we need to tighten up the quantitative techniques that we are using to delineate cohort/generational differences. At present we are using a simple Excel function that considers the highest and lowest values within the distribution specified (0.2 and 0.7 in the case of Figure 6.1) and then fits a grey-scale shading scheme accordingly (giving some indication of high, medium and low values). This is a good descriptive device and one would want to retain the pictorial representation. However, even in cases where there is very little variation in the actual values (from low to high), different shadings would appear – we need some indication of the extent to which there is a statistically significant difference between the different shaded areas.

Developing criteria for a generational 'cut'

To overcome this challenge, we need some indication of (i) the extent to which there is a statistically significant difference between these shading schemes and (ii) we also need an approach that allows for more than three generational categories. Figure 6.2 begins this process by presenting a 'smoothed' data map[3] of the proportion of individuals in the NFS between 1974 and 1997 recorded as vegetarian.[4] For instance, in the top left-hand cell we have zero per cent of those who are 19 in 1974 reporting that they are vegetarian, while by 1981, 0.059 (5.9 per cent) of 19 year olds responsible for the household shop are vegetarian. The major advance from our previous analysis of the BHPS is that we have overcome the limit of having only three categories (which previously forced all shades to be a function of the maximum, minimum and average values in the data and limited the number of identifiable generations to three). Figure 6.2 presents the data as a multi-shaded heat map, where shades are independent of gradients and are a function of absolute values.

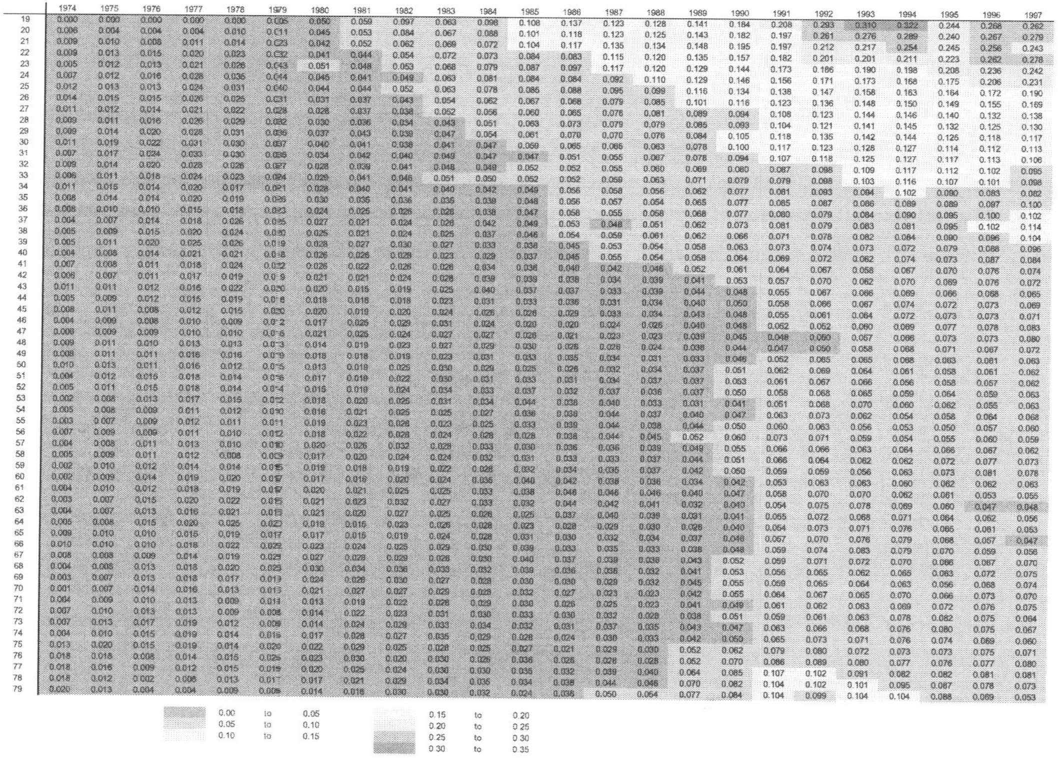

	1974	1975	1976	1977	1978	1979	1980	1981	1982	1983	1984	1985	1986	1987	1988	1989	1990	1991	1992	1993	1994	1995	1996	1997
19	0.000	0.000	0.000	0.000	0.000	0.006	0.050	0.059	0.097	0.063	0.098	0.108	0.137	0.123	0.128	0.141	0.184	0.208	0.293	0.310	0.322	0.244	0.268	0.262
20	0.006	0.004	0.004	0.004	0.010	0.011	0.045	0.053	0.084	0.067	0.088	0.101	0.118	0.123	0.125	0.143	0.182	0.197	0.261	0.276	0.289	0.240	0.267	0.279
21	0.009	0.010	0.008	0.011	0.014	0.023	0.042	0.052	0.062	0.069	0.072	0.104	0.117	0.135	0.134	0.148	0.195	0.197	0.212	0.217	0.254	0.245	0.256	0.243
22	0.009	0.013	0.015	0.020	0.023	0.032	0.041	0.044	0.054	0.072	0.073	0.084	0.083	0.115	0.120	0.135	0.157	0.182	0.201	0.201	0.211	0.223	0.262	0.278
23	0.005	0.012	0.013	0.021	0.026	0.043	0.051	0.048	0.053	0.068	0.079	0.087	0.097	0.117	0.120	0.129	0.144	0.173	0.186	0.190	0.198	0.208	0.236	0.242
24	0.007	0.012	0.016	0.028	0.036	0.044	0.046	0.041	0.049	0.063	0.081	0.084	0.084	0.092	0.110	0.129	0.146	0.156	0.171	0.173	0.168	0.175	0.206	0.231
25	0.012	0.013	0.013	0.024	0.031	0.040	0.044	0.044	0.052	0.063	0.078	0.085	0.088	0.095	0.099	0.116	0.134	0.138	0.147	0.158	0.163	0.164	0.172	0.190
26	0.014	0.015	0.015	0.026	0.025	0.031	0.031	0.037	0.043	0.054	0.062	0.067	0.068	0.079	0.085	0.101	0.116	0.123	0.136	0.148	0.150	0.149	0.155	0.169
27	0.011	0.012	0.014	0.021	0.022	0.028	0.028	0.037	0.038	0.052	0.056	0.060	0.065	0.076	0.081	0.089	0.094	0.108	0.123	0.144	0.146	0.140	0.132	0.138
28	0.009	0.011	0.016	0.026	0.029	0.032	0.030	0.036	0.034	0.043	0.051	0.063	0.073	0.079	0.079	0.085	0.093	0.104	0.121	0.141	0.145	0.132	0.125	0.130
29	0.009	0.014	0.020	0.028	0.031	0.036	0.037	0.043	0.039	0.047	0.054	0.061	0.070	0.070	0.076	0.084	0.105	0.118	0.135	0.142	0.144	0.125	0.118	0.117
30	0.011	0.019	0.022	0.031	0.030	0.037	0.040	0.041	0.038	0.041	0.047	0.059	0.065	0.066	0.063	0.078	0.100	0.117	0.123	0.128	0.127	0.114	0.112	0.113
31	0.007	0.017	0.024	0.033	0.030	0.036	0.034	0.042	0.040	0.049	0.047	0.047	0.051	0.055	0.067	0.078	0.094	0.107	0.118	0.125	0.127	0.117	0.113	0.106
32	0.009	0.014	0.020	0.028	0.026	0.027	0.028	0.039	0.041	0.048	0.048	0.052	0.052	0.055	0.060	0.069	0.080	0.087	0.098	0.109	0.117	0.112	0.102	0.095
33	0.006	0.011	0.018	0.024	0.023	0.024	0.029	0.041	0.046	0.051	0.050	0.052	0.052	0.059	0.063	0.071	0.079	0.079	0.098	0.103	0.116	0.107	0.101	0.098
34	0.011	0.015	0.014	0.020	0.017	0.021	0.028	0.040	0.041	0.040	0.042	0.049	0.056	0.058	0.056	0.062	0.077	0.081	0.093	0.094	0.102	0.090	0.083	0.082
35	0.008	0.014	0.014	0.020	0.019	0.026	0.030	0.036	0.036	0.035	0.039	0.048	0.056	0.057	0.054	0.065	0.077	0.085	0.087	0.086	0.089	0.089	0.097	0.100
36	0.008	0.010	0.010	0.015	0.018	0.023	0.024	0.025	0.026	0.028	0.038	0.047	0.058	0.055	0.058	0.068	0.077	0.080	0.079	0.084	0.090	0.095	0.100	0.102
37	0.004	0.007	0.014	0.018	0.026	0.025	0.027	0.021	0.024	0.026	0.042	0.049	0.053	0.048	0.051	0.062	0.073	0.081	0.079	0.083	0.081	0.095	0.102	0.114
38	0.005	0.009	0.015	0.020	0.024	0.030	0.025	0.021	0.024	0.025	0.037	0.046	0.054	0.059	0.061	0.062	0.066	0.071	0.078	0.082	0.084	0.090	0.096	0.104
39	0.005	0.011	0.020	0.025	0.026	0.019	0.028	0.027	0.030	0.027	0.033	0.038	0.045	0.053	0.054	0.058	0.063	0.073	0.074	0.073	0.072	0.079	0.088	0.096
40	0.004	0.008	0.014	0.021	0.021	0.018	0.026	0.026	0.028	0.023	0.029	0.037	0.045	0.055	0.054	0.058	0.064	0.069	0.072	0.062	0.074	0.073	0.087	0.084
41	0.007	0.008	0.011	0.018	0.024	0.022	0.026	0.022	0.026	0.028	0.034	0.038	0.040	0.042	0.046	0.052	0.061	0.064	0.067	0.058	0.067	0.070	0.076	0.074
42	0.006	0.007	0.011	0.017	0.019	0.019	0.021	0.021	0.024	0.028	0.039	0.039	0.038	0.034	0.039	0.041	0.053	0.057	0.070	0.062	0.070	0.069	0.076	0.072
43	0.011	0.011	0.012	0.016	0.022	0.020	0.020	0.015	0.019	0.025	0.040	0.037	0.037	0.033	0.039	0.044	0.048	0.055	0.067	0.066	0.069	0.066	0.068	0.065
44	0.005	0.009	0.012	0.015	0.019	0.018	0.018	0.016	0.018	0.023	0.031	0.033	0.036	0.031	0.034	0.040	0.050	0.058	0.066	0.067	0.074	0.072	0.073	0.069
45	0.008	0.011	0.008	0.012	0.015	0.020	0.020	0.019	0.020	0.024	0.026	0.028	0.029	0.033	0.034	0.043	0.048	0.055	0.061	0.064	0.072	0.073	0.073	0.071
46	0.004	0.009	0.008	0.010	0.009	0.012	0.017	0.026	0.029	0.031	0.024	0.020	0.020	0.024	0.026	0.040	0.048	0.062	0.052	0.060	0.069	0.077	0.078	0.083
47	0.008	0.009	0.009	0.010	0.010	0.016	0.021	0.026	0.024	0.027	0.027	0.028	0.021	0.023	0.023	0.039	0.045	0.048	0.050	0.057	0.066	0.073	0.073	0.080
48	0.009	0.011	0.010	0.013	0.013	0.013	0.014	0.019	0.023	0.027	0.029	0.030	0.026	0.028	0.024	0.038	0.044	0.047	0.050	0.058	0.068	0.071	0.067	0.072
49	0.008	0.011	0.011	0.016	0.016	0.019	0.018	0.018	0.019	0.023	0.031	0.033	0.035	0.034	0.031	0.033	0.046	0.052	0.065	0.065	0.068	0.063	0.061	0.063
50	0.010	0.013	0.011	0.016	0.012	0.015	0.013	0.019	0.025	0.030	0.029	0.025	0.026	0.032	0.034	0.037	0.051	0.062	0.069	0.064	0.061	0.058	0.061	0.062
51	0.004	0.012	0.016	0.018	0.014	0.016	0.017	0.019	0.022	0.030	0.031	0.033	0.031	0.034	0.037	0.037	0.053	0.061	0.067	0.066	0.056	0.058	0.057	0.062
52	0.005	0.011	0.015	0.018	0.014	0.014	0.015	0.019	0.024	0.034	0.033	0.037	0.032	0.037	0.036	0.037	0.050	0.058	0.068	0.065	0.059	0.064	0.059	0.063
53	0.002	0.008	0.013	0.017	0.015	0.012	0.018	0.020	0.025	0.031	0.034	0.044	0.036	0.040	0.033	0.031	0.041	0.051	0.068	0.070	0.060	0.062	0.055	0.063
54	0.005	0.008	0.009	0.011	0.012	0.010	0.018	0.021	0.025	0.025	0.027	0.036	0.038	0.044	0.037	0.040	0.047	0.063	0.073	0.062	0.054	0.058	0.064	0.068
55	0.003	0.007	0.009	0.012	0.011	0.011	0.019	0.023	0.026	0.023	0.025	0.033	0.039	0.044	0.038	0.044	0.050	0.060	0.063	0.056	0.053	0.050	0.057	0.060
56	0.007	0.009	0.009	0.011	0.010	0.012	0.018	0.022	0.028	0.024	0.028	0.028	0.038	0.044	0.045	0.052	0.060	0.073	0.071	0.059	0.054	0.055	0.060	0.059
57	0.004	0.008	0.011	0.013	0.010	0.010	0.020	0.026	0.032	0.028	0.033	0.030	0.036	0.036	0.039	0.049	0.055	0.066	0.066	0.063	0.064	0.066	0.067	0.062
58	0.005	0.009	0.011	0.012	0.008	0.009	0.017	0.020	0.024	0.024	0.032	0.031	0.033	0.033	0.037	0.044	0.051	0.066	0.064	0.062	0.062	0.072	0.077	0.073
59	0.002	0.010	0.012	0.014	0.014	0.015	0.019	0.018	0.019	0.022	0.028	0.032	0.034	0.035	0.037	0.042	0.050	0.059	0.059	0.056	0.063	0.073	0.081	0.078
60	0.002	0.009	0.014	0.019	0.020	0.017	0.017	0.018	0.020	0.024	0.036	0.040	0.042	0.038	0.036	0.034	0.042	0.053	0.063	0.063	0.060	0.062	0.062	0.063
61	0.004	0.010	0.012	0.018	0.019	0.017	0.020	0.021	0.025	0.025	0.033	0.038	0.046	0.046	0.046	0.040	0.047	0.058	0.070	0.070	0.062	0.061	0.053	0.055
62	0.003	0.007	0.015	0.020	0.022	0.015	0.021	0.023	0.032	0.027	0.033	0.032	0.044	0.042	0.041	0.032	0.040	0.054	0.075	0.078	0.069	0.060	0.047	0.048
63	0.004	0.007	0.013	0.016	0.021	0.013	0.021	0.020	0.027	0.025	0.028	0.025	0.037	0.040	0.039	0.031	0.041	0.055	0.072	0.068	0.071	0.064	0.062	0.056
64	0.005	0.008	0.015	0.020	0.025	0.023	0.019	0.016	0.023	0.026	0.028	0.023	0.028	0.029	0.030	0.026	0.040	0.054	0.073	0.071	0.076	0.066	0.061	0.053
65	0.009	0.010	0.010	0.015	0.019	0.017	0.017	0.015	0.019	0.024	0.028	0.031	0.030	0.032	0.034	0.037	0.046	0.057	0.070	0.076	0.079	0.068	0.057	0.047
66	0.010	0.010	0.010	0.018	0.022	0.022	0.023	0.024	0.025	0.029	0.030	0.039	0.033	0.035	0.033	0.038	0.048	0.059	0.074	0.083	0.079	0.070	0.059	0.056
67	0.008	0.008	0.009	0.014	0.019	0.029	0.027	0.028	0.029	0.028	0.030	0.040	0.037	0.039	0.038	0.043	0.052	0.059	0.071	0.072	0.070	0.066	0.067	0.070
68	0.004	0.005	0.013	0.018	0.020	0.025	0.030	0.034	0.036	0.033	0.032	0.039	0.036	0.036	0.032	0.041	0.053	0.056	0.065	0.062	0.065	0.063	0.072	0.075
69	0.003	0.007	0.013	0.018	0.017	0.013	0.024	0.028	0.030	0.027	0.028	0.030	0.030	0.029	0.032	0.045	0.055	0.059	0.065	0.064	0.063	0.056	0.068	0.074
70	0.001	0.007	0.014	0.016	0.013	0.013	0.021	0.027	0.027	0.029	0.028	0.032	0.027	0.023	0.023	0.042	0.055	0.064	0.067	0.065	0.070	0.066	0.073	0.070
71	0.004	0.009	0.010	0.013	0.009	0.013	0.013	0.019	0.022	0.026	0.029	0.030	0.026	0.025	0.023	0.041	0.049	0.061	0.062	0.063	0.069	0.072	0.076	0.075
72	0.007	0.010	0.013	0.013	0.009	0.008	0.014	0.022	0.023	0.031	0.030	0.033	0.030	0.032	0.028	0.038	0.051	0.059	0.061	0.063	0.078	0.082	0.075	0.064
73	0.007	0.013	0.017	0.019	0.012	0.009	0.014	0.024	0.029	0.033	0.034	0.032	0.031	0.037	0.035	0.043	0.047	0.063	0.066	0.068	0.076	0.080	0.075	0.067
74	0.004	0.010	0.015	0.019	0.014	0.015	0.017	0.028	0.027	0.035	0.029	0.028	0.024	0.030	0.033	0.042	0.050	0.065	0.073	0.071	0.076	0.074	0.069	0.060
75	0.013	0.020	0.015	0.019	0.014	0.020	0.022	0.029	0.025	0.028	0.025	0.027	0.021	0.029	0.030	0.052	0.062	0.079	0.080	0.072	0.073	0.073	0.075	0.071
76	0.018	0.018	0.008	0.014	0.015	0.025	0.023	0.030	0.020	0.030	0.026	0.036	0.026	0.028	0.028	0.052	0.070	0.086	0.089	0.080	0.077	0.076	0.077	0.080
77	0.018	0.016	0.009	0.012	0.015	0.019	0.020	0.025	0.024	0.030	0.030	0.035	0.032	0.039	0.040	0.064	0.085	0.107	0.102	0.091	0.082	0.082	0.081	0.081
78	0.018	0.012	0.002	0.006	0.013	0.017	0.017	0.021	0.029	0.034	0.035	0.034	0.038	0.044	0.046	0.070	0.082	0.104	0.102	0.101	0.095	0.087	0.078	0.073
79	0.020	0.013	0.004	0.004	0.009	0.006	0.014	0.018	0.030	0.030	0.032	0.024	0.036	0.050	0.054	0.077	0.084	0.104	0.099	0.104	0.104	0.088	0.069	0.053

0.00 to 0.05
0.05 to 0.10
0.10 to 0.15
0.15 to 0.20
0.20 to 0.25
0.25 to 0.30
0.30 to 0.35

FIGURE 6.2 Generational map of incidence of vegetarianism (smoothed multi-colour heat map)

The disadvantage of this multi-shaded approach is that our values across the heat map must be user-defined (in this case intervals are defined by steps of 0.05). To provide a better insight into our problem, consider the three-dimensional version of the heat map shown in Figure 6.3. As we can see, the suggestion is that by adopting steps of 0.05 we do not particularly reflect patterns in the data. Rather, what we would want to capture in our delineations is both an apparent generational change through the years studied, but to consider the extent to which such a pattern is significant, relative to the vegetarian 'spike' occurring in the younger age groups in the mid-1990s. In order to examine the extent to which different cohorts are statistically significantly different from each other, we have to compute the associated standard errors around each cell. While the above graphs generated in Excel are relatively easy to interpret, we need to move beyond non-parametric statistical analysis and now take advantage of the functionality of STATA (at the same time retaining an approach that remains visually appealing).

Figure 6.4 sets out the same analysis of NFS data using the STATA inbuilt non-parametric smoothing command; splicing the *z*-axis (cohorts) and then overlaying these.[5] It presents the proportion of individuals who respond that they are vegetarian across the age range for various cohorts. Separate smoothers are estimated for cohorts born every ten years, from the 1920s to the 1970s.[6] Figure 6.4 therefore provides an indication of how we can take arbitrarily defined cohorts (i.e. they are 'cut' every ten years); consider them alongside each other (or 'overlay' them); and then gauge the extent to which we observe one or more of these cohorts constituting a distinct generational category (that is, they exhibit statistically significant differences at various points along the estimated lines).

It is immediately clear from Figure 6.4 that due to data constraints (we only have 23 years of annual survey data) it is not possible to fully follow any single cohort for an entire lifecycle. At best, we can follow individual birth cohorts for a period of approximately two decades – this results in the rather discontinuous picture profile.

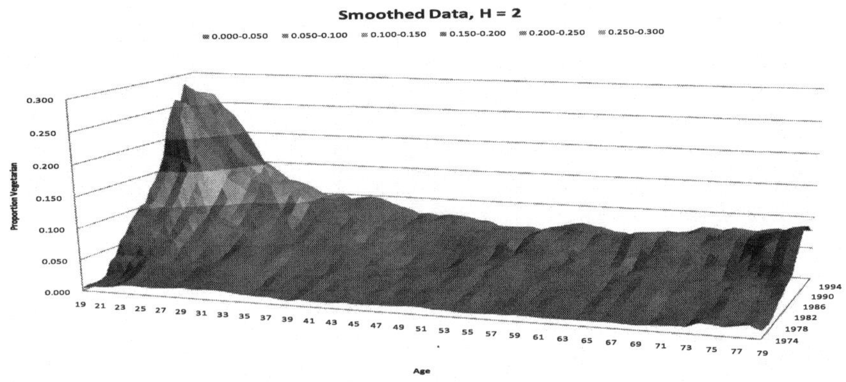

FIGURE 6.3 Generational map of incidence of vegetarianism (smoothed 3D multi-colour heat map)

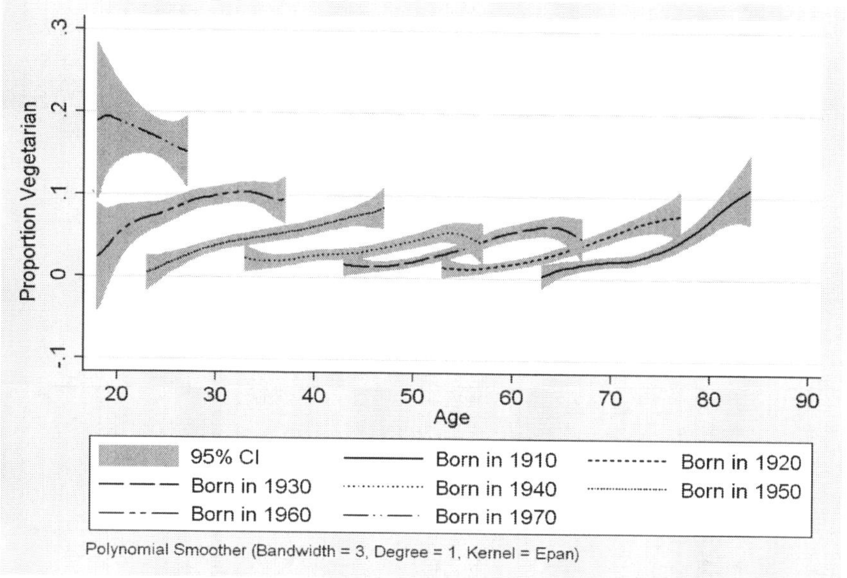

FIGURE 6.4 Generational map of incidence of vegetarianism (smoothed and overlayed cohorts with 95% confidence intervals)

Nonetheless, there are periods of significant overlap for many of the measured cohorts and it is this overlap where significant differences between one generation and the next become apparent. Starting with the birth cohort of the 1910s we can observe that, over the survey period 1974–1997, the proportion of individuals from this cohort reporting that they are vegetarian is relatively low, when they are in their 60s. As the 1910s cohort continues to age the proportion of individuals reporting vegetarianism rises to roughly 10 per cent when aged 80 or more. Comparing this, albeit short, lifecycle profile to the next generation born in the 1920s, the suggestion is that the next cohort follows a remarkably similar trajectory. However, when these two cohorts are aged between their early 60s and late 70s, we can directly compare vegetarianism at the same point in cohort lifecycles. The suggestion is that the 1920s cohort reports (statistically) significantly higher levels of vegetarianism. In other words, when the later generation reaches the same age point as the previous generation, they have a significantly higher proportion of individuals who report being vegetarian.

It is not clear if the rising proportion of individuals in the 1910s and 1920s cohorts that report being vegetarian as they age is due to differential attrition among vegetarians and non-vegetarians at these older ages. It would seem more likely, but there is also a possibility that at such ages individuals do decide to become vegetarian. However, for 1930s and 1940s birth cohorts there is some slight rise in vegetarianism in earlier years, at a (statistically) significantly higher level than the previous cohort, but with some fall in reported vegetarianism as the cohort reaches their mid-50s. Also, it is interesting to note that while the initial levels of vegetarianism seen among the 1970s cohort are significantly higher than the 1960s cohort and the short period of overlap with the 1950s cohort, this is the only cohort (and age group) where we observe a fall in the average levels of vegetarianism in the early years.

Apart from this slight difference for the very latest cohort analysed, there is some indication that differences in vegetarianism in the early years of a cohort's development are most pronounced (i.e. for the more recent cohorts, consideration of those aged between their mid-20s and mid-30s shows the largest gap between cohorts), but in middle age such differences become less significant (for the cohorts that overlap in the 40–50 age groups, there is less of a gap between confidence intervals around the estimated lines). This suggests that cohort effects are predominant in the early years, but then age effects kick in and the different cohorts become less dissimilar in their 40s and beyond. However the suggestion is that, by the time we consider the older cohorts (born in the 1930s, 1940s and 1950s), there is still a significant difference in the enduring levels of vegetarianism throughout the cohort's lifetime, it is just not as pronounced as we might expect in the early years of later cohorts.

These results suggest a pattern of early adoption by younger individuals in each subsequent cohort, but with strong age-effects remaining as the younger adopters within each cohort revert back to the patterns of previous cohorts. Over time, the trend change in behaviour among the younger age group in each subsequent cohort becomes more enduring as they age, and we observe a significant generational change.

As we suggest in the final section of this chapter, this pattern reminds us that the hypothesized differences between generational cohorts are often reflections of more long-term trends in society. Here we observe a long-term trend increase in the proportion of vegetarians in the UK, with 'intermediate' or 'transitional' cohorts (1930s, 1940s and 1950s) exhibiting higher levels of vegetarianism at younger ages, but with more of a tendency to revert back to the behaviours of the previous cohort in later years – it is only with the 1960s cohort that we begin to see a strong generational effect, with much higher levels of vegetarianism in earlier life sustained into mid-life. One can perhaps speculate on an inter-generational transmission mechanism here, where the 'views' of the earlier 1940s and 1950s cohorts do not translate into 'behaviours' for their own household as they age, but work to enforce those of the later 1960s cohort so that the vegetarianism they adopt in earlier years is more likely sustained into older age.

One can see that this final set of analyses has clear strengths, most importantly the ability to identify the point when a cohort exhibits a statistically significant set of behaviours/attitudes to a previous cohort, across key points in the age distribution. However, this approach of 'cutting' is not consistent with the way generations are perceived in the existing literature. For instance, the data suggest that the gap in significance between the 1960s and 1970s cohorts and the previous cohorts is particularly pronounced, but the question then remains of where the intervening cohorts fit within this generational categorization. We suggest that the 1930s, 1940s and 1950s cohorts are perhaps 'transitional' in nature, but it would seem more in keeping with the existing literature to suggest that from the 1960s onwards we have a new generation (with respect to this particular social and economic trend). Clearly a lot of work is still needed, but in pursuing the discussions in this chapter we get a better understanding of the challenges we face if the concept of generations is to be based on a consistent body of theory and empirical evidence.

Emerging conclusions

We start from the general theoretical standpoint that generational difference is driven by a complex combination of birth cohort and a shared experience of historical and political events, collective culture (Mannheim 1952) and the competition for resources (Edmunds and Turner 2002; Eyerman and Turner 1998). However, our approach is to then very much let the data steer the delineation of generational categorizations, rather than speculate on events that may have represented political, economic, social and cultural turning points driving generational difference. The reason for this is simply that (i) the original theory does not provide any insight into the specifics of generational categorizations and (ii) the more recent adoption of the four generational categories cannot be justified on the evidence available and does not (in its essence) take us further forward theoretically. The postulation that there are Gen X, Gen Y, Boomers and Veterans is simply a more specific (unfounded) version of Mannheim and others' suggestion. Even from such a relatively brief consideration of the analysis presented here, there are some interesting potential implications.

For instance, when the literature talks of 'Gen X having attitude A' and 'Gen Y having attitude B', there is a potential to overlook consideration of the more long-term trends driving these differences. When considering the longer-term trend patterns of change, we see (i) the youngest in each subsequent cohort exhibiting changing behaviours (in this case, lower levels of group membership/heightened levels of vegetarianism); (ii) but with less significant differences in cohort effects (as the young in each subsequent cohort revert back to the behaviours of previous cohorts as they age); but eventually, (iii) we see these changing behaviours of the young within each cohort becoming more enduring until a much more pronounced significant difference between cohorts emerges and we can discern generational difference; something that we would claim gives a more tangible foundation to the phenomenon of a 'generation gap' (Inglehart 1990; Quintanilla and Wilpert 1991).

Also there is the potential for generational differences to span generations. For instance, we see quite a decline in group membership among the cohort moving into the age group of between 45 and 60 around 2000–2001. This may simply be a period effect – for instance, suddenly everybody becomes less enthused about politics, but this also highlights the possibility of cross-generational impacts. Rather than differences or generational conflicts, we could have a sudden 'spill-over' of one generation's behaviours to another – the lower levels of group membership seen among the middling-membership generation (who in 2000–2001 were reaching between 26 and 38 years old) could have a sudden impact on the older generation through familial or other ties. The same is possibly happening with generational trends in vegetarianism possibly exerting themselves through some inter-generational transmission mechanisms.

Finally, it is worth noting the need for these next stages of research to recognize the fact that we are treating generational cohorts as being homogeneous despite the fact that identities may be more heterogeneous within cohorts than across cohorts (Dencker *et al.* 2008). Indeed there is some evidence of heterogenity within generational cohorts based on sex (Eskilson and Wiley 1999; Lippmann 2008; Parker and Chusmir 1990), geographical region (Griffin 2004) and education (Schuman and Rogers 2004). Coupled to this, it is quite possible that generational differences are more or less pronounced in different spheres of activity – for instance in the arena of *career and family* they may matter more or less than in the sphere of *politics*. Our approach, which builds an understanding of generational difference from a very inductive perspective, looking at particular groups in society and across issues, seems more suited to accommodate this possible heterogeneity.

In this chapter, our study has focused analysis on two behavioural traits – group membership and vegetarianism. While both of these behaviours are strongly linked to attitudes, in the next stages of analysis we would ideally wish to see how the approach described in this chapter lends itself to data on attitudes (for instance, towards career, education and/or training). However, it is particularly hard to identify datasets containing such information in a way that is consistent across decades. Nevertheless, this chapter provides a useful starting point for developing a methodology that can be used to more accurately identify generational differences.

Notes

1 'Other Group' includes all memberships that do not fit into any of the listed categories and are not community based (ie. their remit/focus is not limited to a local community/region).
2 Because the question is not asked in every wave we have used a two-dimensional uniform smoother with bandwidth 1 to fill in the gaps.
3 We 'smooth' by taking averages around each cell, using a simple two-dimensional uniform kernel smoother, where for each cell the estimated value is given by averaging the values of the nearest M neighbours in both the x-dimension and y-dimension.
4 Where food 'logs' or 'diaries' record that no fish or meat has been acquired for consumption by the head of household.
5 In addition we also make use of a more advanced smoothing technique based on local polynomial regression.
6 Importantly, this approach allows us to estimate confidence intervals around each function.

References

Appelbaum, S., Serena, M. and Shapiro, B. (2005) 'Generation X and the Boomers: an analysis of realities and myths', *Management Research News*, 28(1): 1–33.

Cennamo, L. and Gardner, D. (2008) 'Generational differences in work values, outcomes and person-organisation values fit', *Journal of Managerial Psychology*, 23(8): 891–906.

Chen, P. and Choi, Y. (2008) 'Generational differences in work values: a study of hospital management', *International Journal of Contemporary Hospitality Management*, 20(6): 595–615.

Dencker, J.C., Joshi, A. and Martocchio, J.J. (2008) 'Towards a theoretical framework linking generational memories to attitudes and behaviours', *Human Resource Management Review*, 18: 180–187.

Di Pietro, G., Jack, G., Sturgis, P. and Urwin, P. (2008) 'Measuring the returns to networking and the accumulation of social capital: any evidence of bonding, bridging or linking?', *The American Journal of Economics and Sociology*, 67(5): 941–968.

Edmunds, J. and Turner, B. (2002) *Generational Consciousness, Narrative and Politics*, Lanham, MD: Rowman and Littlefield.

Eskilson, A. and Wiley, M. (1999) 'Solving for the X: aspirations and expectations of college students', *Journal of Youth and Adolescence*, 28(1): 51–70.

Eyerman, R. and Turner, B. (1998) 'Outline of a theory of generations', *European Journal of Social Theory*, 1(1): 91–106.

Filipczak, B. (1994) 'It's just a job: Generation X at work', *Training*, 31(4): 21–27.

Griffin, L. (2004) 'Generations and collective memory revisited: race, religion and memory of civil rights', *American Sociological Review*, 6: 544–577.

Inglehart, R. (1990) *Culture Shift*, Princeton, NJ: Princeton University Press.

Jurkiewicz, C. (2000) 'Generation X and the public employee', *Public Personnel Management*, 29(1): 55–74.

Jurkiewicz, C. and Brown, R. (1998) 'GenXers vs. Boomers vs. Matures: generational comparisons of public employees' motivation', *Review of Public Personnel Administration*, Fall: 18–37.

Kupperschmidt, B. (2000) 'Multigenerational employees: strategies for effective management', *The Health Care Manager*, 19(1): 65–76.

Lippmann, S. (2008) 'Rethinking risk in the new economy: age and cohort effects on unemployment and re-employment', *Human Relations*, 61: 1259–1292.

Lyons, S., Duxbury, L. and Higgins, C. (2007) 'An empirical assessment of generational differences in basic human values', *Psychological Reports*, 101: 339–352.

Mahoney, J. (1976) 'Age and values: the generation non-gap', *Psychological Reports*, 39: 62.

Mannheim, K. (1952) 'The problem of generations', in P. Kecskemeti (ed.) *Essays on the Sociology of Knowledge*, London: Routledge and Kegan Paul, pp. 276–322.

Mason, W.H. and Wolfinger, N.H. (2001) *Cohort Analysis*, California Centre for Population Research, University of California, LA, CCPR-005-01.

Parker, B. and Chusmir, L. (1990) 'A generational and sex-based view of managerial work values', *Psychological Reports*, 66: 947–950.

Parry, E. and Urwin, P. (2009) *Tapping into Talent: The Age Factor and Generation Issues*, London: Chartered Institute of Personnel and Development.

Parry, E. and Urwin, P. (2011) 'Generational differences in work values', *International Journal of Management Reviews*, 13(1): 79–96.

Quintanilla, S.A. and Wilpert, B. (1991) 'Are work meanings changing?', *European Work and Organizational Psychologist*, 1(2/3): 91–109.

Rhodes, S. (1983) 'Age-related differences in work-attitudes and behaviour: a review and conceptual analysis', *Psychological Bulletin*, 93(2): 328–367.

Schuman, H. and Rogers, W. (2004) 'Cohorts, chronology and collective memories', *Public Opinion Quarterly*, 68: 217–254.

Strauss, W. and Howe, N. (1991) *Generations: The History of America's Future, 1584–2069*, New York: William Morrow.

Turner, B. (1998) 'Ageing and generational conflicts: a reply to Sarah Irwin', *British Journal of Sociology*, 49(2): 299–304.

Twenge, J.M., Campbell, S.M., Hoffman, B.R. and Lance, C.E. (2010) 'Generational differences in work values: leisure and extrinsic values increasing, social and intrinsic values decreasing', *Journal of Management*, 36: 1117–1142.

Wong, M., Gardiner, E., Lang, W. and Coulon, L. (2008) 'Generational differences in personality and motivation: do they exist and what are the implications for the workplace?', *Journal of Managerial Psychology*, 23(8): 878–890.

PART III

New empirical evidence about generations

7

INTERGENERATIONAL COOPERATION IN TEAMS AS A DRIVER OF TEAM COMMITMENT AND LOYALTY

Ans De Vos

Introduction

In this chapter I approach generational diversity from the viewpoint of intergenerational cooperation in teams. I thereby consider generational diversity as both a surface-level and a deep-level dimension of diversity. In addition I also include diversity "in the eyes of the beholder," namely team members' perceptions of the quality of intergenerational cooperation in their team. I study team process factors affecting these three facets of intergenerational cooperation in teams, and relate them to outcomes in terms of team members' commitment to the team and their intentions to stay.

The "greying of the workforce," together with young employees entering the workplace as Baby Boomers retire, make generational diversity an important dimension of workplace demography (Wong et al. 2008). As a consequence, interest from management practitioners in intergenerational differences and generation management has increased substantially over the past decade (e.g. Hewlett et al. 2009). One of the concerns by human resource (HR) managers is that presumed differences in work attitudes and values between generations might hinder effective intergenerational cooperation in the workplace (Howe and Strauss 2000). Research on stereotypes employees hold about the attitudes and values of employees from other generations suggests that this might be a valid concern (Deal 2007; Smola and Sutton 2002; Wong et al. 2008).

This concern was also the point of departure for the case study I describe in this chapter. This case study took place in three federal government institutions in Belgium, in which both qualitative and quantitative techniques were used to empirically address the topic of intergenerational cooperation in teams in order to draw conclusions and formulate advice for better managing intergenerational cooperation. The main question was: *whether and how generational diversity was a factor affecting cooperation within teams as well as team members' commitment to their team.*

In this chapter I describe the process we followed to address this question and the lessons drawn from research in terms of implications for HR and team leadership. In addition to presenting the findings, I also comment on the processes developed together with the organization to facilitate intergenerational cooperation. The study consisted of 21 focus groups and a survey conducted among 78 teams (659 employees and their team leaders) – teams in varying degrees of generational diversity. By looking at generations through the lens of diversity and cooperation within teams, I provide a fresh perspective on the literature on managing generations. In what follows, I first briefly elaborate on teamwork and cooperation within teams in general, departing from the literature on teams. Next, I address generational diversity in teams, thereby distinguishing between deep-level and surface-level diversity as well as perceived quality of intergenerational cooperation. I then proceed by describing the case study and a discussion of the findings.

Teamwork in organizations

Teams are units of two or more individuals who interact interdependently to achieve a common objective (Baker and Salas 1997). Teams allow for the completion of tasks that require more than one individual (Bell 2007). With economic and technological changes placing increasingly higher demands on organizations, teams are seen as an important way to achieve organizational objectives. The idea of the effectiveness of teams over individuals is well summarized in the expression that a team is "more than the sum of its parts." Because team members interact interdependently in order to be successful, team members must engage in a number of team processes to achieve collective goals (Marks et al. 2001). Many process variables have been found to play a role in affecting team cooperation and outcomes (LePine et al. 2008). The study addressed four process variables that have been found to be significant predictors of team cooperation: team leader coaching, team reflexivity, communication, and workload sharing.

First, *team leader coaching* refers to the leader's "direct interaction with a team to help members make coordinated and task-appropriate use of their collective resources in accomplishing the team's work" (Hackman and Wageman 2005: 269). Overall, team coaching has been shown to influence team processes and outcomes (e.g. Edmondson 2003; DeRue et al. 2010). Second, I include *team reflexivity* (Schippers et al. 2008), or "the extent to which group members overtly reflect on, and communicate about the group's objectives, strategies and processes, and adapt these to current or anticipated circumstances" (West 2000: 3). Studies have shown that team reflexivity plays a significant role in team performance (De Jong and Elfring 2010; Schippers et al. 2008). Third, *communication* was included. By communication I refer to the extent to which team members openly exchange information with each other about their role, the approach they take, their underlying reasons, and other information that is important for attaining a qualitative team result (Campion et al. 1993). Fourth, *workload sharing* refers to "the extent to which members of a team do a fair share of the team's work" (Erez et al. 2002: 930).

Workload sharing has been found to be beneficial for team cohesion as well as team effectiveness (e.g. Campion et al. 1993). The main argument in this research is that workload sharing produces a process gain, by reducing social loafing or free-riding (Campion et al. 1993; Stewart and Barrick 2000). Research on teams has provided evidence for the importance of these team process variables for teamwork in general. Given our interest in intergenerational cooperation within teams, the study addressed whether these variables affect diversity in team members' psychological contracts and perceived quality of intergenerational cooperation in teams.

Diversity in teams

Team composition, or the configuration of member attributes in a team (Levine and Moreland 1990), is conceived as a factor having powerful influence on team processes and outcomes (Kozlowski and Bell 2003). Surface-level composition variables refer to overt demographic characteristics that can be reasonably estimated after brief exposure, such as age, race, education level, and organizational tenure. Deep-level composition variables refer to underlying psychological characteristics such as personality factors, values, and attitudes. Much of the research on surface-level composition variables has focused on how demographic heterogeneity may lead to differences in team performance (e.g. Bunderson and Sutcliffe 2002; Pelled et al. 1999). Studies have found that, over time, surface-level diversity is less important and deep-level diversity is more important in explaining team processes and outcomes such as conflict or performance (Bell 2007; Harrison et al. 1998, 2002). The category of deep-level composition variables includes a range of psychological variables on which people differ, including context-dependent variables (e.g. attitudes) as well as relatively enduring team member individual differences such as personality factors, values, and abilities (Bell 2007; Mohammed and Angell 2004; Stewart 2006). One dimension of team composition is the team's composition in terms of generations to which team members belong. Generation can be considered as a surface-level composition variable, while underlying characteristics that are supposed to vary with generational membership (e.g. work values) can be seen as a deep-level composition variable.

Generational diversity as a surface-level dimension of team diversity

A generation is referred to as a cohort of individuals born in the same period, who show the effects of one or more discontinuous macro-changes in their behavior, which its members have experienced during their formative period (Deal 2007). A generation represents a unique type of social location based on the dynamic interplay between being born in a particular year and the socio-political events that occur throughout the life course of the birth cohort, particularly when the cohort comes of age (McMullin et al. 2007). Hence, generational differences are conceived as being the result of significant economic, political, and social events people from the same birth cohort experience during the formative years of their childhood (Deal 2007; Costanza et al. 2012; McMullin et al. 2007). One particular setting in which these differences receive considerable attention, mainly in the popular press, is the workplace (Costanza et al. 2012), where generalized differences among groups such as generations are used as a criterion for segmentation in HR practices. In this sense, we can conceive generational cohorts as a surface-level dimension of diversity within the workplace.

Classification of generations

Although there are differences among researchers as to the birth years that define generations (Benson and Brown 2011), some consensus has emerged about the broad classification. Baby Boomers are generally classified as being born after the Second World War and up to the mid-1960s. The second group, Generation X, was born between the mid-1960s and late 1970s. Third, Generation Y was born in the 1980s and 1990s. Today's workplace includes employees with a broad range of ages and generational membership (Costanza et al. 2012). In this chapter I use the classification in terms of generational membership to study intergenerational cooperation in work teams. I thereby do not aim to clarify whether the observed findings are indications of the existence or non-existence of generational over age effects but we see these categorizations as relevant when looking at workforce diversity and studying its implications for management.

Generational differences in psychological contracts as a dimension of deep-level diversity

The topic of generational diversity might be relevant for organizations if it turns out that this surface-level dimension of diversity reflects an underlying deep-level dimension of diversity (i.e. differences in work values and attitudes toward work) between employees belonging to different generations. If this is indeed the case, managers have to take these generational differences into consideration if they want to manage their teams effectively. Although a recent meta-analysis by Costanza et al. (2012) cast doubt on the findings regarding these sorts of differences, writings about these differences are still very common in the popular press. Moreover, observed differences in work values or attitudes between employees from different age cohorts reported in most peer-reviewed studies only reflect an age factor, not a generation factor, with generations simply being a category of employees being in the same stage of their lives and careers (Benson and Brown 2011; Smola and Sutton 2002). The question as to whether differences in work attitudes and values between employees from different age cohorts reflect a "generational component" or an "age component" is timely and relevant from a scientific perspective. On the other hand, for managers, this scientific debate is less relevant. The challenge is rather how to effectively manage these differences if they affect team cooperation and commitment, no matter whether they are the result of generational factors or merely age-related differences. In this chapter, I look at possible deep-level intergenerational differences through the lens of the psychological contract.

The psychological contract refers to employees' perceptions of the terms of their employment relationship; that is, their promise-based beliefs about the contributions they should make to their employer and the inducements they expect to receive from their employer in return (Rousseau 1995). Research on the outcomes of the psychological contract have shown that employees' evaluations of psychological contract fulfillment affect important work-related attitudes and behaviors including commitment, intention to stay, and organizational citizenship behavior (e.g. Rigotti 2009; Robinson and Morrison 2000; Zhao et al. 2007). Psychological contracts are conceived as an individual's subjective beliefs, which are subject to personal interpretations and which are affected by individual characteristics such as personality or work values (e.g. De Hauw and De Vos 2010; Raja et al. 2004) (see Chapter 3 of this book for a more detailed discussion of the psychological contract).

One of the reasons why generational differences in the workplace are of managerial interest is the idea that employees from different generations have different psychological contracts. In part this is due to the fact that the meaning of careers has changed substantially over the past decades and that organizations can no longer offer employment security (Dries et al. 2008). On the other hand, it is assumed that as a consequence of differences in work values and work attitudes, generations differ in the importance they attach to the inducements being part of their psychological contract (Dries et al. 2008; Smola and Sutton 2002; Twenge and Campbell 2008). In other words, psychological contracts are not only affected by individual characteristics but also by factors related to time and context, like generational membership. Generational differences in psychological contracts can hence be conceived as a deep-level dimension of diversity in the workplace.

Earlier studies support the idea that differences in work attitudes and values exist between employees from different generations. For example, Jurkiewicz (2000) found that Baby Boomers more strongly valued chances to learn new things and freedom from pressures to conform compared to their colleagues from Gen X, while the latter valued freedom from supervisors more than Baby Boomers did. In addition, Smola and Sutton (2002) found that Gen X attached more importance to promotion. The implication for managing teams is that when employees from different generations work together, these differences in work values form a dimension of deep-level diversity that might affect the quality of team cooperation and performance.

Our own study used the framework of the psychological contract to look at possible differences between generations in the beliefs employees have regarding the terms of the exchange agreement with their employer. The study addressed whether these underlying beliefs, which are significant predictors of work-related attitudes and behaviors such as commitment, performance, extra-role behavior, and intention to stay (Zhao et al. 2007), differ between colleagues belonging to different generations. Looking at the team level, the question is whether the presumed existence of differences in psychological contracts between team members from different generations also affects the actual cooperation within their team.

Generational diversity in the eye of the beholder: perceived quality of intergenerational cooperation

In addition to surface-level and deep-level diversity, we also studied intergenerational cooperation by including team members' perceptions of the quality of intergenerational cooperation within their team. By adding this dimension, we consider whether and to what extent generational diversity affects perceptions of the quality of cooperation and whether generational diversity affects employees' team commitment and loyalty when controlling for the perceived quality of intergenerational cooperation. Adding this dimension is also relevant given the evidence that members from one generation tend to have stereotypical views on work attitudes and behaviors of members from other generations (Deal et al. 2010). Even though these perceptions differ substantially from reality (Deal 2007), in the workplace these might impact how individuals interact with colleagues belonging to another generation and hence how they experience the quality of intergenerational cooperation.

Figure 7.1 provides a summary of the variables addressed in the study and the expected relationships between them. To sum up, I look at team composition from a generational perspective, thereby including both surface-level and deep-level generational diversity. In addition to team composition I also look at team process variables: first, general team process variables; and, second, the process of intergenerational cooperation.

While generational diversity is a team composition factor that can be used as a criterion when forming teams, the other two facets of intergenerational cooperation (psychological contract diversity and perceived quality of cooperation) are factors that can be influenced by the way the team works together and is being managed by the team leader.

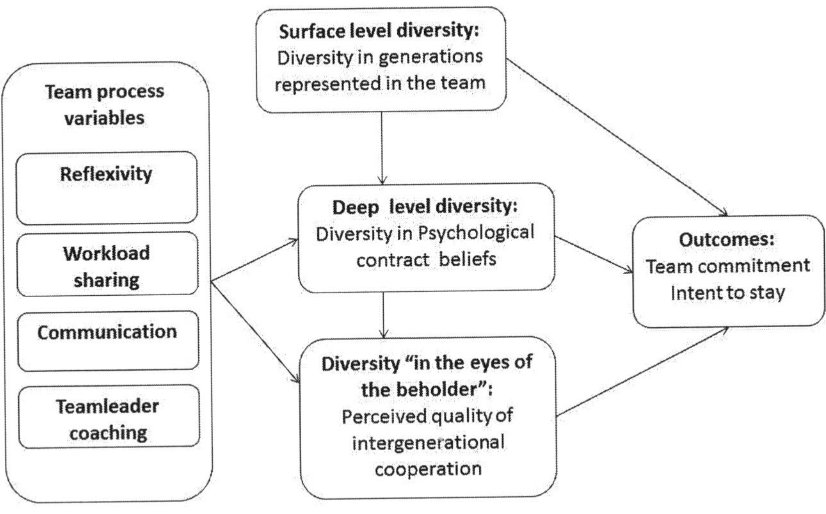

FIGURE 7.1 Model used for studying intergenerational cooperation in teams

The study context

Today the 50+ generation forms 45 percent of the workforce employed within the Belgian federal government (www.pdata.be, accessed 1 January 2013). Baby Boomers going into retirement are being replaced by young graduates, leading to a significant increase of Generation Y employees. Furthermore, workforce demographics reveal that the Generation X population, which can be seen as the generation connecting Generation Y and Baby Boomers, is small compared to both Generation Y and Baby Boom employees. This demographic development is facing the federal government with a series of challenges that reach further than simply anticipating the outflow of a large number of employees. Challenges that were mentioned by the management of the organization included the following: knowledge sharing and exchange of experience between older and younger generations, providing a motivating workplace for all employees regardless of their age; and taking into account a diversity of expectations. In view of this, the HR department aimed to develop an HR policy that stimulates cooperation between different generations in teams and leverages the advantage of generational diversity within teams.

Method

The method followed in the study consisted of three phases: (1) interviews and six focus groups with a sample of team members and supervisors within each of the three participating institutions (see below); (2) a survey among 659 employees from 78 teams across the three institutions; and (3) 15 focus groups in which the survey findings were presented and possible avenues for facilitating intergenerational cooperation were addressed.

Selection criteria for participating institutions

The Belgian federal government is a complex organization that has a very large number of employees, distributed across a variety of institutions. Three institutions were selected to participate in this research, namely (1) the National Employment Office, (2) FPS Health, Food Chain Safety and Environment, and (3) the National Archives. These three institutions differ in degree of geographical centralization as well as types of occupations being employed, but all three have a highly diverse workforce as far as generational diversity is concerned. Teamwork in all three institutions was concerned with different sorts of tasks, but teams were similar in that there was a high degree of face-to-face interaction between team members to get their tasks done – mainly the processing of files and dossiers from citizens related to unemployment or health, and historical data.

Phase 1: exploratory interviews and focus groups

First, interviews were conducted with HR managers from the three participating institutions. In addition, in each institution two focus groups were organized, one with team members and one with team leaders. For every focus group, ten participants were invited to engage in an open conversation on the topic of intergenerational cooperation. This enabled the study's authors to record experiences in practice, bottlenecks, and expectations and to include these in the quantitative research. The two main selection criteria for the employees who were invited to this focus group were variability in age and being part of, or leading, a team consisting of employees from different generations, with a representation of employees from as many different teams as possible.

Phase 2: quantitative study – survey among team members and team leaders

Based on the input from the focus groups and the literature on intergenerational cooperation, psychological contracts, and teamwork, a questionnaire was constructed for a survey within a sample of teams (team members and their team leaders). In each organization the sampling for heterogeneity criterion was used to select teams that differed in their degree of intergenerational diversity (surface-level dimension of diversity).

Measures

All answers were provided using Likert scales ranging from 1 = strongly disagree to 5 = strongly agree. *Team leader* coaching was measured with three items from Edmondson (1999). A sample item is: "Our supervisor initiates meetings to discuss the team's progress" (alpha reliability = .74). *Workload sharing* was measured with three items from Campion et al. (1993). A sample item reads: "Everyone on my team does their fair share of the work" (alpha reliability = .90). *Communication* was measured using three items developed by Edmondson (1999). A sample item reads: "Colleagues in our team are always willing to share information about their work with others" (alpha reliability = .83). Team reflexivity was measured with four items from Schippers et al. (2008) (alpha reliability = .79). A sample item reads: "We regularly discuss whether the team is working effectively together." *Psychological contract – perceived employer obligations* were assessed using 12 items (e.g. career perspective, challenging job, work–life balance) based on De Vos et al. (2003, 2005) (alpha reliability = .88). *Quality of intergenerational cooperation* was assessed using eight items that were developed for this study. A sample item reads: "In this team there is respect for everyone's way of working, independent of their age" (alpha reliability = .85). *Commitment to the team* was measured using a four-item scale developed by Van der Vegt et al. (2000). A sample item reads: "I feel proud to belong to this team" (alpha reliability = .84). *Intention to stay* was assessed using two items, "I could easily continue doing my current job until my retirement" and "I perceive sufficient perspectives within this organization to stay here until I retire" (alpha reliability = .73). The *control variables* were gender (1 = male, 2 = female), employment status (1 = full-time, 2 = part-time job), and team seniority (number of years within the team). Seniority was also assessed, but as there was a strong correlation (r = .75) between age and seniority, the study's authors did not include seniority as a control variable in further analyses.

Sample characteristics

The final sample comprised 659 individuals from 78 teams, with an average of nine members per team (SD = 3.61, range = 3–17 members). Of all respondents, 20 percent belonged to Generation Y (1980–2003), 20 percent to Generation X (1968–1979), and 60 percent were Baby Boomers (1945–1976). Because of the large proportion of Baby Boomers, subgroups were created: "Baby Boom 40" (1957–1967, 31 percent of the sample) and "Baby Boom 50" (1945–1956, 29 percent of the sample). Sixty-six percent of the respondents were female. The majority (49 percent) had a high school degree and 35 percent had a bachelor or higher degree. Forty-two percent had an organizational seniority of more than ten years and 46 percent were members of the current team for more than five years.

Phase 3: exploration and implications of survey findings via focus groups

Although a quantitative survey gives first indications of possible actions, the results are often insufficient for drawing up an in-depth action plan. This is why in each of the three institutions, five focus groups were organized with the aim of further exploring the results and putting them into a framework for formulating advice to the organization. One focus group was held with team leaders, and four with employees grouped per generation (Generation Y, Generation X, Baby Boom 40 and Baby Boom 50). In each focus group, between six and ten employees were brought together to share their opinions and experiences related to intergenerational cooperation, and to further discuss the findings from the survey (Krueger and Casey 2000). Each session lasted two hours. To limit the possible biasing influence of group conformity or social desirability, the Delphi method was used, a structured communication technique (Linstone and Turoff 1975). Before starting the discussion about each question, participants were asked to write down their individual views anonymously, which were subsequently shared in the group, moderated by the researchers, who also collected the written responses and fed these back to the group. In line with the literature on best practices for organizing focus groups, use was made of the "funnelling approach" (Krueger and Casey 2000). The focus groups were started with more general questions to get the discussion going (e.g. "Do you recognize the results based on the questionnaire?" and "Can you give examples to make the results concrete?"), and then gradually went over to more specific questions about the survey findings in view of the research model.

Analyses

Content analysis techniques were used to analyze the data obtained from the interviews and focus groups. The data obtained from the quantitative research were analyzed using hierarchical regression analyses in SPSS (Statistical Package for the Social Sciences). All scales were collected at the individual level. Then they were aggregated to the team level since there was sufficient agreement within teams. The median ranged from .72 (workload sharing) to .83 (commitment to the team).

Results

Significance of surface-level diversity

Interestingly, during the exploratory focus groups, participating employees admitted that age stereotypes might exist in the workplace, but they did not experience these as a factor hindering effective cooperation within their own teams. In other words, the perceptions they had about the work values or attitudes of colleagues from other generations did not affect their perception of the quality of the working relationship they have with these colleagues. Many of them indicated that the overall quality of team leadership was the single most determining factor of their team commitment rather than the composition of their team in terms of generational diversity.

The findings from the survey confirm this observation. The authors first performed a number of analyses at the individual level, across the 78 teams. First, they looked at whether employees from different generations differed significantly in terms of their psychological contract beliefs (i.e. relationship between surface-level and deep-level diversity). As shown in Table 7.1, there were significant differences between generations in terms of psychological contract beliefs. In general Gen Yers and Gen Xers believed the organization had made more promises to them in terms of the inducements they could expect, hence supporting findings from earlier studies that younger generations tend to have higher expectations regarding their employment relationship (De Hauw and De Vos 2010). Also employees' perceptions of the quality of intergenerational cooperation within their team differed significantly between generations, with Gen Y and Gen X employees being more positive about this cooperation than Baby Boomers. Finally, surface-level diversity itself appeared to be unrelated to outcomes. Employees from different generations did not differ significantly in terms of their reported commitment to the team or their intentions to stay.

Figure 7.2 summarizes the main findings from the regression analyses conducted to assess relationships between team process variables, diversity dimensions, and outcomes at the team level (n = 78). The standard deviation was used as a measure of dispersion indicating the degree of generational diversity and diversity in psychological contract beliefs in each team.

TABLE 7.1 Differences in psychological contract beliefs, perceived quality of intergenerational cooperation and outcomes as a function of generational cohort

	Gen Y	*Gen X*	*Baby Boom 40*	*Baby Boom 50*	*Significance*
Perceived employer inducements	4.14 (.57)	4.17 (.57)	3.89 (.63)	3.83 (.67)	$p < .001$ GX, GY > BB40, BB50
Quality of intergenerational cooperation	3.81 (.63)	3.76 (.64)	3.65 (.65)	3.59 (.72)	$p < .01$ GX, GY > BB40, BB50
Team commitment	3.76 (.74)	3.75 (.78)	3.65 (.79)	3.64 (.80)	ns
Intent to stay	3.05 (1.09)	3.26 (.98)	3.49 (.97)	3.32 (1.09)	ns

Descriptive statistics: Average scores on five-point Likert scales and standard deviations (between brackets) are given; standardized beta-coefficients are reported
** $p < .01$; * $p < .05$

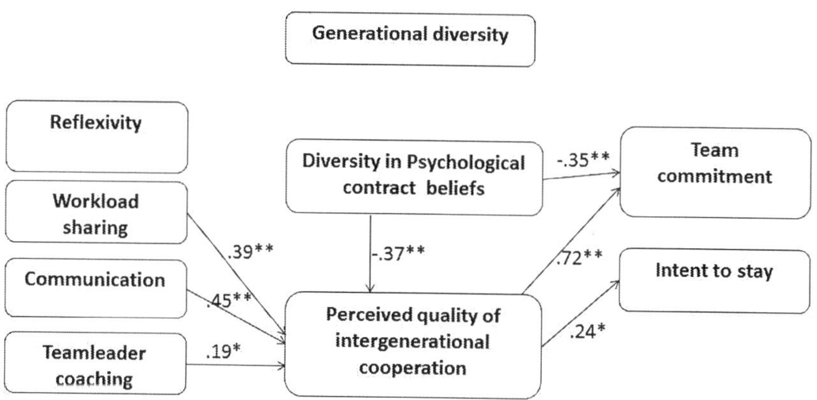

n = 78 teams
Note: standardized beta-coefficients are reported; non-significant relationships are not reported; only direct relationships are reported in the model
** $p < .01$; * $p < .05$

FIGURE 7.2 Results from the regression analyses

Generational diversity: associations between the three dimensions and relationship with outcomes

Regression analyses conducted at the team level reveal that surface-level diversity, i.e. diversity in generations represented in a team, is not significantly related to diversity in psychological contract beliefs ($\beta = .05$, $p > .05$) or to perceived quality of intergenerational cooperation ($\beta = -.05$, $p > .05$). In addition, no significant associations were found between generational diversity and team commitment or intention to leave. Diversity in psychological contract beliefs was significantly and negatively associated with perceived quality of intergenerational cooperation ($\beta = -.37$, $p < .001$) and with team commitment ($\beta = -.35$, $p < .001$) but not with intention to stay. However, when perceived quality of intergenerational cooperation was added to the regression equation, the relationship between diversity in psychological contract beliefs and team commitment was no longer significant. There was a significant and positive direct association of perceived quality of intergenerational cooperation with team commitment ($\beta = .72$, $p < .001$) and intention to stay ($\beta = .24$, $p < .05$). This suggests that perceived quality of intergenerational cooperation can reduce the negative association between diversity in psychological contract beliefs and team commitment.

To sum up, the results show that surface-level generational diversity does not play a significant role in explaining either deep-level diversity or perceived quality of intergenerational cooperation, nor does it affect outcomes in terms of team commitment and intention to stay. Interestingly, although the study found differences among generations in terms of their psychological contract beliefs when looking at the individual level of analysis, diversity in psychological contract beliefs within a team is not related to outcomes of team commitment and loyalty when controlling for quality of intergenerational cooperation. In other words, this element of deep-level diversity does not affect team outcomes – although at an individual level individual employees' psychological contracts were found to affect their individual commitment to the team and intention to stay.

Team processes and generational diversity

Teams reporting higher levels of team leader coaching, communication, reflexivity, or workload sharing did not report significantly more or less diversity in psychological contract beliefs, but perceived quality of intergenerational cooperation was significantly affected by these team process variables. Communication ($\beta = .45$, $p < .001$) and workload sharing ($\beta = .39$, $p < .001$) were significantly and positively associated with higher levels of perceived quality of intergenerational cooperation. The association with team leader coaching was marginally significant ($\beta = .19$, $p = .059$), while the association with team reflexivity was not significant. In other words, those teams in which the team members experienced better communication and team leader coaching, and reported a better workload sharing, were more positive about cooperation across generations.

Discussion

Together, the findings suggest that looking at generational differences might be relevant for managers if they want to consider the psychological contract with their employees at an individual level. It is important to be aware that employees from different generations might place more or less value on certain elements of this psychological contract, as indicated in Table 7.1, just as other factors such as gender or personality might explain differences (e.g. Raja et al. 2004). Given the abundance of research on the outcomes of the psychological contract, paying attention to those factors explaining psychological contract perceptions might be important for managers in order to ensure employee commitment and retention (De Hauw and De Vos 2010). As shown by the study's findings, the dynamics of the psychological contract are mostly an individual-level phenomenon, with potentially important consequences for individual motivation. When looking at cooperation between individuals from different generations, the perceived quality of this cooperation is negatively affected by apparent differences in psychological contracts. So the diversity in psychological contracts that might exist among colleagues working within the same team is a factor that should be taken into account by team leaders, but which can be overcome by ensuring that intergenerational cooperation is good. And this, in turn, can be realized by general team process variables such as communication and workload sharing.

This also implies that, even though generations might have stereotypical views on what drives members from other generations, these stereotypes do not necessarily play out in the way that colleagues cooperate on a daily basis. This is in line with the observations during the exploratory focus groups in phase 1 of the research. The perceived quality of this cooperation across generations is significant and important to address from a managerial perspective, as the study found that those teams who were more positive about this cooperation also reported higher levels of team commitment and intention to stay. Team process variables were significant in explaining this perceived quality of cooperation, not age diversity as a surface-level team composition variable or psychological contract diversity as a deep-level team composition variable. This implies that it is important for team leaders to ensure that they create a team climate in which they pay attention to coaching their team members, to facilitate communication among team members and to ensure that team members share the workload in a fair way.

Validation of findings via focus groups and implications for team management

In this case study, the findings were subsequently used from the survey as input for the focus groups organized with employees throughout the three participating institutions. Per generation, four focus groups were organized (three with employees and one with supervisors), in which their interpretations of the findings and possible avenues for solutions to foster intergenerational cooperation in teams were discussed. This resulted in a list of action points, which were subsequently validated with the HR directors of each institution. An action plan was then worked out and validated by the management committee of each institution. The study's authors thereby departed from the existing HR policies and people management approach to highlight current strengths in terms of facilitating intergenerational cooperation, point out possible weaknesses, and formulate suggestions for remediating/adjusting existing policies in view of stimulating better intergenerational cooperation and adding some new ones. Specific suggestions were formulated to enhance the three team process variables that were found to have a significant influence on quality of intergenerational cooperation: team leader coaching, communication, and workload sharing. Special attention was thereby given to supporting team leaders in their role and actions to better prepare future team leaders in this role of facilitator of intergenerational cooperation. This advice included (1) programming regular team meetings to facilitate communication and address possible avenues for adjustments in work approach and workload sharing; (2) actively stimulating knowledge sharing, especially between colleagues from different generations – thereby considering knowledge sharing as a two-way process; (3) paying attention to competencies developed through experience, both as a criterion for task division but also as an opportunity for mutual learning between generations; and (4) using experience not age as a criterion when setting individual goals, but also including knowledge sharing – both for young and older generations – as an explicit individual and team goal.

Contribution to the study of generational differences

Rather than focusing on generational differences in terms of work attitudes or values, or employees' perceptions of these differences, in this chapter I addressed cooperation within teams and the extent to which this cooperation is affected by generational differences. As teams are an important unit in organizations, and many employees work together in teams on a daily basis, it is important to increase our understanding of what generation management might mean at the team level. By conducting a study on generational diversity from the angle of surface- versus deep-level diversity, I provide new insights into this topic. The approach I followed (i.e. a mixture of qualitative focus groups and a survey) might also be used as an example for other organizations to get a grip on intergenerational cooperation within their context and to draw lessons for their HR management practices.

Conclusion

Managing generations is an important challenge in contemporary HR management. Given the ageing of the workforce and the increasing importance of teams in organizations, studying intergenerational cooperation within teams is a timely topic. The findings suggest that, at least in the organization the author studied, stereotypes about other generations ("the outgroup") do not significantly affect cooperation between generations within a team. On the contrary, team processes including team leader coaching are important in making the team something to unite rather than divide generations. It is important for organizations and team leaders to use these dynamics of teamwork processes to leverage intergenerational cooperation in order to obtain high levels of team commitment, which should ultimately result in high team performance.

Despite disagreements about the validity of speaking in terms of generations versus age cohorts, on a daily basis organizations are confronted with employees working together to obtain organizational objectives. It is the diversity employees bring into a working relationship that is expected to be one of the benefits of teamwork but on the other hand this diversity also brings challenges in overcoming differences that might hinder effective cooperation. The study suggests that organizations should not limit themselves to capturing and managing possible differences in work attitudes or values existing within their workforce, but instead pay more attention to how to ensure the quality of cooperation between generations within teams by making sure that teams are managed in an effective way. This places some burden on the team leaders, but with the positive message that team leaders who succeed in installing a healthy team climate through team processes such as communication, workload sharing, and coaching will also reap the benefits of better intergenerational cooperation.

References

Baker, D.P. and Salas, E. (1997) 'Principles and measuring teamwork: a summary and look toward the future', in M.T. Brannick, E. Salas and C. Prince (eds) *Team Performance Assessment and Measurement: Theory, Methods, and Applications*, Mahwah, NJ: Erlbaum, pp. 331–355.

Bell, S.D. (2007) 'Deep-level composition variables as predictors of team performance: a meta-analysis', *Journal of Applied Psychology*, 92(3): 595–615.

Benson, J. and Brown, M. (2011) 'Generations at work: are there differences and do they matter?', *The International Journal of Human Resource Management*, 22(9): 1843–1865.

Bunderson, J.S. and Sutcliffe, K.M. (2002) 'Comparing alternative conceptualizations of functional diversity on management teams: process and performance effects', *Academy of Management Journal*, 45: 875–893.

Campion, M., Medsker, G.J. and Higgs, A.C. (1993) 'Relationship between work group characteristics and effectiveness: implications for designing effective work groups', *Personnel Psychology*, 46: 823–850.

Costanza, D.P., Badger, J.M., Fraser, R.I., Severt, J.B. and Gade, P.A. (2012) 'Generational differences in work-related attitudes: a meta-analysis', *Journal of Business and Psychology*, 27: 375–394.

Deal, J.J. (2007) *Retiring the Generation Gap: How Employees Young and Old can Find Common Ground*, San Francisco, CA: Josey-Bass.

Deal, J.J., Altman, D.G. and Rogelberg, S.G. (2010) 'Millennials at work: what we know and what we need to do (if anything)', *Journal of Business and Psychology*, 25: 191–199.

De Hauw, S. and De Vos, A. (2010) 'Millennials' career perspective and psychological contract expectations: does the recession lead to lowered expectations?', *Journal of Business and Psychology*, 25(2): 293–302.

De Jong, B.A. and Elfring, T. (2010) 'How does trust affect the performance of ongoing teams? The mediating role of reflexivity, monitoring, and effort', *Academy of Management Journal*, 53: 535–549.

DeRue, D.S., Barnes, C.M. and Morgeson, F.P. (2010) 'Understanding the motivational contingencies of team leadership', *Small Group Research*, 41: 621–651.

De Vos, A., Buyens, D. and Schalk, R. (2003) 'Psychological contract development during organizational socialization: adaptation to reality and the role of reciprocity', *Journal of Organizational Behavior*, 24(5): 537–599.

De Vos, A., Buyens, D. and Schalk, R. (2005) 'Making sense of a new employment relationship: psychological contract-related information seeking and the role of work values and locus of control', *International Journal of Selection and Assessment*, 13(1): 41–52.

Dries, N., Pepermans, R. and De Kerpel, E. (2008) 'Exploring four generations' beliefs about career: is satisfied the new successful?', *Journal of Managerial Psychology*, 23(8): 907–928.

Edmondson, A. (1999) 'Psychological safety and learning behavior in work teams', *Administrative Science Quarterly*, 44: 350–383.

Edmondson, A.C. (2003) 'Speaking up in the operating room: how team leaders promote learning in interdisciplinary action teams', *The Journal of Management Studies*, 40, 1419–1452.

Erez, A., LePine, J. and Elms, H. (2002) 'Effects of rotated leadership and peer evaluation on the functioning and effectiveness of self-managed teams: a quasi-experiment', *Personnel Psychology*, 55: 929–948.

Hackman, J.R. and Wageman, R. (2005) 'A theory of team coaching', *Academy of Management Review*, 30: 269–297.

Harrison, D.A., Price, K.H. and Bell, M.P. (1998) 'Beyond relational demography: time and the effect of surface- versus deep-level diversity on group cohesiveness', *Academy of Management Journal*, 41: 96–107.

Harrison, D.A., Price, K.H., Gavin, J.H. and Florey, A.T. (2002) 'Time, teams and task performance: changing effects of surface- and deep-level diversity on group functioning', *Academy of Management Journal*, 45: 1029–1045.

Hewlett, S.A., Sherbin, L. and Sumberg, K. (2009) 'How Gen Y & Boomers will reshape your agenda', *Harvard Business Review*, July–August: 71–76.

Howe, N. and Strauss, W. (2000) *Millennials Rising: The Next Great Generation*, New York: Knopf Doubleday Publishing Group.

Jurkiewicz, C.L. (2000) 'Generation X and the public employee', *Public Personnel Management*, 29: 55–74.

Kozlowski, S.W.J. and Bell, B.S. (2003) 'Work groups and teams in organizations', in W.C. Borman and D.R. Ilgen (eds) *Handbook of Psychology: Industrial and Organizational Psychology*, New York: Wiley, pp. 333–375.

Krueger, R.A. and Casey, M.A. (2000) *Focus Groups: A Practical Guide for Applied Research*, London: Sage Publications.

LePine, J.A., Piccolo, R.F., Jackson, C.L., Mathieu, J.E. and Saul, J.R. (2008) 'A meta-analysis of teamwork processes: tests of a multidimensional model and relationships with team effectiveness criteria', *Personnel Psychology*, 61: 273–307.

Levine, J.M. and Moreland, R.L. (1990) 'Progress in small group research', *Annual Review of Psychology*, 41: 585–634.

Linstone, H.E. and Turoff, M. (1975) *The Delphi Method: Techniques and Applications*, Reading, MA: Addison-Wesley.

Marks, M.A., Mathieu, J.E. and Zaccaro, S.J. (2001) 'A temporally based framework and taxonomy of team processes', *Academy of Management Review*, 26: 356–376.

McMullin, J., Comeau, T. and Jovic, W. (2007) 'Generational affinities and discourses of difference: a case study of highly skilled information technology workers', *British Journal of Sociology*, 58: 297–316.

Mohammed, S. and Angell, L.C. (2004) 'Surface and deep-level diversity in workgroups: examining the moderating effects of team orientation and team process on relationship conflict', *Journal of Organizational Behavior*, 25: 1015–1039.

Pelled, L.H., Eisenhardt, K.M. and Xin, K.R. (1999) 'Exploring the black box: an analysis of work group diversity, conflict, and performance', *Administrative Science Quarterly*, 44: 1–28.

Raja, U., Johns, G. and Ntallanis, F. (2004) 'The impact of personality on psychological contracts', *Academy of Management Journal*, 47: 350–367.

Rigotti, T. (2009) 'Enough is enough? Threshold models for the relationship between psychological contract breach and job related attitudes', *European Journal of Work and Organizational Psychology*, 18(4): 442–463.

Robinson, S.L. and Morrison, E.W. (2000) 'The development of psychological contract breach and violation: a longitudinal study', *Journal of Organizational Behavior*, 21: 525–546.

Rousseau, D.M. (1995) *Psychological Contracts in Organizations: Understanding Written and Unwritten Agreements*, Thousand Oaks, CA: Sage.

Schippers, M.C. and Den Hartog, D.N., Koopman, P.L. and van Knippenberg, D. (2008) 'The role of transformational leadership in enhancing team reflexivity', *Human Relations*, 61: 1593–1616.

Smola, K.W. and Sutton, C.D. (2002) 'Generational differences: revisiting generational work values for the new millennium', *Journal of Organizational Behavior*, 23: 363–382.

Stewart, G.L. (2006) 'A meta-analytic review of relationships between team design features and team performance', *Journal of Management*, 32: 29–54.

Stewart, G.L. and Barrick, M.R. (2000) 'Team structure and performance: assessing the mediating role of intrateam process and the moderating role of task type', *Academy of Management Journal*, 43: 135–148.

Twenge, J.M. and Campbell, S.M. (2008) 'Generational differences in psychological traits and their impact on the workplace', *Journal of Managerial Psychology*, 23(8): 862–877.

Van der Vegt, G.S., Emans, B.J.M. and Van de Vliert, E. (2000) 'Affective responses to intragroup interdependence and job complexity', *Journal of Management*, 26: 633–655.

West, M.A. (2000) 'Reflexivity, revolution and innovation in work teams', in M.M. Beyerlein, D.A. Johnson and S.T. Beyerlein (eds) *Product Development Teams*, Stamford, CT: JAI Press, pp. 1–29.

Wong, M., Gardiner, E., Lang, W. and Coulon, L. (2008) 'Generational differences in personality and motivation: do they exist and what are the implications for the workplace?', *Journal of Managerial Psychology*, 23(8): 878–890.

Zhao, H., Wayne, S.J., Glibkowski, B.C. and Bravo, J. (2007) 'The impact of psychological contract breach on work-related outcomes: a meta-analyis', *Personnel Psychology*, 60: 647–680.

8

TOWARD AN IDENTITY-BASED PERSPECTIVE OF GENERATIONS

Michael J. Urick and Elaine C. Hollensbe

Introduction

Popularization of the term "generation" in contemporary discourse has resulted in confusion and dilution regarding what it really means (Pilcher 1994). Adding to the confusion is the fact that "generations" have been described in multiple ways in the academic literature as well. In many organizational studies, age cohorts have served as a proxy for one's generation (see, for example, Twenge et al. 2010). Most recently, some scholars have suggested that generations can be understood as identities (Joshi et al. 2010), or composites of values and beliefs with which individuals identify (Finkelstein et al. 2001). An identity-based approach can provide a more robust explanation of generations by shifting the focus from groupings to identities and identification. Thus, this chapter asks the question: how might identity and identification be useful to understanding generations? After reviewing definitional aspects of generations, we draw on a cross-generational qualitative study to explore generations, identity, and identification. Our study contributes to understanding "generation" by elaborating four ways in which individuals relate to generations through an identity framework: strong identities (in which generational categories are perceived to possess unique and identifiable traits), identification (in which individuals strongly define themselves as a member of a particular generational category and its perceived traits), disidentification (in which individuals state that they do not define themselves by a particular generational category), and de-prioritization (in which individuals place their generation low on a list of possible identities by which they define themselves).

Definitions of generations

Generations have become a common topic for popular business publications and corporate training events (Costanza et al. 2012), despite no clear agreement on the definition of generations (Joshi et al. 2011; Parry and Urwin 2011). Joshi and colleagues (2011) note several ways that generations might be understood in an organizational context: collective consciousness, genealogy, life stage, and biological age, which we outline below. However, as will be shown, each definition has drawbacks.

First, *collective consciousness* suggests that a generation is created when a group of individuals experience the same (often large-scale) historical event, which is assumed to impact a group of individuals who are subjected to it in the same way (Mannheim 1970). However, a problem with this definition is that psychological and emotional development rates are not the same across everyone who shares a historical event; individuals experiencing the same event may vary in their awareness of (or caring about) the event. *Genealogy* refers to kinship or lineage. In a business context, genealogy can pertain to generational succession within particular organizational roles, such as successive CEOs. However, exploring generation as genealogy is difficult given that each organization has unique generational groupings, limiting generalizability. *Life stage* proposes that a generation is comprised of a group of individuals who all reach a level of maturity at the same time. In a business context, life stage refers to groups of individuals achieving milestones at a particular time, e.g. organizational entry, promotion, etc. Once again, a drawback is that this definition assumes social groupings unique to an organization. Finally, *biological age* is the most common definition of generation used by researchers (Costanza et al. 2012); generations are often understood by age groupings, such as Generation Y, Generation X, Baby Boomers, and Veterans (Smola and Sutton 2002; Society for Human Resource Management 2005). A problem with this definition is that it assumes that traits exist within (and differences between) individuals of certain age groupings with little consideration of situational factors. That is, situational factors such as upbringing (e.g. values deriving from the way an individual was raised) or workplace characteristics (e.g. the work environment or industry) may influence the way an individual behaves more than his or her biological age does.

An alternative to the above definitions is to view generations through an identity framework. According to Joshi et al. (2010: 393), generational identities are "an individual's knowledge that he or she belongs to a generational group/role, together with some emotional and value significance to him or her of this group/role membership." With this framework, generation is based on the way in which individuals define themselves (or others) by drawing on their membership in various social groupings that have significance to them. Thus, unlike other definitions, it is not confined to particular events, roles, cohorts, or age groups. Individuals can draw upon multiple aspects in defining generation and incorporating it into their self-definitions. Also, as will be shown later in this chapter, individuals often discuss aspects of belonging and self-definition when describing generation, increasing its importance and relevancy. Finally, understanding generations as social identities allows researchers to discuss the emergence of generational in- and out-groups and how they form, as social identities are pivotal in the development of inter-group relations inside and outside organizations (Hogg et al. 2012).

Generations as social identities

A key feature in Joshi et al.'s (2010) definition of generational identity is the word "membership." Membership has been explained by social identity and self-categorization theories, which state that people seek to classify themselves (Tajfel and Turner 1985) and perceive identification or oneness with a group (Ashforth and Mael 1989). Generations can be seen as social identities, or "that part of an individual's self-concept which derives from his knowledge of his *membership* in a social group (or groups) together with the value and emotional significance attached to that *membership*" (Tajfel 1978: 63; italics added). Thus, individuals might be likely to identify closely with a particular generation as a result of seeing membership of a certain group as being consistent with their views of who they are as a person. For example, when defining themselves, individuals could draw on an age group in which collective memories are shared (age-based generation identity); this membership category could therefore become the basis of their definition of generation.

Individuals can also identify with roles (rather than just with collectives) (Ashforth et al. 2008; Sluss and Ashforth 2007). When individuals draw on relationships with those who have preceded or succeeded them in a particular role (genealogy-based generation identity) in defining themselves, this membership category forms the basis for their definition of generation. Finally, when individuals draw on a set of organizational experiences and outcomes that they share with a group of new recruits in an organization (life stage-based generation identity) (Ashforth and Mael 1989; Brickson 2000), this membership forms their generational definition.

Such social identification stems from several things including the categorization of individuals as members of certain groups or roles; the distinctiveness and prestige of the individual's group or role (known as the in-group); and the recognition and salience of other different non-overlapping groups or roles (known as the out-groups) (Ashforth and Mael 1989). Identification occurs when an individual values a group or role and perceives it as contributing to a sense of self. Because the attachment of value and emotion to a group or role is part of identification (Ashforth et al. 2008), individuals may perceive similar values between generational members and themselves, which will continue to make their identification with a generation stronger. If one highly identifies with the group or role, the individual will readily draw on it as an identity in defining self (Haslam 2004).

With regard to generations, individuals often use socially accepted generational categories (such as Baby Boomer or Generation X designations) to identify with and define self. From these categories, individuals can group themselves and others into certain generational designations. Self-categorization theory (Ashforth et al. 2008) postulates that such categorization fulfills two basic human needs: inclusion and differentiation (Brewer and Brown 1998). It is related to social identity theory because both theories have been used to explain one's concern for membership in social groups and comparisons individuals make between in- and out-group members. In sum, people classify themselves (and others) into generational groups as a result of perceived oneness with the thoughts, values, and stereotypes popularly associated with members of particular groups.

It should also be noted that individuals can perceive a psychological bond (or identification) with a group or role even in the absence of physical contact (Deaux 1996). As an example, an individual may closely identify with the prototypical characteristics of a particular generation yet not have much interaction in the workplace with others in that generation. As Mannheim (1970) notes, even though there may not be a close personal social bond between members of generations, individuals may identify with a generation because of a shared consciousness stemming from similar experiences within a larger social group (i.e. society). From this discussion, theory suggests the usefulness of viewing the concept of generation as an identity. We now draw on a study of generation identity and identification with the goal of better understanding and illustrating these concepts.

A study of generation identity and identification

To examine generation through an identity framework, we conducted a qualitative study in which we began by asking a sample of professionals diverse in age, occupational role, industry experience, educational level, gender, length in the workforce, and career stage to tell us to what generation they belonged. The professionals we studied were drawn from two different pools: a young professional sample participating in a leadership training program conducted by the Chamber of Commerce in a large Midwestern city; and a group of mature professionals who volunteer at a not-for-profit small business consulting organization in a Mid-Atlantic city.

The first sample was comprised of 28 participants with the age range of 24 through 35 and with 2–18 years in the workforce. Industries and jobs represented included human resources, higher education, government, finance, legal, and marketing among others. The highest level of education varied from bachelor's degree to doctorate. The second sample was comprised of 32 participants with the age range of 55 through 84 and with 25–60 years in the workforce. Industries and jobs represented included healthcare, engineering, manufacturing, procurement, clergy, and retail among others. The highest level of education varied from some college to doctorate. We deliberately chose these two samples (an older and a younger group) for two reasons. First, individuals of these ages have been understudied in generations research as much of the extant literature has focused on what is termed Generation X and the Baby Boomer generation, which are widely classified as having members with ages between 36 and 54 (the excluded ages in this study). The second reason for choosing these samples is that these groups represent bookend generations currently in the workforce: one is the source of most new job entrants and the other the source of significant cumulative organizational knowledge. As such, understanding these groups' perspectives is particularly important as we view their perspectives to be both interesting and insightful in gaining a broader understanding of generational phenomena.

In total, we conducted 60 semi-structured interviews (approximately one hour each) with members of our samples, and our interview protocol included questions regarding our participants' perceptions of and experiences with generations. Examples of some of our questions include:

- When someone says the word "generation," what do you think of?
- What does this word mean to you?
- What are some ways to describe your generation?
- Does this fit or not fit you?
- What do you believe are some differences between generations?
- What are some similarities?

In our interviews, we deliberately did not define the term "generation" nor did we suggest that generations could be identities.

Our interviews were professionally transcribed, and we coded and analyzed them using a grounded theory approach (Strauss and Corbin 1998). Because the interviews were semi-structured, details of each conversation varied, though some common questions were asked of all interviewees. Therefore, though we had some common questions, there was ample opportunity to probe on interesting concepts and allow interviewees to highlight concepts that they felt were important regarding certain phenomena, allowing ideas and themes to emerge in the interviews. We also analyzed data concurrently with interviewing to ensure we could follow up in subsequent interviews on interesting emergent themes.

To analyze the data in each interview, we used a two-step, fine coding system in which two coders worked independently and then cooperatively in order to validate themes and minimize bias. In the process that we used, both researchers identified relevant themes (called codes) independently from the data to build a dictionary of codes that served as a record and document of their precise meanings. Then, transcripts were discussed in cooperative meetings at which time the independent codes were negotiated, explained, and agreed upon in order to assign a final set of codes for each transcript. This approach models that of others who have used grounded theory techniques (e.g. Ashforth et al. 2007; Corley and Gioia 2004; Kreiner et al. 2006). Following this process, we then used the NVivo 10 software to enter all codes, perform searches of text, and analyze relationships between codes.

Findings

In the analysis of our interviews, we coded many passages related to generation identity and identification with generations. Major themes that emerged from our interviews include: generations as strong identities; identification with generation identities (including age-based generation identities); and disidentification with and de-prioritizing of generation identities.

Generations as strong identities

The term "identity" implies a self-referential description that answers the questions "who am I?" (individual identity) or "who are we?" (collective identity) (Ashforth et al. 2008). As mentioned earlier, individuals draw on group membership in developing a sense of who they are (Tajfel and Turner 1985). In order for an individual's identity to be influenced by a "group," that group must have features that resonate with an individual's beliefs and values. Interestingly, in our study, we found that participants perceived generations as having unique identities, which in some cases were perceived to be quite strong (i.e. clear, easily recognizable). The quote below suggests that Generation X,[1] for example, does not have a clear identity, while others do.

> I almost think of [Generation X] as being a generation without a great sense of identity – just like the name Generation X. The Veterans generation has a clearly defined historical implication and the Baby Boomers of building our country into the modern US that we know today, whereas Generation X, I don't think of like that. There's not a major historical event that I wrap around that generation or identify with that generation.
>
> (Male, age 26)

In this participant's view, the Veteran and Baby Boomer generations have clearer identities than does Generation X due to being anchored to major historical events. This participant draws on multiple categories in this passage (e.g. age-based categories and events), in framing his generation definition through an identity lens. The larger point, however, is that from his perspective, at least some of the popular generational designations have clear identities.

As another example of younger generational categories not having clear identities, one older male participant noted: "Generation X and Generation Y are man-made identities. I recognize them but I don't really accept those designations". This quote reinforces the idea that popular categorizations of generations are a collection of labels that, though "man-made," are recognizable social groupings. Though this particular participant does not accept the identities, he recognizes them all the same.

While we included the latter quote as an interesting exception, most participants in our study were able to clearly articulate traits and characteristics associated with generation identities. For example, some common descriptors of "younger generations"[2] included "entitled," "me-focused," and "short term-oriented." Unlike the perceived identities of older generations, which were often based on particular events, the perceived identities of younger generations were most often based on stereotypical traits or characteristics that members of the groups were often assumed to possess, even though recent research suggests that many of these traits are not supported by clear evidence (Costanza et al. 2012; Parry and Urwin 2011). Therefore, with regard to at least some generation identities, things that people might *believe* to be a defining feature of a generation may, in fact, be based on perceptual errors.

To summarize, participants reported various aspects of particular groups as defining of those groups. We provided examples of this when our participants explicitly labeled generations as identities (even if the groupings or associated stereotypes were not agreed upon). Identities of generations have been reinforced either through perceptions (or misperceptions) of specific traits, behaviors, or linkages to historic events. However, we also noted that some (primarily younger) generational groupings did not have as strong or recognizable identities as others. Based on the above discussion, we propose:

> **P1:** Generations are perceived as having identities that vary in strength (clarity or recognizability).

Next we will move from how individuals define generations as identities to how individuals draw on generation identities to form their own identity.

Identification with generations

Identification occurs when individuals attach part of their self-definition to a larger group. They perceive themselves as having characteristics similar to the prototypical characteristics of that group (Ashforth et al. 2008; Ashforth and Mael 1989). When asked to discuss their definitions of generations, some participants in our study noted that generations are groups with which individuals can identify or find a connection. Consider, for example, the following quote:

> Well, it's [generation] what you understand and what you can identify with in life. It's the place you were at that time. The place can be where you grew up. The place can be where you raised your children. The place can be where you go to church. The place can also be history.
>
> (Female, age 76)

Note here that, according to this participant, identification with a generation need not be influenced only by biological age or historic events. Though this quote includes the latter membership category, it includes many others, including physical location, as a basis for identifying with a generation. This makes sense when considering whether or not similar generational categorizations exist in different geographic regions (e.g. the United States and China) as generational perceptions, generational groupings, generational characteristics, and even the definition of the word "generation" differs based on physical location. Additionally, it is often assumed that generations are based on formative years or when an individual "grew up." While the above participant mentions this basis, she mentions many other sources as well.

However, an example in which a participant relates to a generation because of when he grew up (in an era of technology usage) is noted below:

> I belong to Generation Y… it's [technology] just the kind of language that we speak because all of these things developed right as we were at the age – probably 12 or 13 – where we could get online at home. So, I think as these technologies were developing, we were developing with them.
>
> (Male, age 25)

In his response, this interviewee clearly links his perception that Generation Y is adept at using technology with himself; he identifies with this generation because he is also good with technology. Note the regular usage of the word "we" when discussing Generation Y as further evidence of this participant's identification. Our participants regularly discussed various traits or collective characteristics they associated with particular generations, as well as the extent to which they accepted and internalized those traits and characteristics.

To summarize the above discussion, individuals can identify with generations. If a generational category has prototypical characteristics that are appealing or familiar, individuals draw on these characteristics in defining themselves. In our interviews we consistently noted instances in which individuals clearly stated that they identified or connected with a particular generation. Therefore, we propose:

> **P2:** Individuals' identities are informed by perceived traits and characteristics of a generation through identification with those traits and characteristics.

Based on the prevalence of the literature suggesting age as a basis for defining generations (Costanza et al. 2012; Joshi et al. 2011), one might assume that age would also be a basis for identifying with a particular generation. However, some of our interviewees indicated that they do *not* identify with their particular birth-year generation or that they identify with a generation *other* than the one into which they were born. In other words, they viewed their generation as purely an identity-based (rather than a chronologically based) grouping. As an example of alternative (non-birth-year) generation identification, the participant in the quote below has a biological age suggesting Generation Y; however, she identifies instead with Generation X.

> I think in terms of ideology or emotionally I feel more connected to Generation X because I had older siblings; so, I picked up on their cultural and social cues … And then Generation Y… the thing I don't identify with is the sense of entitlement. I don't feel like I'm entitled to certain things in the workplace.
>
> (Female, age 30)

As can be seen in this quote, even though this individual understands herself as being part of an age-based generational grouping (Generation Y), she does not feel closely identified with its assumed characteristics. Rather, she identifies with another generational grouping (Generation X). Thus, in some cases, knowledge of *other* generational groupings' perceived characteristics allows individuals to identify with generational groupings *other than* what one's biological age might suggest. Therefore, we propose:

> **P3:** Individuals' identities can be informed through identification with any generation (not necessarily one that corresponds with biological age).

Disidentification with and de-prioritizing of generation identities

Similar to identification with a non-age-based generation, individuals may also *dis*identify with a generation. Disidentification is when an individual defines oneself as *not* having the same attributes that he or she believes define a particular group (Elsbach and Bhattacharya 2001). We saw this phenomenon in statements in which individuals criticized, rejected, or disavowed aspects of a generation into which they saw themselves falling (often with regard to their biological age). In many cases, interviewees made statements along the lines of "that's my generation, but not me." The following is an example in which a participant suggests that his generation is known for being poor with technology but he is not – thereby disidentifying with this generational feature.

> You're going to have a lot of people of my generation who won't touch a computer. I was an accountant so I had to get heavily into the use of Excel and some of the products that came in before that.
>
> (Male, age 69)

This participant, who describes his generation as "people … who won't touch a computer," describes how he, in fact, was engaged "heavily" in technology. He was not alone with his statement in distancing himself from a trait that some would perceive to be a characteristic of his generation. In our analysis, we saw many instances in which participants disidentified with their generation on the basis of level of laziness, job performance, community involvement, and other characteristics. In every instance, participants would state that their *generation* behaved in a certain manner but *they* did not. As an additional example, in the quote below, a member of an older generation disidentifies from her generation because she perceives members do not respect younger colleagues.

> Just because a person's young, that doesn't mean they should be less respected. They don't always understand the nature of life, and therefore there's no reason for us to assume that they do, so you have to be rather gentle about it …

> Let the younger person ask questions and encourage them to ask questions. Sometimes the older person lays down laws, "This is it," whether it's the boss or [not] … I think the older person has to understand that the younger person is going to stumble, just as we did, and that's okay. That's a part of growing.
>
> (Female, age 78)

This older participant criticizes her generation for not supporting, mentoring, or respecting younger generations. Throughout our conversation with her, though, she clearly provided examples of how she personally did support and attempt to understand those in a younger generation, thus disidentifying with her perception of her generation.

In summary, generation identities can be so well recognized that individuals might acknowledge their prototypical traits, yet distance themselves from these characteristics. The two examples highlighted above illustrate instances in which participants disidentified with certain perceived traits of their age-based generation. Hence, we propose:

> **P4a:** Individuals may choose to disidentify with an age-based generation by emphasizing characteristics that run counter to common perceptions of it.

Finally, in some cases participants established a hierarchy of identities, valuing some memberships more than others. For example, in this quote, a participant describes how he would feel if someone criticized his generation: "If your entire self-worth is wrapped up in what your generation is then you're going to take that criticism much more personally, but I don't think most people only define themselves by what year they were born" (male, age 33).

From this quote, we again see that one's generation is but one of potentially many ways in which a person might define himself. In his response, this participant places generation low on the list of things important to who he is. Thus, by establishing an identity hierarchy, individuals may disavow association with a generation's perceived features in lieu of other more valued identities.

Similarly, another participant stated:

> When I think of me and all the boxes I'd put myself in to describe me it's not my generation. There're so many more. So I guess it [criticism] wouldn't affect me as much because I don't concern myself with Gen Y or anything like that.
>
> (Female, age 28)

Here, the participant again mentions her generation as being less important than other "boxes I'd put myself in to describe me." Additionally, though, she is clear about distancing herself from (not being concerned about) Generation Y.

As suggested in the literature on social identity theory, individuals do not solely define themselves by one group in which they belong. In other words, individuals maintain a variety of social and personal identities on which they draw to create their concept of self. According to Kreiner et al. (2006), personal identity boundaries can overlap with those of group identities and individuals pull from multiple groups to which they belong in order to create a holistic understanding of their identity – in effect prioritizing some, but deprioritizing others, creating a hierarchy. As illustrated in the above quotes, some participants state that they do not draw upon their generation at all to define themselves. Therefore, we propose:

> **P4b:** Individuals establish a hierarchy of identities and may choose to de-prioritize an age-based generation identity by distancing themselves from generational labels or prototypical characteristics.

From the above quotes and analysis, it is clear that many of our interviewees included membership in particular generations in their self-definitions. In some cases, they discussed generation as a strong identity, identified with generations (though not necessarily age-based ones), or chose to disidentify with or de-prioritize generation as part of their identity. In the next section, we consider the contribution and implications of our findings.

Discussion

Generations in the workforce are a hot topic among business people though a clear definition of generations has been elusive and an academic understanding of generational phenomena has fallen short (Costanza et al. 2012). Stereotypes of generational traits and supposed trends about generations have proliferated in publications and training; however, there is little in the way of academic research to back them up. In our study, we take a first step in exploring the different ways in which individuals define generations and use them in their self-definition. Interestingly, our study participants drew on stereotypes in defining generations as identities. These perceived generation identities then reinforce generational stereotypes as employees enact them in organizations and use them to inform their interactions with others. This phenomenon suggests practical and theoretical implications for why it is important to understand generations as identities within the context of business including: clarification of the connection between self and generation; a closer examination of intergenerational interactions; and improvement in human resource practices.

The first implication is that generation identities allow us to explain individual differences that exist between people; generations are social identities that each person can choose to incorporate (Ashforth and Johnson 2001; Serpe 1987). Our study supports recent statements made by theorists such as Joshi and colleagues (2010) that generations can be viewed as important identities in organizational contexts. Furthermore, our study moves researchers a step closer to understanding the complexities of the generation construct. Practically, understanding how one's identification with a generation influences behavior is important within organizations as well. Employers should seek to understand the social identities that define employees in order to better understand and manage their values, beliefs, and behaviors. In other words, rather than assume that an older co-worker is reluctant to change or a younger employee has a sense of entitlement (two often-stated generational stereotypes), managers and colleagues should seek to understand whether these prototypical generational characteristics actually influence those individuals. In addition to organizational or team identities that employees use in defining themselves, generation identity is another important social identity to consider in organizational interactions and policies.

Second, generation identities allow us to better understand the tensions that occur between members of different generations. Social identity and self-categorization theories suggest that intergenerational conflict can be based on perceptions of in- and out-group differences in values, beliefs, and behaviors, whether or not these differences are actually supported in work-related activities. Key here is that clear generation identities allow employees to group themselves and others into generational categories (in- and out-groups) in order to make sense of and predict their behavior. Classification into such groupings can lead to decreased respect, lower trust, and other negative aspects of interactions with out-groups (Tsui et al. 1995) when values, beliefs, and behaviors are believed to be incompatible. It is in the best interest of managers and organizations to understand the nature of these intergenerational interactions so that they can better manage them.

Lastly, examining generations as identities allows for a more accurate assessment of generational effects that can be used for improving human resource practices. By taking an identity-based perspective of generations, a clearer representation of generation – beyond just age cohorts – is possible. This identity-based approach would advocate for less age stereotyping in organizations, as mentioned earlier. Instead, coworkers and managers should understand that not everyone of a certain age exhibits stereotypical traits and, therefore, organizations should not engage in training that proliferates generational stereotypes. Instead, in training employees, organizations should examine the implications that perceptions of generational differences have on interactions rather than focus on generational trends or differences between generations. Organizational implications, however, are not just limited to training. Organizations should also ensure that they avoid stereotypical traits of generations in hiring and in assigning tasks. As shown here, individuals may identify and incorporate traits inconsistent with those of their biological age-based generation, making hiring or task assignment based on assumed traits ineffective.

Though this chapter is based on a qualitative study of a diverse sample, it is not without its limitations. While we were able through our qualitative method to better understand how participants perceive generations, we did not explore in depth how those perceptions are formed. Therefore an area for future research would be to consider how generation identities and identification with them form. We have considered one factor – popular stereotypes – however, it is likely there are other important factors to consider in understanding how generation identities form and identification occurs. For example, Haslam and Reicher (2006) noted that support derived from strong social identities helps individuals resist stressors. Thus, generation identification may be a response to stress associated with organizational challenges.

In addition, we have found that individuals may identify or disidentify with their age-based generation. Future process-oriented research might explore the bases for this (dis)identification. For example, are individuals who are on the cusp between two generations more likely to show latitude in "choosing" an alternative generation identity and disidentifying with their biological one? Is (dis)identification with a generation identity wholesale, or do individuals pick and choose particular aspects of generation identities with which they (dis)identify? Our data suggest the latter, though this would be an interesting question for future research.

Finally, we have suggested propositions derived from our qualitative study that can be explored (qualitatively) or tested (quantitatively) in future research. Based on our study, we support movement away from solely age-based considerations of generations toward identity-based ways of defining generations to better understand why and how individuals draw on generational identities in defining who they are. This chapter contributes to the literature on both identity and generations by showing that generations can be strong identities with which individuals identify or disidentify and that individuals prioritize generation identities differently. Thus, it provides an entry point for researchers seeking to examine intergenerational interactions. It suggests practical reasons for focusing less on generational stereotypes and more on individuals and what generation identities they choose to incorporate.

Acknowledgments

The chapter presented here is part of a larger study on intergenerational interactions. Funding was provided in part by Siddall funds from the University of Cincinnati Management Department in the Lindner College of Business. We wish to acknowledge the help and participation of the anonymous interviewees in our two samples.

Notes

1 Our participants often used generational labels popularized by the media, e.g. Generation X, Generation Y, Baby Boomers, and Veterans, terms that appear in the quotes we include here.

2 Some of our participants chose to refer to generations in broad groupings, e.g. "younger generation" and "older people" in the interviews. In unpacking their quotes in the text, we have retained the language they used.

References

Ashforth, B.E., Kreiner, G.E., Clark, M.A. and Fugate, M. (2007) 'Normalizing dirty work: managerial tactics for countering occupational taint', *Academy of Management Journal*, 50: 149–174.

Ashforth, B.E., Harrison, S.H. and Corley, K.G. (2008) 'Identification in organizations: an examination of four fundamental questions', *Journal of Management*, 34: 325–374.

Ashforth, B.E. and Johnson, S.A. (2001) 'Which hat to wear? The relative salience of multiple identities in organizational contexts', in M.A. Hogg and D.J. Terry (eds) *Social Identity Processes in Organizational Contexts*, Philadelphia, PA: Taylor & Francis, pp. 31–48.

Ashforth, B.E. and Mael, F. (1989) 'Social identity theory and the organization', *Academy of Management Review*, 14: 20–39.

Brewer, M.B. and Brown, R. (1998) 'Intergroup relations', in D. Gilbert, S. Fiske and G. Lindzey (eds) *The Handbook of Social Psychology*, 4th edn, Boston, MA: McGraw-Hill, pp. 554–594.

Brickson, S. (2000) 'The impact of identity orientation on the individual and organizational outcomes in demographically diverse settings', *Academy of Management Review*, 25: 92–101.

Corley, K.G. and Gioia, D.A. (2004) 'Identity ambiguity and change in the wake of a corporate spin-off', *Administrative Science Quarterly*, 49: 173–208.

Costanza, D.P., Badger, J.M., Fraser, R.L., Severt, J.B. and Gade, P.A. (2012) 'Generational differences in work-related attitudes: a meta-analysis', *Journal of Business Psychology*, 27: 375–394.

Deaux, K. (1996) 'Social identification', in E.T. Higgins and A.W. Kruglanski (eds) *Social Psychology: Handbook of Basic Principles*, New York: Guilford Press, pp. 777–798.

Elsbach. K.D. and Bhattacharya, C.B. (2001) 'Defining who you are by what you're not: organizational disidentification and the National Rifle Association', *Organization Science*, 12: 393–413.

Finkelstein, L.M., Gonnerman, M.E. and Foxgrover, S.K. (2001) 'The stability of generation identification over time and across contexts', *Experimental Aging Research*, 27: 377–397.

Haslam, S.A. (2004) *Psychology in Organizations: The Social Identity Approach*, Thousand Oaks, CA: Sage.

Haslam, S.A. and Reicher, S.D. (2006) 'Stressing the group: social identity and the unfolding dynamics of stress', *Journal of Applied Psychology*, 91: 1037–1052.

Hogg, M.A., van Knippenberg, D. and Rast, D.E. (2012) 'Intergroup leadership in organizations: leading across group and organizational boundaries', *Academy of Management Review*, 37: 232–255.

Joshi, A., Dencker, J.C., Franz, G. and Martocchio, J.J. (2010) 'Unpacking generational identities in organizations', *Academy of Management Review*, 35: 392–414.

Joshi, A., Dencker, J.C. and Franz, G. (2011) 'Generations in organizations', *Research in Organizational Behavior*, 31: 177–205.

Kreiner, G.E., Hollensbe, E.C. and Sheep, M.L. (2006) 'Where is the "me" among the "we"? Identity work and the search for optimal balance', *Academy of Management Journal*, 49: 1031–1057.

Mannheim, K. (1970) 'The problem of generations', *Psychoanalytic Review*, 57: 378–404.

Parry, E. and Urwin, P. (2011) 'Generational differences in work values: a review of theory and evidence', *International Journal of Management Reviews*, 13: 79–96.

Pilcher, J. (1994) 'Mannheim's sociology of generations: an undervalued legacy', *British Journal of Sociology*, 45: 481–495.

Serpe, R.T. (1987) 'Stability and change in self: a structural symbolic interactionist explanation', *Social Psychology Quarterly*, 50: 44–55.

Sluss, D.M. and Ashforth, B.E. (2007) 'Relational identity and identification: defining ourselves through work relationships', *Academy of Management Review*, 32: 9–32.

Smola, K.W. and Sutton, C.D. (2002) 'Generational differences: revisiting generational work values for the new millennium', *Journal of Organizational Behavior*, 23: 363–382.

Society for Human Resource Management (2005) *SHRM Generational Differences Survey Report: A Study by the Society for Human Resource Management* (SHRM surveys series), Alexandria, VA: Society for Human Resource Management.

Strauss, A. and Corbin, J. (1998) *Basics of Qualitative Research: Techniques and Procedures for Developing Grounded Theory*, 2nd edn, Thousand Oaks, CA: Sage.

Tajfel, H. (1978) 'Social categorization, social identity and social comparison', in H. Tajfel (ed.) *Differentiation Between Social Groups: Studies in the Social Psychology of Intergroup Relations*, London: Academic Press, pp. 61–76.

Tajfel, H., and Turner, J.C. (1985) 'The social identity theory of intergroup behavior', in S. Worchel and W.G. Austin (eds) *Psychology of Intergroup Relations*, 2nd edn, Chicago, IL: Nelson-Hall, pp. 7–24.

Tsui, A.S., Xin, K.R. and Egan, T.D. (1995) 'Relational demography: the missing link in vertical dyad linkage', in S.E. Jackson (ed.) *Diversity in Work Teams: Research Paradigms for a Changing Workplace*, Washington, DC: American Psychological Association, pp. 97–129.

Twenge, J.M., Campbell, S.M., Hoffman, B.J. and Lance, C.E. (2010) 'Generational differences in work values: leisure and extrinsic values increasing, social and intrinsic values decreasing', *Journal of Management*, 36: 1117–1142.

9

KEEN, GROOVY, WICKED, OR PHAT, IT IS ALL COOL

Generational stereotyping and social identity

Katherine J. Roberto and John R. Biggan

"What is the younger generation coming to?" begs the first line of a *Time Magazine* article (Time Magazine 1956). Another article begins "It [the workplace] won't look the same … It will be run by a generation with new values" (Fisher et al. 2009). They could both be talking about one of the hottest topics today – the newest generation in the workplace. Only, the first article was written over 50 years ago, the second just four.

The popular press seems obsessed with the notion of generational differences. For over 80 years, *Time Magazine* has published more than 50 articles on the various generations and their differences. Since 2008, *BusinessWeek* magazine has published over 45 articles on the different generations. This is not a new phenomenon. There seems to be a pervasive need to identify, explain, and categorize those younger groups hot on the older generations' heels. But are they really that different from each other? Joel Stein (2013: 28) begins his *Time* cover article with an interesting observation: "I am about to do what old people have done throughout history: call those younger than me lazy, entitled, selfish, and shallow."

Recent empirical research has not found meaningful differences between generations (Gentry et al. 2011; Real et al. 2010). Twenge (2010: 207) postulates: "Many people probably perceive generational differences as stronger than they actually are. Some of this might be the natural human tendency to generalize." Though generational differences may not be as strong as perceived, the conversation persists generation to generation – providing stereotype after stereotype. If we understand the content of generational stereotypes, we can then work to understand why we may behave differently (Ng and Feldman 2012) and why we seem to have the same conversation with every new generation. The aim of this chapter is to examine the stereotypes that individuals hold about their own and other generations. Specifically, the prevalence of stereotypes held and the degree to which members of any generation hold any given stereotype. Furthermore, we examine the rate of positive and negative traits associated with each generation and its relationship with generational identification.

Literature

Generations

To understand differences between generations, we must first define what we mean by generation. Kupperschmidt (2000: 66) defined a generation as an "identifiable group that shares birth years, age location, and significant life events at critical developmental stages." This definition provides not only a way to group individuals (by birth years and age), but more importantly by classifying them together by the events that were experienced at a pivotal developmental stage. It is during an individual's early adolescence through early adulthood that many life-defining events occur (Macky et al. 2008), and individuals begin to form the collective memory of their generation. The recollection of these enduring collective memories shapes one's values and beliefs (Joshi et al. 2011), which remain relatively stable throughout his or her adult life (Macky et al. 2008). The values and understandings of the world that developed as a result of these collective memories create differences in the generations (Joshi et al. 2011). Though differences arise due to the exposure to diverse events during these critical years, authors warn that "not all members of each generation will be exactly the same; however, there are certain qualities inherent in the majority based on their collective life experiences of the group that develop" (Carver and Candela 2008: 986).

Currently, there are three primary generations in the workforce: the Baby Boomers (Boomers), Generation X (Gen Xers), and Millennials. Also called the "Me Generation," Boomers were born between 1946–1964 (Lancaster and Stillman 2002). The literature describes Boomers as optimists and idealists who constantly seek self-improvement. They are extremely competitive individuals, defining themselves by the things they have accomplished (Frandsen 2009).

Characterized by their "live to work mentality" (Carver and Candela 2008), they bring dedication, experience, and knowledge to the workplace (Lockwood 2009). They work hard and expect others to work hard, often "going the extra mile" for their organization (Zemke et al. 2000), giving them the characterization of workaholics (Pekala 2001). Status is important to them (Busch et al. 2008), as expressed through public recognition such as promotions, titles, and premier office real estate (Kupperschmidt 2000).

Born between 1965 and 1980, Generation X (Lancaster and Stillman 2002) is classified as independent, resilient (Frandsen 2009), pragmatic, adaptable, and self-reliant; a diverse group that prefers balance, fun, and informality (Zemke et al. 2000). However, the literature also describes them as cynical, arrogant, demanding, and impatient (Carver and Candela 2008).

Gen Xers embody the work-to-live mentality (Carver and Candela 2008). As results-oriented people (Deeken et al. 2008), they focus on productivity, not hours worked (Houlihan 2008), which often leads to them being called "slackers" (Zemke et al. 2000). Watching the Boomers sacrifice to get ahead, they prefer organizations that allow for work–life balance (Frandsen 2009). They will work until the job is done putting in their 40 hours, but little beyond (Pekala 2001). They are willing to sacrifice to reach their own personal achievements, but less likely to sacrifice for the organization (Carver and Candela 2008).

Born between 1981 and 2000, Millennials, or Generation Y (Lancaster and Stillman 2002), grew up not only with computers in both their homes and schools, but also the internet – allowing instant access to information and communication (Carver and Candela 2008). The literature describes Millennials as family- and team-oriented (Deeken et al. 2008; Frandsen 2009). They are highly educated, comfortable with diversity, and incredibly active (Zemke et al. 2000). However, they demonstrate higher levels of narcissism and self-esteem (Twenge and Campbell 2008), placing greater value on extrinsic characteristics such as money and fame (Twenge et al. 2012).

Driven to learn and grow (Connor and Shaw 2008), Millennials abide by a "work smarter, not harder" mentality (Buhler 2008), seeking out opportunities for meaningful work (De Hauw and De Vos 2010). They prefer flexible working environments and expect to achieve work–life balance (Carver and Candela 2008). They have a greater tolerance for the permeability of boundaries between work and family life due to the 24/7 nature of technology (Whinghter 2009). Ultimately, however, this generation sees work as less central to their lives, placing a greater value on leisure time (Twenge 2010), meaning they are less likely to make sacrifices for the company at the expense of their personal lives (Remo and Kwantes 2009).

Stereotypes

Clearly, there is a myriad of characteristics ascribed to each generation, which can set the generations at odds with each other. These characteristics are stereotypes, defined as "a set of beliefs about personal attributes of a group of people" (Ashmore and Del Boca 1981: 16). We create "pictures in our heads" of what other groups are like and how they behave, which elicit various emotional responses from us, the observer (Ashmore and Del Boca 1981). We want to know what to expect, so we stereotype. We want to know how to treat people, so we stereotype. However, when we stereotype, we often treat people accordingly which can lead to self-fulfilling prophecies (Chen and Bargh 1997). For example, one study found that when negative stereotypes were primed, older workers were less motivated to learn and develop new skills; but when positive stereotypes were primed, this effect was mitigated (Gaillard and Desmette 2011).

Stereotyping allows individuals to compress large quantities of social information into smaller, more manageable amounts. It allows one to infer appropriate and expected behaviors, and permits categorization of others into particular social categories (Kunda and Spencer 2003).

Thus, this chapter first examines the following questions:

Research question 1: Do individuals classify themselves into the age groups often given in the literature?

Research question 2: What stereotypes do working adults hold about each generation?

Research question 3: How similar are the stereotypes across generations?

According to Kunda and Spencer (2003), people may stereotype to accomplish two possible goals: comprehension (the need to understand the social situation around them and reduce the complexity of information and attitudes) and self-enhancement (the need to maintain or enhance self-esteem and preserve one's self-concept). This can be explained through the lens of social identity theory.

Social identity theory

Tajfel and Turner (1986: 16) define social identity as the "aspects of an individual's self-image that derive from the social categories to which he perceives himself belonging." When individuals become part of a social group, they merge their emotional and psychological experiences into a cohesive identity that is magnified or diminished based upon the social group they are currently occupying (Turner et al. 1987).

Social identity theory makes three basic assumptions. First, individuals seek to enhance their self-esteem by attempting to view themselves in a positive light according to a positive self-concept (Tajfel and Turner 1986). Therefore, individuals are motivated to see the groups that they belong to and identify with in a positive light to the extent that they modify their interpretation of the group to maintain this perception (Turner et al. 1987). Oakes (1987) found that when a participant discriminated against the outgroup, it increased his or her self-esteem relative to the ingroup, which demonstrates his or her desire for a positive social identity. Second, social groups inherently have both positive and negative qualities associated with them (Tajfel and Turner 1986). Third, in order to maintain the positive feeling about one's own group, the individual must compare his or her ingroup to a referent outgroup that is perceived to be negative in relation to the ingroup (Turner et al. 1987).

These assumptions lead to two general predictions about behavior within an ingroup. People want to achieve a positive social identity (Tajfel and Turner 1986); therefore, they will find positive distinctions between their ingroup and the referent outgroup (Turner et al. 1987). Individuals will increase their adherence to the stereotypical behavior of the ingroup while simultaneously amplifying the stereotypes of the outgroup. Though not necessarily accurate, this will create discriminatory incidents that allow the ingroup to maintain necessary distinction (Hogg et al. 1995).

Thus, in accordance with social identity theory, the self-enhancement motivation of stereotyping reflects the need to maintain or enhance self-esteem and preserve one's self-concept. This motivates individuals to form beliefs about others in their social situation, often negative in order to establish feelings of superiority and a higher sense of self-worth. When an individual feels exposed by another in the environment, he or she is more likely to activate negative stereotypes of the individual while aggressively suppressing positive stereotypes about them. This enhances their perceived superiority over the disparaged other (Kunda and Spencer 2003). Therefore, in order to maintain a positive sense of self in relation to one's generation, individuals would be motivated to disparage other generations while promoting their own. As such, we would hypothesize that individuals will use more positive stereotypes about the generations they classify themselves into, and more negative stereotypes about the generations to which they do not belong. Furthermore, the greater the identification with their given generation, the more positive stereotypes about their own generation they will provide in relation to the negative stereotypes about their own generation.

The chapter further examines the following questions:

Research question 4: Which groups have more positive and negative terms associated with them?

Research question 5: What is the relationship between positive and negative stereotypes both between and within each generation?

Methods

This study was conducted in order to gain a better understanding of what stereotypes people have about generations. As recommended by Denzin (1978) and Jick (1979), both quantitative and qualitative data were collected in order "to enrich our understanding by allowing for new or deeper dimensions to emerge" (Jick 1979: 603).

Sample

Participants were recruited using a snowball sample. The authors sent out an email invitation to complete an online survey[1] utilizing personal and professional contacts. After completion, these individuals were asked to forward the email and survey link to others who would be likely to participate. A total of 175 responses were received. After eliminating surveys in which respondents did not list any stereotypes for the generations, 144 were analyzed.

The majority of the sample was female (58.3 percent) and described themselves as white/Caucasian (88.9 percent). All participants were employed full-time and worked in a variety of industries: education (14 percent), technical (11 percent), sales (11 percent), medical/healthcare (8 percent), consulting (6 percent), professional (7 percent), government (5 percent), and marketing (5 percent). Forty-four percent of the participants classified themselves as Boomers, with 19 percent identifying as Gen Xers and 36 percent as Millennials.

Upon further examination of the data, 11 percent of the responses were from international (northern Europe) respondents. After conducting a χ^2 test ($\chi^2(2)=5.24$, $p = .07$), the US and European samples were not found to be significantly different, and were combined for analyses.

Measures

Participants responded to an open-ended survey asking the following question: "Please type in all the stereotypes (or perceived characteristics) that come to mind when you think about ______ group." This was asked three times: once for the Boomers, once for Generation X, and once for Generation Y/Millennials. Except in the consent form, which noted that Boomers were the oldest generation in the workforce, followed by Generation X, then Millennials, no other information about the generations (including age/date ranges) was given so as not to bias the possible stereotypes given.

Analysis

Following Corbin and Strauss's (1990) model of open coding, traits of the generations were recorded by two experienced independent coders and compared for similarities and differences. As it is difficult to analyze many traits separately, Corbin and Strauss (1990) recommend grouping concepts into larger, more meaningful categories that may be compared and analyzed. After assessing the traits, themes began to emerge for each generation.

Examination of the first set of research questions

The first questions examined were, first: do individuals classify themselves into the age groups often given in the literature? Second, what are the stereotypes that working individuals hold about each generation? Lastly, are the stereotypes similar across generation?

First, we considered whether or not individuals correctly classified themselves according to the generational divides in the literature. There is no consensus in the literature as to the starting and ending points for the generations. Lancaster and Stillman (2002) divided the generations according to birth years as follows: Boomers, 1946–1964; Generation X, 1965–1980; and Millennials, 1981–1999. Carver and Candela (2008) divided them as follows: Boomers, 1943–1960; Generation X, 1961–1981; and Millennials, 1982–2000. Due to this we allowed for some overlap (i.e. for two people born in 1980, if one categorizes themselves as X and one as Millennial, both would be considered correct identifications) in order to accommodate this inconsistency. Interestingly, all overlaps came from participants born between 1980 and 1982. Participants were coded as incorrect if, for example, they were born in 1985 and classified themselves as a member of Generation X.

The majority of the sample (88 percent) correctly identified themselves as belonging to the generation indicated by the literature. For Boomers, 95 percent correctly identified themselves; the remaining three individuals identified themselves as members of Generation X. Ninety percent of Generation X members correctly identified themselves. Three of the remaining participants identified themselves as Boomers (all born in the late 1960s), and the other as Millennial (born in the mid/late 1970s). However, only 77 percent of Millennials correctly identified themselves. The rest (whose birth years ranged from 1983–1989) all classified themselves as Generation X. This may be due to a generally negative perception of Millennials, in which members of this generation might prefer to identify with an earlier generation to separate themselves from the negative stereotypes.

To address the second research question, we examined the number of stereotypes given for each of the three generations. For Boomers, participants listed 718 (M = 4.99, SD = 2.83) traits falling into 24 overarching categories (with a 93 percent agreement rate in categorization). Participants listed 641 (M = 4.45, SD = 2.54) traits for Generation X for a total of 25 categories (94 percent agreement). For Millennials, 689 (M = 4.79, SD = 3.32) traits were given, resulting in 25 categories (88 percent agreement; see Table 9.1 for categories).

Upon examination, some stereotypes were found to be similar across generations. The stereotype that Millennials are "entitled/spoiled" is one that was frequently given by survey respondents and concurs with the literature. However, this stereotype is only presented for Millennials in the literature, but appears for each generation, increasing linearly in frequency from Boomer (10 percent) to Gen X (16 percent) to Millennials (30 percent) in the survey data. Also in concurrence with the literature, a positive stereotype that emerged, which increases in magnitude across generations, is highly educated (Boomers – 6 percent, Gen X – 11 percent, and Millennials – 12 percent). Two stereotypes emerged for all three generations that are rarely mentioned in the literature for any group – self-centered and materialistic (see Twenge and Campbell 2008; Twenge et al. 2012 for discussion of narcissism across generations). Nine percent of respondents stereotyped Boomers as self-centered, increasing to 16 percent for Gen X then decreasing to 12 percent for Millennials. Materialistic was mentioned by 7 percent of respondents for Boomers, 5 percent for Gen X, and 6 percent for Millennials. Generational differences are often seen as stark differences with unique traits associated with specific groups, but these findings suggest that in some cases these differences may be more in the magnitude of the stereotype rather than the stereotype itself.

A linear trend also emerges for certain stereotypes that could be considered ends of a spectrum. A large number of respondents made mention of age for each generation. Forty percent of respondents stereotyped Boomers as old, getting old, or aging. Eleven percent characterized Millennials as young. For the most part, in terms of age, little was mentioned for Gen X; less than 5 percent called this generation young and none called them old (or even middle-aged as would be the more accurate description). The stereotype of old or young brings with it a larger idea of who and what these generations are capable of – connotations within the

TABLE 9.1 Comparison of categories of stereotypes about the generations

Baby Boomers		*Generation X*		*Generation Y/Millennial*	
Literature	*Survey*	*Literature*	*Survey*	*Literature*	*Survey*
Workaholics (83%)	Aging/old (40%)	Independent (75%)	Tech astute (23%)	Tech savvy (70%)	Tech savvy (34%)
Hard-working (45%)	Hippies/drugs (22%)	Negative disposition (70%)	Lazy (21%)	Work–life balance (68%)	Entitled/spoiled (30%)
Loyal (43%)	Hard-working (21%)	Adaptable (53%)	Independent (19%)	Civic-minded (55%)	Lazy (14%)
Competitive (43%)	Activists (18%)	Work–life balance (48%)	Entitled/spoiled (16%)	Adaptable (40%)	Tech-dependent (14%)
Activists (43%)	Retired/retiring (18%)	Tech astute (45%)	Self-centered (16%)	Efficient/multi-taskers (40%)	Educated (12%)
Tech illiterate (28%)	Conservative (16%)	Lack loyalty (43%)	Work–life balance (14%)	Educated (40%)	Self-centered (12%)
	Wealthy (12%)	Hard-working (33%)	Educated (11%)	Needy (38%)	Lack people skills (11%)
	Rigid (12%)		Adaptable (10%)	Ambitious (33%)	Young (11%)
	Time period reference (12%)		Lack loyalty (10%)	Confident/arrogant (30%)	Lack focus (10%)
	Tech illiterate (11%)			Team-oriented/social (30%)	
	Entitled/spoiled (10%)			Lack focus (28%)	
	Loyal (10%)			Diverse (25%)	
	Traditional values (10%)				

Baby Boomers		*Generation X*		*Generation Y/Millennial*	
Literature	*Survey*	*Literature*	*Survey*	*Literature*	*Survey*
5–24.9% cut	5–9.9% cut	5–24.9% cut	5–9.9% cut	5–24.9% cut	5–9.9% cut
Rigid (23%), educated (20%), optimistic (18%), experienced (15%), status/recognition (15%), impatient (13%), independent (13%), team players (13%), work–life balance (13%), poor health (8%), liberal spending (8%), personal growth (8%), respect authority (8%)	Self-centered (9%), liberal (8%), goal-oriented (8%), optimistic (8%), responsible (7%), materialistic (7%), educated (6%), frugal (6%), independent (5%), large group (5%), strain on social security (5%), militaristic (5%)	Educated (23%), lazy (23%), "latch key" (15%), career-focused (15%), efficient/multi-taskers (15%), fun (13%), loyal (13%), team players (13%), want feedback (13%), career security (10%), impatient (8%), informal (8%), personal fulfillment (8%), problem solvers (8%)	Negative disposition (8%), decline in traditional families (8%), greedy (8%), ambitious (7%), apathetic (7%), informal (7%), music important (7%), tech consumers (7%), hard-working (6%), not familiar with Gen x (6%), impatient (5%), liberal (5%), materialistic (5%), poor work ethic (5%), sex/drugs (5%), tolerant (5%)	Entitled (23%), independent (23%), lazy (23%), lack loyalty (20%), optimistic (20%), seek structure (18%), career-focused (13%), like a challenge (13%), like change (10%), loyal (8%), meaningful work (8%), inexperienced (5%)	Dependent (9%), work–life balance (9%), non-conformists (8%), not financially stable (8%), informal (8%), team-oriented/social (8%), lack work ethic (7%), needs attention (7%), tolerant (7%), ambitious (6%), impatient (6%), indifferent (6%), materialistic (6%), liberal (5%), optimistic (5%), inexperienced (5%)

Only categories reported in 5% (minimum) of the samples from the literature and survey are included.

stereotype itself (Ashmore and Del Boca 1981), attributes such as slow or rigid subsumed under old and inexperienced or reckless, within the concept of young.

If work ethic is seen as a continuum (anchors of hard-working and poor work ethic), this stereotype changed linearly across generations, such that 21 percent stereotyped Boomers as hard-working, where 7 percent stereotyped Millennials as having a poor work ethic – with neither alternative stereotype discussed for the alternative group. However, Gen Xers were labeled both hard-working (7 percent) and as having a poor work ethic (5 percent). In the opposite direction, technological functioning exhibits a positive linear change from Boomers being classified as illiterate (11 percent) to Gen Xers as astute/capable (23 percent) and Millennials as savvy (34 percent). These may not necessarily be truly different stereotypes, rather different ends of a spectrum – a positive and negative way to view the same stereotype. Over time, as generational positions change (youngest becoming oldest), these perceptions too may change – those who are lazy today may be hard-working when compared with younger, lazier generations.

These stereotypes, however, were not reported evenly from the generations. For example, the stereotype that Gen Xers are hard-working came from Gen Yers with Baby Boomers stereotyping Gen Xers as having a poor work ethic. Interestingly, Gen Xers were split between the two. This highlights the need to then examine the polarization of stereotypes about generations by different groups.

Examination of the second set of research questions

The second set of research questions asked: which groups have more positive and negative terms associated with them? What is the relationship between positive and negative stereotypes both between and within each generation? Specifically, we looked at whether individuals used more positive stereotypes about the generations they classified themselves into, and more negative stereotypes about the generations they did not believe they belonged to.

The same raters coded each stereotype as having a positive connotation, a negative connotation, or as neutral indicating no connotation could be interpreted from the stereotype. A positive stereotype would be "hard-working" or "caring," where a negative stereotype would be "workaholic" or "self-centered." Neutral comments could include referencing music popular during that generation's formative years – like the Beatles or 80s pop. Stereotypes, such as liberal and conservative, were coded as neutral stereotypes, as the raters could not assume whether the participant meant the term to be positive or negative. However, where a reasonable assumption could be made as to the participants' perception of the term, such as "liberal whack-jobs," the stereotype was coded accordingly (in this example – negative).

An analysis of the average number of responses for each group showed that Millennials provided a similar number of stereotypes (744; $M = 14.31$, $SD = 7.12$) for all three groups as did members of Generation X (371; $M = 13.25$, $SD = 7.43$) and Boomers (956; $M = 14.94$, $SD = 8.07$), $F(2, 141) = .48$, $p = .62$.

First, we examined which groups had more positive and negative ratings in general. Each generation had roughly the same percentage of positive stereotypes given

– 27 percent of stereotypes about Boomers, 30 percent about Generation X, and 25 percent about Millennials were positive. For neutral and negative comments, this was not true. The majority, 39 percent, of the stereotypes about Boomers were coded as neutral. Less than 25 percent of comments for either Generation X (24 percent) or Millennials (21 percent) were rated as neutral. The most dramatic differences were in the negative stereotypes given about the generations. Thirty-three percent of the Boomer's stereotypes were coded negative, where 46 percent of Generation X's and over half (54 percent) of all stereotypes given about Millennials were negative.

This indicates that overall people ascribe relatively general positive stereotypes to each generation, some similar (i.e. highly educated) and some different (i.e. tech savvy for younger generations and hard-working for older generations). The steady increase in negative stereotypes could be a reflection of the lower amount of time spent with younger generations. Allport's (1954) intergroup-contact theory would argue that intergroup contact can lead to positive reevaluations of negative stereotypes of members of an outgroup. If a Millennial is spending more time around Boomers in the workplace or at home with family, then they may have fewer negative stereotypes about Boomers; whereas Boomers, who may interact with fewer Millennials in general, may have more negative stereotypes due to lack of contact. The participants were asked how often they interacted with each group. A majority, 84 percent, of participants reported they interacted with a Boomer on a regular (daily/weekly) basis, where only 74 percent interacted with Millennials regularly. However, this may only be part of the story as more participants (88 percent) reported interacting with Xers than Boomers although they were viewed more negatively than Boomers.

The next step was to examine, based on their own classification of their generation (regardless of whether it matched with the dates described in the literature), if, as social identity theory would suggest, individuals would give their perceived ingroup more positive stereotypes, and the outgroups more negative stereotypes. Participants, for their generation, gave nearly 40 percent positive stereotypes, 23 percent neutral, and 37 percent negative. As Tajfel and Turner (1986) suggested, people may have a realistic understanding that their group has both positive and negative qualities associated with it. For the other generations, however, 27 percent of the comments were positive, 29 percent were neutral, but 44 percent were negative (see Figure 9.1).

Next, we examined the degree of identification to a generation and the number of positive and negative stereotypes given about their own and other generations. Using a five-point Likert scale (1 being "Do not identify with at all" and 5 "Identify with completely"), participants were asked to what degree they identified with a generation (see Figure 9.2). Far more negative stereotypes were given by those who said they did not identify with a generation at all (52 percent) or somewhat did not identify with a generation (61 percent) compared to positive stereotypes (17 and 20 percent, respectively). However, more positive stereotypes were given by those who identified completely with a generation (43 percent) or somewhat identified with a generation (41 percent) than negative stereotypes (31 and 32 percent, respectively).

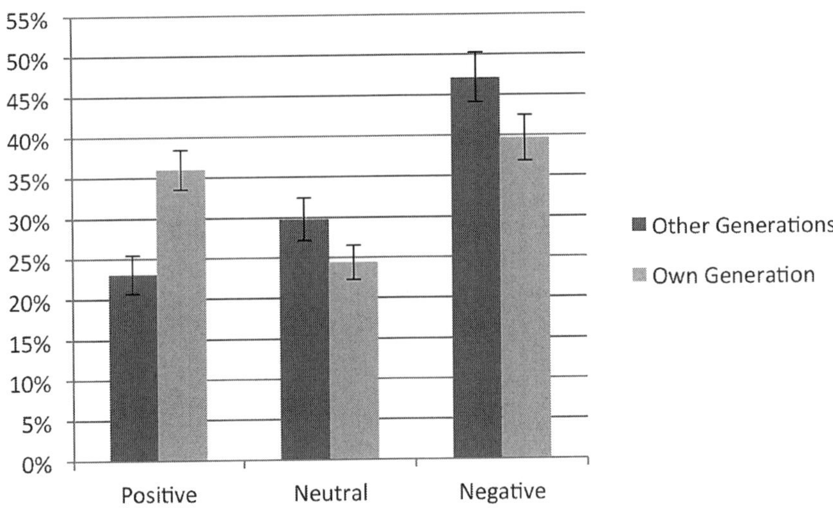

FIGURE 9.1 Percentage of stereotype responses for own and other generations

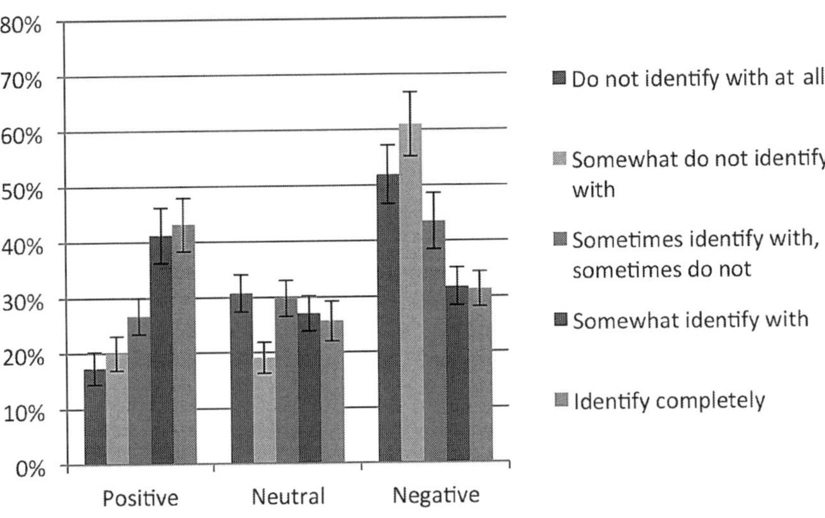

FIGURE 9.2 Percentage of stereotype responses by strength of group identification

Thus, participants were more likely to give positive stereotypes about generations they identified with, while giving disparaging stereotypes about generations they did not identify with – supporting the social identity approach that an individual's level of identification with a group guides his or her feelings about how positive or negative the group is. This may help partially explain why so many Millennials incorrectly categorized themselves – if they hold strong negative stereotypes about their actual generation, they may actively choose to identify with a generation they perceive to have more positive stereotypes.

Another area examined was trends across time (Boomers–Millennials) for the three types of stereotypes (positive, neutral, and negative). Responses from all three groups were combined and analyzed (see Figure 9.3). Across all groups, a linear increase from Boomers to Millennials is seen in the number of negative responses that are provided, with Boomers receiving the least negative responses (37 percent) and Millennials the most (61 percent). This increase seems to come from a shifting of neutral responses to negative responses rather than positive responses shifting to negative responses. For instance, only a small decline in positive responses is seen from Boomers (23 percent) to Millennials (18 percent). However, neutral responses decline dramatically from Boomers (40 percent) to Millennials (21 percent).

This was further explored by examining the types of responses members of each group provided for all three groups (Figure 9.4). When done for individuals who correctly identified their cohort, a pattern emerged. As expected, individuals gave the most positive stereotypes to their own group and the least positive stereotypes to members of other groups. However, the results were not a simple "us" and "them" structure, but rather individuals provided the second highest number of positive responses to the group adjacent to their own (e.g. for Baby Boomers, Generation X) and the lowest number of stereotypes to the group farthest from their own, in time (e.g. for Baby Boomers, Generation Y). The reverse was true for negative stereotypes, except in the case of Millennials where members provided the highest number of positive stereotypes as well as the highest number of negative stereotypes about their own group. It is possible that this finding for Millennials was influenced by the age of the respondents. Whereas birth years for Boomers and Gen Xers spanned the entire generation, Millennials only spanned the first half of the generation because those in the latter half are too young to participate. There could be a dissociation between the perceptions of the early and later halves of the generation – as sometimes observed with the Boomers (Almeida et al. 2006).

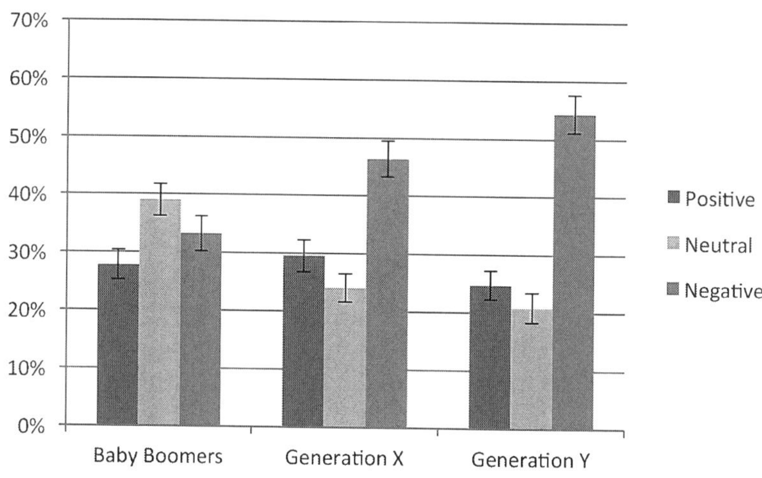

FIGURE 9.3 Percentage of stereotype responses about each generation

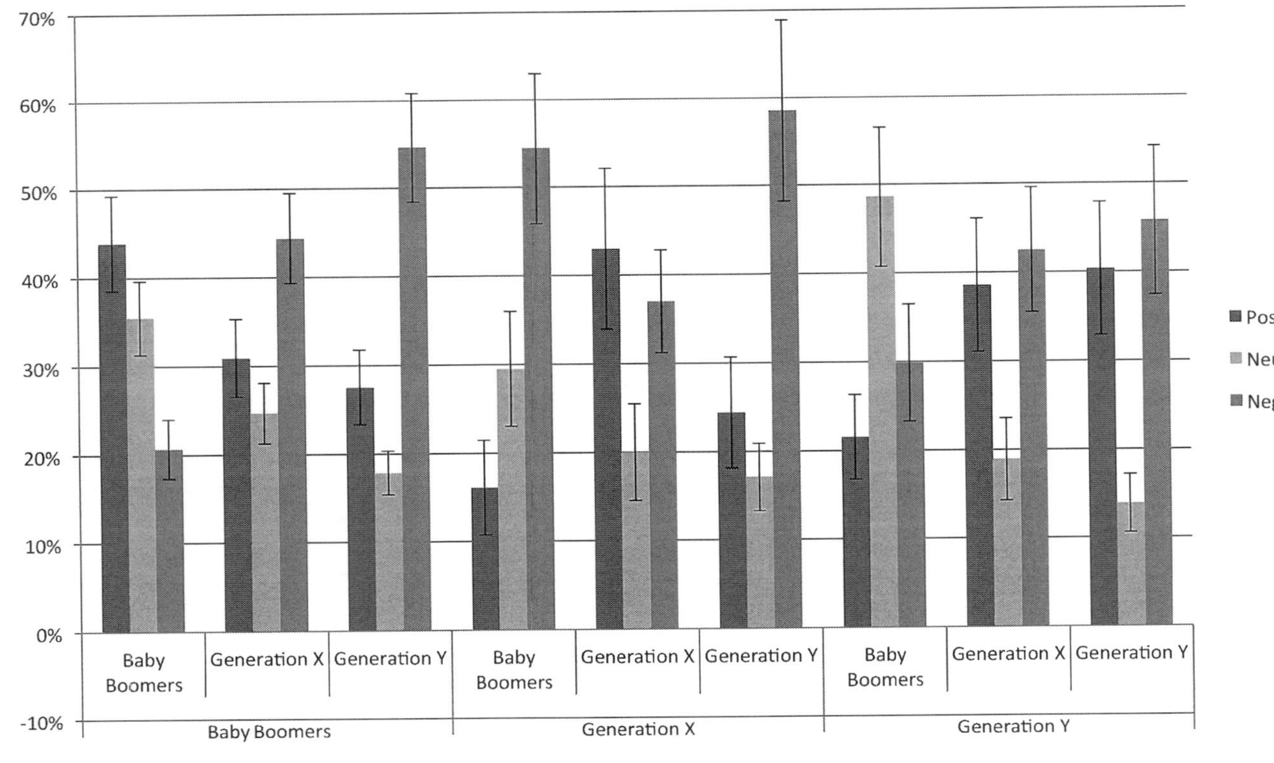

FIGURE 9.4 Percentage of stereotype response about each group (top) by the generation that stereotyped them (bottom)

Note: only participants who correctly identified their generation were included.

To examine this and further explore how generational positioning (the distance, in years, of an individual from the center of the generation) may influence beliefs about other generations, the distance from the center of each generation (Boomers = 1952, Generation X = 1972, and Millennials = 1990) was computed for all participants using their birth year. Next, the number of positive, neutral, and negative responses was correlated with generational position. We found that as individuals' generational position increases, the number of positive stereotypes they provided decreased ($r = -.20$, $p < .001$) and the number of negative stereotypes increased ($r = .12$, $p < .05$), but the number of neutral terms remained stable ($r = -.03$, $p = .58$; see Figure 9.5). Future research should consider the degree of separation between those participating in the research and the target group of the research.

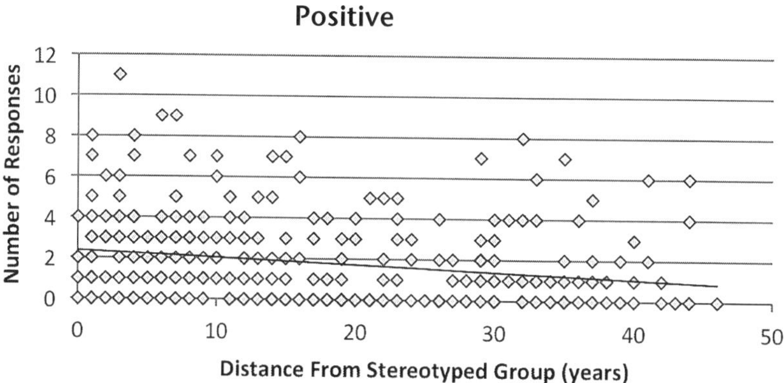

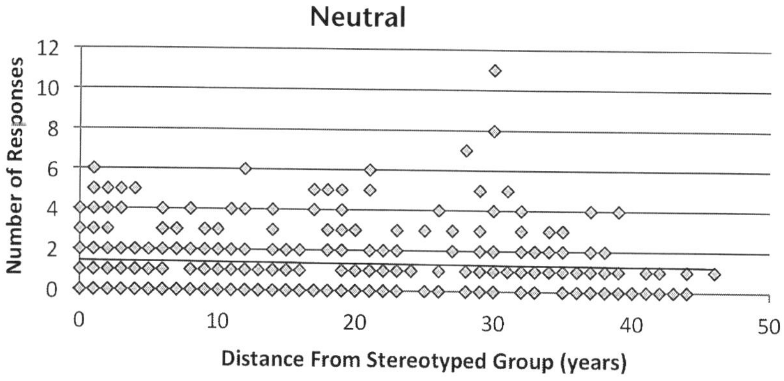

FIGURE 9.5 Relationship between distance (years) from the stereotyped group and type of response

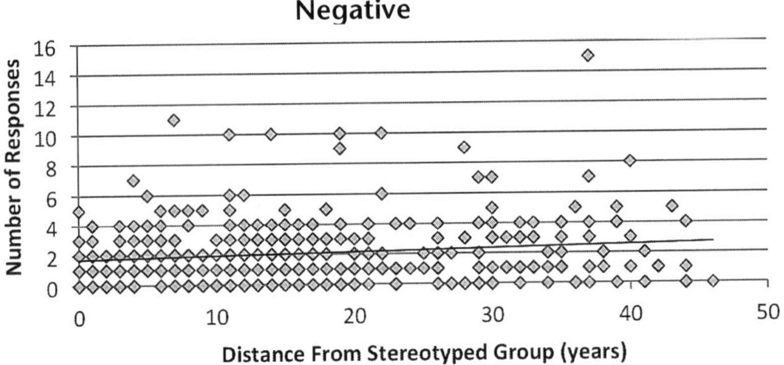

FIGURE 9.5 *Continued*

Note: positive ($r = -.20$, $p < .001$), neutral ($r = -.03$, $p = .58$), and negative ($r = .12$, $p < .05$).

Conclusions

Overall, our results suggest that not only do we identify with particular generations, but when juxtaposed with other generations we promote positive stereotypes about our ingroup and negative stereotypes about the outgroups (Tajfel and Turner 1986). Furthermore, the stereotypes held about generations are not necessarily unique to any one generation, but rather contingent upon generational positioning, often viewing younger generations more negatively than older generations. Stereotypes about any generation may not exclusively be due to the generation itself, but more so because of the number of years separating the observer and his or her target in a different generation.

We are more positive about those closer to our birth year than we are about others more distant, such that as the spacing increases so does our negativity about those others. This indicates that when we are confronted with someone who is either much older or much younger than ourselves, we are more likely to ascribe more negative and fewer positive characteristics about them. The effect sizes for generational position were small and did not account for all of the differences between the groups, but they were significant.

Two potential limitations should be discussed. First, the utilization of a snowball sample beginning with associates of the researchers could result in a non-representative sample. However, the full sample yielded respondents from various races and genders, all generations of interest, and across multiple countries beyond the direct contact of the researchers. Second, due to the nature of the survey (being online with open-ended questions), there is the possibility that participants could have researched traits and characteristics of generations through web searches while taking the survey. However, after some examination the likelihood seems relatively minimal. The top site found on several search engines when typing in each generation's name is Wikipedia. Having identified the most common traits on those pages, and searching participants' responses, no participant was found to use the same wording, order, or list of traits found on each page for each generation.

From a practical perspective, this research indicates that in situations with high generational conflict, distance in age should be taken into account. The wider the distance in age between employees, the more physically noticeable it may be and therefore more easily identifiable. Thus, when employees 40 years apart, for example, interact and their generational identity is activated, they may unwittingly set themselves up for a more negative interaction due to their negative stereotypes about each other. This means that managers should address not only generational stereotypes, but also non-specific age stereotypes when addressing conflict between employees.

As we progress as a field, the use of generational position should be considered in addition to, not in lieu of, the generations themselves, as it may help elucidate why some research finds differences between generations while other research fails to do so. This may also affect the degree to which generational identity is activated – in situations of high birth year separation, the noticeable differences between individuals should more acutely activate one's generational identity. Combined, this will lead to a richer understanding of generations and why perceptions of differences persist.

Over 100 years ago an article in *The Atlantic* noted "teachers are saying that never in their experience were young people so thirstily avid of pleasure as now ... so selfish" (cf. Stein 2013). Research may be having a difficult time identifying meaningful differences (Gentry et al. 2011; Real et al. 2010) because what we think of each generation – the stereotypes we hold – are not that different. We create pictures of a group in our heads to explain those who are chronologically more distant from us whether they are truly different or not, perhaps changing how we behave toward them. Which prompts the question... What are these generations coming to?

Note

1 For the full survey, please contact the first author, Katherine J. Roberto at katherine.roberto@mavs.uta.edu.

References

Allport, G.W. (1954) *The Nature of Prejudice*, Reading, MA: Addison-Wesley.

Almeida, D.M., Serido, J. and McDonald, D. (2006) 'Daily life stressors of early and late baby boomers', in S.K. Whitbourne and S.L. Willis (eds) *The Baby Boomers Grow Up: Contemporary Perspectives on Midlife*, Mahwah, NJ: Lawrence Erlbaum.

Ashmore, R.D. and Del Boca, F.K. (1981) 'Conceptual approaches to stereotypes and stereotyping', in D.L. Hamilton (ed.) *Cognitive Processes in Stereotyping and Intergroup Behavior*, Hillside, NJ: Erlbaum.

Buhler, P.M. (2008) 'Managing in the new millennium: managing the Baby Boomers', *Supervision*, 69: 19–21.

Busch, P., Venkitachalam, K. and Richards, D. (2008) 'Generational differences in soft knowledge situations: status, need for recognition, workplace commitment and idealism', *Knowledge and Process Management*, 15(1): 45–58.

Carver, L. and Candela, L. (2008) 'Attaining organizational commitment across difference generations of nurses', *Journal of Nursing Management*, 16: 984–991.

Chen, M. and Bargh, J.A. (1997) 'Nonconscious behavioral confirmation processes: the self-fulfilling consequences of automatic stereotype activation', *Journal of Experimental Social Psychology*, 33: 541–560.

Connor, H. and Shaw, S. (2008) 'Graduate training and development: current trends and issues', *Education and Training*, 90(5): 357–365.

Corbin, J. and Strauss, A. (1990) 'Grounded theory research: procedures, canons, and evaluative criteria', *Qualitative Sociology*, 13: 3–21.

Deeken, J., Webb, P. and Taffurelli, V. (2008) 'We are all winners: training silents to Millennials to work as a team', *The Serials Librarian*, 54: 211–216.

De Hauw, S. and De Vos, A. (2010) 'Millennials' career perspectives and psychological contracts expectations: does the recession lead to lowered expectations?', *Journal of Business Psychology*, 25: 293–302.

Denzin, N.K. (1978) *The Research Act*, 2nd edn, New York: McGraw-Hill.

Fisher, A., Godin, S. and Fitzpartick, L. (2009) 'The future of work,' *Time Magazine*, 14 May.

Frandsen, B.M. (2009) 'Leading by recognizing generational differences', *Long-Term Living: For the Continuing Care Professional*, 58: 34–35.

Gaillard, M. and Desmette, D. (2011) '(In)validating stereotypes about older works influences their intentions to retire early and to learn and develop', *Basic and Applied Social Psychology*, 32: 86–98.

Gentry, W.A., Griggs, T.L., Deal, J.J., Mondore, S.P. and Cox, B.D. (2011) 'A comparison of generational difference in endorsement of leadership practices with actual leadership skill level', *Consulting Psychology Journal: Practice and Research*, 63: 39–49.

Hogg, M.A., Terry, D.J. and White, K.M. (1995) 'A tale of two theories: a critical comparison of identity theory with social identity theory', *Social Psychology Quarterly*, 58: 255–269.

Houlihan, A. (2008) 'The new melting pot: how to effectively lead different generations in the workplace', *Construction News*, January: 8–9.

Jick, T.D. (1979) 'Mixing qualitative and quantitative methods: triangulation in action', *Administrative Science Quarterly*, 24: 602–611.

Joshi, A., Denker, J.C. and Franz, G. (2011) 'Generations in organizations', *Research in Organizational Behavior*, 31: 177–205.

Kunda, Z. and Spencer, S.J. (2003) 'When do stereotypes come to mind and when do they color judgment? A goal-based theoretical framework for stereotype activation and application', *Psychological Bulletin*, 129: 522–544.

Kupperschmidt, B.R. (2000) 'Multigeneration employees: strategies for effective management', *Health Care Manager*, 19: 65–76.

Lancaster, L. and Stillman, D. (2002) *When Generations Collide*, New York: Harper Business.

Lockwood, N.R. (2009) 'The multigenerational workforce: opportunity for competitive success', *Society for Human Resource Management Research Quarterly*, First Quarter: 1–10.

Macky, K., Gardner, D. and Forsyth, S. (2008) 'Generational differences at work: introduction and overview', *Journal of Managerial Psychology*, 23: 857–861.

Ng, T.W.H. and Feldman, D.C. (2012) 'Evaluating six common stereotypes about older workers with meta-analytic data', *Personnel Psychology*, 65: 821–858.

Oakes, P.J. (1987) 'The salience of social categories', in J.C. Turner, M.A. Hogg, P.J. Oakes, S.D. Reicher and M.S. Wetherell (eds) *Rediscovering the Social Group*, Oxford: Basil Blackwell.

Pekala, N. (2001) 'Conquering the generational divide', *Journal of Property Management*, 66: 30–38.

Real, K., Mitnick, A.D. and Maloney, W.F. (2010) 'More similar than different: millennials in the US Building trades', *Journal of Business and Psychology*, 25: 303–313.

Remo, N. and Kwantes, C.T. (2009) 'Generation Y's attitudes towards contemporary human resource practices', paper presented at 24th Annual Society of Industrial Organizational Psychology Conference, New Orleans.

Stein, J. (2013) 'The new greatest generation: why Millennials will save us all', *Time Magazine*, 20 May.

Tajfel, H. and Turner, J.C. (1986) 'The social identity theory of intergroup behavior', in S. Worchel and W.G. Austin (eds) *Psychology of Intergroup Relations*, Chicago, IL: Nelson-Hall Publishers.

Time Magazine (1956) 'Bobby-soxers' Gallup,' *Time Magazine*, 13 August, http://www.time.com/time/magazine/article/0,9171,865481,00.html (accessed 10 December, 2011).

Turner, J.C., Hogg, M.A., Oakes, P.J., Reicher, S.D. and Wetherell, M.S. (1987) *Rediscovering the Social Group*, Oxford: Basil Blackwell.

Twenge, J.M. (2010) 'A review of the empirical evidence on generational differences in work attitudes', *Journal of Business and Psychology*, 25: 201–210.

Twenge, J.M. and Campbell, S.M. (2008) 'Generational differences in psychological traits and their impact on the workplace', *Journal of Managerial Psychology*, 23: 862–877.

Twenge, J.M., Campbell, W.K. and Freeman, E.C. (2012) 'Generational differences in young adults' life goals, concern for others, and civic orientation, 1966–2009', *Personality Processes and Individual Differences*, 102(5): 1045–1062.

Whinghter, L.J. (2009) 'Acting your age at work: do generational differences really matter?', paper symposium presented at the 24th Annual Society for Industrial Organizational Psychology Conference, New Orleans.

Zemke, R., Raines, C. and Filipczak, B. (2000) *Generations at Work: Managing the Clash of Veterans, Boomers, Xers, and Nexters in Your Workplace*, New York: American Management Association Publications.

10

LAUNCHING A CAREER

Inter-generational differences in the early career stage based on retrospective accounts

Sean T. Lyons, Eddy S. Ng and Linda Schweitzer

Introduction

Launching a career is one of the critical challenges of early adulthood. The early career stage, which generally occurs by age 30 (Shindul-Rothschild 1995) is a period of tremendous psychological changes, including organizational and occupational socialization, gaining professional competence and self-efficacy and earning the acceptance and respect of peers (Lynn et al. 1996). This foundational career stage is when career entrants form initial career expectations that may or may not be consistent with the reality of their subsequent experiences. Recent literature concerning generational differences (e.g. Twenge et al. 2010) and the changing nature of careers (e.g. Briscoe and Finkelstein 2009; Sullivan and Baruch 2009) suggests that the nature and experiences of today's career entrants differ notably from previous generations. If so, traditional career counseling and life planning models may not be consistent with more contemporary career experiences (Burke and Ng 2006), requiring a new conception of the career cycle.

In this qualitative study, we compare the early career experiences of members of three distinct generations (Baby Boomers, Generation Xers, and Millennials) of Canadian workers. In order to overcome the limitations of cross-sectional research as a method of studying inter-generational career patterns, we employed in-depth interviews to attain guided retrospective narratives of the early careers of people from various generations. This study illustrates a useful means of qualitatively assessing generational differences. It contributes to the literature concerning generations and careers by analyzing first-hand accounts of the early career experiences of people who launched their careers in various historical eras, providing contextual evidence about the changing nature of careers through the words of career actors.

Generational cohorts

Shifting social patterns can be investigated through the examination of differences in the experiences and perceptions of successive generational cohorts (Glenn 1977; Howe and Strauss 2007). Generational theory posits that the shared formative experiences of a cohort of people born and raised in the same historical era form the basis for shared values and personality traits (Mannheim [1928] 1952; Twenge 2006). There is considerable variation in the way that today's generational groups have been categorized in the management literature (Parry and Urwin 2011). In this study, we define the cohorts using birth-year boundaries that are reflective of Canadian research: Baby Boomers were born between 1945 and 1964; Generation Xers were born between 1965 and 1979; and Millennials were born in 1980 or later (Barnard et al. 1998; Foot 1998; Lancaster and Stillman 2002).

The earliest of the Baby Boomers entered the full-time adult labor force in the mid-1960s, when unemployment rates hovered around 5 percent (Gower 1992). With these opportunities available to them, Baby Boomers are said to have worked intently to build "stellar careers" in an era of economic expansion and low unemployment during their early-career phase (Lancaster and Stillman 2002).

When the first of the Generation Xers entered the labor force in the early 1980s, they faced the dual challenges of weak job prospects resulting from outsourcing and poor job growth, and increasing "credentialism" as the rate of post-secondary education continued to rise (Lancaster and Stillman 2002; Moses 1997). People of this generation have been characterized as "job-hoppers," changing jobs and employers frequently to gain new skills to pursue opportunities, even if lateral moves were required (Lancaster and Stillman 2002).

The millennial generation began entering the labor force in the late 1990s, when unemployment rates were lower than 8 percent, the most favorable labor market since the late 1970s (Canada Employment Insurance Commission 2010). Although the millennial generation is relatively new to the labor market, commentators have suggested they will be highly mobile and will expect great change and variety in their job assignments (Lancaster and Stillman 2002). They are purported to be impatient in terms of advancement (Ng et al. 2010), and willing to change employers frequently to advance their careers (Corporate Leadership Council 2005). They are also said to place great emphasis on work–life balance, and are willing to sacrifice career advancement in favor of lifestyle (Lancaster and Stillman 2002).

Few studies to date have empirically investigated differences in the career experiences of different generational cohorts. In a sample of 380 Belgian university students and employees, Dries et al. (2008) found that Generation Xers and Millennials were less likely than the silent generation (born before 1946) and Baby Boomers to have "bounded" careers (i.e. that follow the traditional upward linear career path), and were more likely to have "homeless" careers (i.e. mobility due to an inability to attain stability, even though it is desired) and "staying" careers (i.e. multiple previous job and organization changes, despite seeking security and stability with their current employer). More recently, Lyons et al. (2012) examined the objective career moves of the various generations and reported that younger generation workers changed jobs more frequently, made more upward and lateral career moves, and made more career changes than previous generations. These findings suggest there are indeed shifts in the career patterns among the various generations. However, they offer little in the way of explanation for why these changes are occurring. What is needed is a qualitative investigation of the experiences of each generation as a means of contextualizing and interpreting the inter-generational differences that have been examined. In particular, by examining the early career experiences of each generation, we gain an understanding of the foundational experiences that set them on differing career paths.

The early career stage

Career researchers have long recognized that individuals progress through predictable developmental stages throughout their careers. Super's (1957) seminal theory of career development argued that career development is a continuous process of learning and growth in which an individual develops and refines his/her career self-concept in the context of various life roles, and educational and work experiences. Super argued that people progress through four age-based career development stages: the early career stages of exploration and establishment; and the late career stages of maintenance and decline. In this chapter, we focus on the *exploration* and *establishment* stages, which have been completed by members of all three generations of workers in the present workforce and thus provide a basis for direct comparison of the generations. These early stages are indeed foundational, as one's early career experiences have subsequent implications for future career opportunities and ultimately career success.

The exploration stage is primarily focused on development of self-awareness and the exploration of career options through trial-and-error reality testing (Super 1957). It begins with a tentative period (ages 15–17), in which needs, interests, values, and abilities are considered in conjunction with future opportunities, and tentative choices are made that lay the foundation for future career decisions, including one's introduction to work via a first part-time job (Niles and Harris-Bowlsbey 2005). This is followed by a transition period (ages 18–21), in which the individual's growing perceptions of his/her competencies and labor market opportunities shape his/her self-concept and career decisions. The exploration phase concludes with a trial period (ages 22–24), in which the individual secures an entry-level job in his/her chosen occupational field and tries it out to determine if it is suitable as a profession. This stage also allows us to assess the degree of confidence, optimism, and self-efficacy when entering the labor market.

In the *establishment* stage, the individual seeks employment, settles into a career pattern that will carry him/her throughout the remainder of his/her career, and learns to integrate the roles of worker, spouse, and parent. Arthur et al. (1999) call this a period of "informed direction" in which the individual identifies a means to achieving career and life objectives, solidifies family relationships, and makes specialization choices that steer the direction of the career moving forward. The establishment stage begins with a trial period (ages 25–30) in which the individual adjusts in response to unsatisfactory employment situations, in search of his/her "life's work." Super (1957) noted that this is often a period of "floundering" for young people, as they move around geographically and occupationally, seeking through trial and error to find their career niche. Super also noted that careers become more stable as one matures, so job changes after age 30 are normally the exception rather than the rule. Thus, the establishment stage concludes with a stabilization period (ages 31–44) in which the individual works to secure a permanent place in a profession by becoming a dependable producer and establishing a strong reputation (Niles and Harris-Bowlsbey 2005). The establishment stage allows us to capture how individuals agree with their careers, capitalize on opportunities, and further their careers.

The present study

A limitation of Super's life-stage theory is that it did not acknowledge the potential for historical shifts in the developmental process. More recent career theories (e.g. Mitchell and Krumboltz's (1996) social learning theory of career decision making or Lent et al.'s (1996) social cognitive career theory) explicitly acknowledge the role of environment in shaping careers. This suggests that historical shifts in the social and economic conditions will result in changes in the nature of careers. Although, as noted above, there is some evidence of changing career patterns, there is little understanding of the qualitative nature of those changes or their underlying causes. This study thus qualitatively investigates the early career experiences of Millennials, Gen Xers, and Baby Boomers in order to gain insights into how career patterns may be changing and, more importantly, why.

Methods

Savickas's (2005: 43) career construction theory contends that a career is more than just a chronology of jobs and organizations; it is the patterning of career experiences into a cohesive whole that "produces a meaningful story" in the mind of the career actor. From this perspective, careers must be viewed in the context in which they were enacted, as they represent adaptations to an employment environment rather than mere enactments of maturation processes (Savickas 2005). We thus contend that the most appropriate way to assess potential generational differences in early career experiences is through the qualitative analysis of career narratives. "Narrative psychology" (Sarbin 1986) is part of a broader field of discourse analysis, useful for understanding the world from the perspective of those studied (informants) (Boyce 1995). Using career narratives allows us to explore, not just the parts of a career, but how those parts are related (Cochran 1990), providing insights about the internal and external factors that shaped early careers.

Informants in this study were guided through the narrative of their careers through in-depth, oral history interviews. An oral history allows informants to provide a detailed retrospective account of their experiences (Yow 1994). In an oral history interview, informants provide a retrospective account of their experiences, guided by an interviewer who may use complementary data to probe or focus on specific events (Yow 1994). In this study, interviewers used résumés of informants (interviewees) to guide the emerging career narratives. Résumés were deemed to be an appropriate source of complementary data, as they are created and maintained by individuals throughout their careers for the purposes of job search and promotion. Savickas (2005) notes that writing or updating a résumé requires the individual to re-construct his/her career history, making the résumé a natural point of reflection on one's career experiences. We acknowledge that some of the older workers may not remember all of their career experiences given time lapse. However, by reviewing informants' detailed résumés prior to the interviews, the interviewers were able to identify gaps in the respondents' career histories and pose probing questions to guide the emerging career narratives, focusing on career decisions and seeking details.

Participants

Participants in the present study (n = 84) were identified through snowball sampling. The researchers recruited a small sample of professional workers from their extended networks of friends, family, acquaintances, and colleagues. These initial respondents were asked to provide the names of individuals in their own extended networks who might be interested in participating in the study. The researchers continued sampling in this fashion until a minimum of ten participants was obtained for each of the generational cohorts. The sample was expanded during the analysis in order to ensure sufficient data to reach a point of saturation (Glaser and Strauss 1967), where we uncovered no unique career themes with additional members of a cohort. A number of the millennial respondents were eliminated from this study because they were under the age of 25 and had not accumulated significant career experience at the time of the interviews. The final sample was composed of 23 Baby Boomers, 40 Generation Xers, and 21 Millennials. The sample consisted of 44 women (52 percent) and 40 men. The participants worked in a variety of occupations: six worked in administrative or clerical positions (7 percent), ten worked in front-line or production jobs (12 percent), 23 worked in supervisory or middle-management positions (27 percent), 24 worked in professional, technical, or specialist positions (29 percent), and 21 were in senior management or executive positions (25 percent). Eighty-six percent of respondents were born in Canada.

Interview procedure

Data were obtained through in-depth oral history interviews guided by the researchers, who were informed by the respondent's objective career data (résumé). Prior to the interviews, respondents completed questionnaires[1] containing various demographic questions and a summary of the respondents' educational and work history, including a listing of all jobs and employers, starting with their first "career job." Respondents indicated whether each job change was upward, lateral, or downward in terms of status in pay, or a change of track entirely. Interviewers reviewed the pre-questionnaire responses for any gaps and inconsistencies in the historical data and sought clarification and probed for further information during interviews. Respondents were asked to "tell the story" of their careers, with prompts from the interviewers as needed to expand or clarify information, based on the résumé provided. Interviews were audio recorded and transcribed for analysis.

Data analysis

The interview transcript (career narratives), career history data, and demographic information for each respondent were compiled for analysis. The researchers independently reviewed a common set of data from five respondents (from all three generations) and discussed them to ensure a common understanding of the career narratives. The researchers then drafted short *career cases* that summarized the details of the transcripts and career histories and captured important quotes from the respondents. This served to focus the researchers on the salient career points identified by the respondents and helped to clarify their meaning in the context of this study. The career cases were then compared across the researchers to identify and address any discrepancies in the interpretation of the transcripts and in the depth and breadth of the career cases. Once a common strategy for drafting the career cases was reached, the remaining dossiers were divided among the researchers and career cases were drafted for all respondents.

The full analysis involved the researchers' reviewing the career cases on a generation-by-generation basis (based on the generational boundaries identified above) to identify themes that were both common to the generational cohorts and unique to individual cohorts. Representative quotes were collected to illustrate each theme, and are presented below.

Results and discussion

The career cases of all three generations revealed the typical struggles of the early career, such as choosing a university major, adjusting to working life, and developing one's career self-concept (i.e. one's vocational preferences and competencies). All three generations began working full-time at age 22 on average, though men started working full-time approximately one year sooner on average than women of their generation. The family status of the various generations during their early careers differed markedly. Of those respondents who reported having been married at least once, only 25 pe cent of the Millennials were married by age 30, compared to 50 percent of Gen Xers and 76 percent of Boomers. Only 12.5 percent of Millennials and Gen Xers had children by age 30, compared to 40 percent for the Boomers. However, there were notable differences in the ways that the early career stage was experienced by each generation. These differences are described in the following subsections.

Baby Boomers

The career cases of the early Baby Boomers (born prior to 1960) reflected a traditional upward, linear career path, often with a single employer. They spoke of the relative ease with which they found jobs in the earlier stages of their careers as well as the opportunities for advancement. Fred[2] is a typical example; he accepted an entry-level job with a company right out of university and within a year was promoted to a management position. He was promoted twice more before the age of 30. Another example is Olivia, a 59-year-old self-employed human resource consultant, who was hired out of high school into a clerical position with a large public utility company where she worked for 29 years. Within her first six years of employment she was promoted six times and was in a supervisory role by age 25. She continued to advance, receiving seven promotions by age 30 and ten by age 41. A sample of quotes illustrative of this theme is given in Table 10.1.

Most of the Boomer informants indicated that they did not have great expectations or a clear career plan when they started working. However, their lack of career planning often reflected a pattern of assessing opportunities as they emerged, rather than carefully plotting a course to follow. Many of the Boomers indicated that promotions in their early careers were unsolicited. However, despite an abundance of options, the Boomers expressed a general desire to stay with their employers throughout their early careers unless they had reasons to leave. The Boomers' early career cases reveal significant ambition and optimism, generally as a result of their successes, which gave them confidence moving forward. Some quotes indicative of this theme are given in Table 10.1.

The career cases of the late Boomers (born in the early 1960s) are similar in nature to those of the Generation Xers, as discussed below, indicating difficulty getting established in their careers. This suggests that, when considering career experiences, the generational boundary of 1961 (cf. Foot 1998) may be a more appropriate dividing line between the Boomer and Generation X cohorts.

TABLE 10.1 Themes and illustrative quotes from Baby Boomers

Theme 1: abundance of opportunities
Back in the 70s and even early 80s when you got tired of it you just moved on to the next town. Or if you had a partner and the partner decided to go somewhere you just pick up and find a new job in a couple of weeks. Those boom days for jobs are all gone. And that's sort of the way it is. Andy, 60, psychologist
School wasn't such a big thing when I [was young], not like it is today where you need a college education, because I could have quit my job on a Wednesday and had a new job on a Thursday. Abby, 51, retired auto worker
There was a great deal of work around and available for a young person … I had probably five different job offers at more or less the same time. Fred, 60, corporate managing director
My mother knew a gentleman who had pull. And I think at that time that's how you got a job. I literally went in and started the next day. I didn't go through any testing they didn't have testing back then. It was just you met that person who was with personnel and he said "we'll start you here." Rachel, 54, administrative assistant
Theme 2: upward career progression by seizing available opportunities
I would say that my career has happened by accident rather than by design. It was serendipitous events and going where you are needed. I seldom interviewed for jobs, but have been requested to join teams or change jobs. Veronica, 57, school psychologist
If you applied yourself and demonstrated that you had a good work ethic and were competent at your job, there were opportunities for you to apply to different positions all along the way. In some cases, particularly at lower levels, you were encouraged to apply for jobs that happened to come up. Olivia, 59, self-employed human resource consultant
Theme 3: self-confidence gained through experience
When I was an analyst I thought "I could be a manager now." When I became a manager of analysts, I thought "I could be a vice president of the corporation." When I became a senior vice president of marketing, I was managing a team of 107 people, and I thought, "well I could be an executive vice president." Rick, 61, CEO of a financial services company
When I first started, for women certainly … expectations were not very high. If you could get into an office that was pretty good. When I started working, my expectations changed completely. I was working in law firms and accounting firms and the accounting firm suggested I do vocational tests and … I got a university degree, which changed things. Emily, 60, legal assistant

Generation Xers

The linear, upward career patterns that were common among the early Boomers were not as evident among the Gen Xers, fewer of whom worked for a single employer throughout their earlier careers. Several of the Gen X informants entered post-secondary education, but then dropped out to go to work, often going back to complete their education at a later time, or completing a second degree to further their credentials and increase their opportunities. Others completed post-secondary education and had no clear plans for how their careers would unfold after they graduated, often because they were the first in their families to achieve such levels of education.

Like the Boomers, the career cases of the Generation Xers reveal little planning in their early careers. Unlike the Boomers, however, whose lack of a career plan largely coincided with a "wait-and-see" approach to emerging opportunities, the Gen Xers' lack of planning reflected difficulty in identifying relevant opportunities, despite having obtained educational credentials. One example of this phenomenon is Nate, a 38-year-old occasional teacher, who had no clear plan and pursued a variety of different avenues throughout his early career, including working in real estate and studying science, business administration, and computer science in university and college before he eventually pursued education and work in teaching. Another example is Alex, a 40-year-old policy analyst, who struggled to find work out of university in the early 1990s and ended up driving a truck to make ends meet, returning to university almost a decade later to obtain a master's degree.

Like the Baby Boomers, the Gen Xers also expressed low expectations for their initial careers. However, these low expectations were not attributed to unknown career prospects, but to a perceived lack of opportunities to get established. Many willingly started their careers in less-than-ideal jobs in order to get started and pay their bills. Although most of our interviewees had post-secondary education, it was common for them to start in positions that were not related to their education or for which they could be deemed overqualified. The lack of opportunities and low confidence in their initial abilities is demonstrated in Table 10.2.

TABLE 10.2 Themes and illustrative quotes from Generation Xers

Theme 1: absence of opportunities
I found it was very difficult to find a job in the field. I tried only professional jobs and then I decided that I needed to pay the bills … so I decided to get any job. I got a few administrative jobs and then I tried to get in to the federal government, so I accepted a clerical job. Within three years, I changed three different positions and now, probably two years ago, I got where I feel I'm supposed to be in terms of my education. Marta, 35, public servant
I think I'm a typical Gen Xer, where you go to university and you get out and there was just nothing. There was no job and nobody wanted you. I remember, you know, you wanted to build some experience, people wouldn't even have you volunteer, they just didn't want you there in the building even. It's easy to look back and say, "well that was a blip," but as a group we went through it this way and when you're living it, that's your reality. It's pretty limiting, it's bleak … your expectations were so low and trying to see beyond that was just difficult at the time … but the mindset then was just if you can get out there and put a roof over your head and get the basics and a couple hundred bucks in your pocket at the end of the year. Alex, 40, policy analyst
I have never really had a plan. Yes, so I never really said I want to be a director and this is what I want to do. I've always just done the best job that I can at the time in the job I'm doing … I've never had a path to say "yeah, this is what I'm aiming for." When I first started my career, I was really just focused on foot in the door. I would have worked for free. I just wanted the experience and I started off at a really piddly salary … I was just so happy to have the opportunity. Christine, 31, HR director
Theme 2: lack of confidence
When I joined the public service I didn't necessarily think that I would be able to get to where I am as quickly as I have … there [are] a lot of really smart people around who sort of blow your mind when you speak to them and when you see them in action. You sort of think that you know, maybe one day down the road I could be at that … It's really tough to visualize fresh out of school. Nathan, 31, public policy analyst
I was really unsure of my capabilities. I never thought I could be one of those people that was managing other people, or one of those people that was even making a salary per se. You know, I just didn't, I had no idea what I was capable of. Really, I had low self-confidence at that point until it was tested. Christine, 31, HR director
I was 25, 26 … you know at the point you're not really sure what your capabilities are and they approached me and said "what do you think would be interested [in a managerial position]?" And I said "yeah sure, if you guys have the confidence, I'll do it." But, you know, looking back, it was really too much. I had no people management skills whatsoever. I'd been a sales person, a successful sales person but I had no people management skills and that's really what was the difficult part of it … I then took a step back and just sort of rebuilt and went back and learned all the things that people just assumed that I knew before and didn't. Laura, 41, senior sales manager

Millennials

As with the older generations, the career cases of the Millennials suggested little career planning – particularly in the long term. Millennials' stories suggested high mobility and a restlessness in their early career stages. As shown in the first theme in Table 10.3, Millennials were ambitious and eager to advance rapidly in earnings and status. A number of the career cases indicate a desire to continuously advance and a willingness to change jobs and employers after only a short time in order to move up. An example of this is Jessica, a 30-year-old human resources specialist, who indicated that she had intended to advance rapidly. Following a series of temporary positions in low-paying service jobs, Jessica applied for a human resources position for which she was not hired. She attributes her not being hired to her honest insistence that this position would be a "stepping stone" for her (see Table 10.3).

A second type of restlessness relates to a desire to accumulate a variety of life experiences and to live in a desired location (see Table 10.3). A number of the Millennials indicated that they pursued career opportunities in order to travel or live in a specific country or region. In most cases, these opportunities were intended to be temporary. For instance, André, a 28-year-old learning coach, recounts how he ended up working at a resort hotel: "I thought I would stay only for the summer at the beginning, but my passion, basically skiing, [brought me to] the middle of the Rockies … I fell in love with rock-climbing so it kept me here."

Another common theme among the Millennials was a short-term perspective on career planning. Many indicated that they were in perpetual job search and rather unwilling to stay in one place for too long if they were feeling unsatisfied. The traditional notion of "paying one's dues" by working one's way up in the company is not reflected in their cases. Rather, they appear to view external opportunities as the most viable route to career advancement. Many, like Jessica mentioned above, accepted jobs that they viewed to be "stepping stones" to more desirable positions. For instance, Haley, a 28-year-old analyst for a law-enforcement organization, indicated that she accepted an entry-level administrative position upon graduating with her master's degree, but continued searching and moved into a more senior job within three months. The Millennials indicated an acceptance of the temporary nature of entry-level jobs, such as co-op positions, term jobs, and management training programs as necessary steps in the early career process today.

Although some Millennials did not express a strong desire to change jobs and employers, they tended to show indifference, rather than patience. For instance, when we asked Chase, a 25-year-old employee of an accounting firm, how he saw his career unfolding between now and his retirement, he said: "I haven't actually thought about it, I have no idea. I'll probably stay here until I decide that I don't want to. Or I win the lottery."

TABLE 10.3 Themes and illustrative quotes from the Millennials

Theme 1: eagerness for advancement
When I first started … I just kind of figured that two years would be an appropriate time to work there and gain experience, and you know kind of figure out where I belong … I would say within the next year or two years, I will probably look for something, another experience, more so than leave the company, just look for another experience … I do tend to like to move up and advance my career as much as I can. Whether that means moving up or moving laterally, it makes no difference to me. Zakiya, 25, retail pharmacy employee
I read somewhere [that] if young people aren't being promoted within two years of the company, then they feel like they're wasting their time. And I've been promoted three times in twenty months, so … The first time it took a long time, took a year, to get there, but after that it definitely exceeded my expectations. Marvin, 25, machine operator
They decided not to hire me in that position because they weren't sure that I would stay for a lengthy period of time, because I had indicated that I wanted to grow my career and that I wanted to move onwards and upwards, and that I wanted to use it as a step to move onwards … that was the feedback that I got. Jessica, 30, human resources specialist
Theme 2: eagerness for variety
I understand that I am in a very fortunate position but it doesn't change the fact that I'm willing to leave if something better comes around, which I guess is inherent to my generation … I want international work experience very badly, and I think that a position in China or India would be very beneficial for me in the future. Eric, 25, IT consultant
I would be very interested in moving … that's one of the reasons I chose to work in the hospitality industry because you're able to move from coast to coast or even around the globe depending on the company. Jody, 26, human resource recruiter
Well I've worked with small organizations, I've worked in the provincial government, I felt like federal experience was something that I needed for my long-term career aspirations. I'm not necessarily going to stay in the federal government, but just to see what it was like. Chris, 25, policy analyst
Theme 3: willingness to leave employers
For the short amount of time I've been out of school, I've had a lot of changes so I always say I never know where I'm going to be in the next year, I can't really predict. Haley, 28, policy analyst
I'm really challenged right now and they're developing me … But if they let me stand for a while I'm going to start looking elsewhere. I keep my options open … if there's something better somewhere else, for sure, I'll move. André, 28, learning coach
I think people should be as loyal to their company as their company is loyal to them. You know, I have been here so many years, basically sacrificing so much of my personal life. Annie, 29, hotel housekeeping manager

General discussion

The career cases examined here reveal that, although all three generations faced the developmental challenges that are expected in the early career stage, the nature of those challenges differed among generations, as did their adaptations to them. The themes that emerged for each of the generations and how their early career patterns are different are summarized in Table 10.4. All three generations indicated that the early career period was a time of exploration and trial-and-error as they sought to establish their career self-constructs. None of the generations indicated that they had clear plans at the outset of their careers. However, the early Boomers' lack of planning was not an impediment to their success, as opportunities abounded for them. In contrast, the Generation Xers' (and late Boomers') lack of planning coincided with a paucity of opportunity that required them to be adaptive and take whatever jobs came their way and make the best of them through subsequent education and training. The Millennials' lack of a plan does not seem to have inhibited their ambition and there is much evidence in their career cases to suggest that they know when their needs are not being met and are willing to move on, sometimes in the absence of other opportunities.

Baby Boomers experienced a relatively easy transition to work, followed by linear upward progress. Gen Xers described difficulties establishing their careers and were more mobile than the Boomers (out of necessity). Millennials were even more mobile than Gen Xers and expressed restlessness and eagerness for advancement.

The cases of the Baby Boomers and the Generation Xers reflected a lack of confidence early in their careers. This theme was not evident in the Millennials' cases. In the case of the Boomers, their lack of initial confidence was offset by the opportunities that they were afforded to rapidly advance and develop; opportunities that often came in the form of unsolicited promotions and job offers. The Generation Xers' cases indicate that their initial lack of confidence was overcome through their resilience and their ability to learn and develop, often without clear advancement opportunities.

TABLE 10.4 Comparison of themes across generations

Baby Boomers	*Generation Xers*	*Millennials*
Abundance of opportunities	Absence of opportunities	Eagerness for advancement
Upward career progression by seizing available opportunities	Lack of confidence	Eagerness for variety
Self-confidence gained through experience		Willingness to leave employers

Another similarity is that an upward, linear career pattern predominated the cases of all three generations. However, the overall upward career trajectories did not always take place within single organizations and the younger generations described successively more mobility in their early career trajectories. The younger two generations were less likely to have worked for a single employer throughout their early careers stage.

The results suggest that the economic and labor conditions faced by the Boomers allowed them the confidence to take chances and exploit the abundant opportunities available to them, while rising steadily in their early careers. In contrast, a tougher economy and less hospitable labor market provided fewer opportunities for Gen Xers, likely eroding their confidence and causing them to seek out alternate approaches to their careers and build resilience. Improvements in the economy, combined with a labor market that is well aware of the skills gap that will be created by the retiring Baby Boomers, may have contributed to their restlessness and eagerness for advancement and variety. As generational theory suggests, the shared career-related environmental conditions of the generational cohorts would seem to form the basis for shared career experiences.

Conclusion and limitations

The use of career cases allowed us to investigate the careers of members of the three generations in a qualitative sense, through the perspectives of the informants' career narratives. Although still cross-sectional in nature, the use of career narratives allowed us to compare the early career histories of each generation. Retrospective accounts may introduce some bias, however, and the differing ages of the three generations in this study translate into different time lapses in retrospection (Baby Boomers were reflecting on career decisions made almost 50 years ago). However, the process of oral history interviews allowed us to contextualize the events of individuals' career histories, bringing life to the objective data contained in their résumés. The patterns revealed in these narratives suggest that the early career stages of successive generations have differed in important ways that had lasting impacts on their subsequent career trajectories. Future research should seek to verify the themes observed here in a larger representative sample in order to assess their generalizability. However, these preliminary findings suggest that the life-stage model of career development, while still valuable, must be interpreted within the historical context of opportunities and challenges in which the life stages are enacted.

Notes

1 The pre-interview questionnaire data were analyzed by Lyons et al. (2012).
2 All names are pseudonyms.

References

Arthur, M.B., Inkson, K. and Pringle, J.K. (1999) *The New Careers: Individual Action and Economic Change*, London: Sage.

Barnard, R., Cosgrove, D. and Welsh, J. (1998) *Chips and Pop: Decoding the Nexus Generation*, Toronto: Malcolm Lester.

Boyce, M.E. (1995) 'Collective centring and collective sense-making in the stories and storytelling of one organization', *Organization Studies*, 16(1): 107–137.

Briscoe, J.P. and Finkelstein, L.M. (2009) 'The "new career" and organizational commitment: do boundaryless and protean attitudes make a difference?', *Career Development International*, 14: 242–260.

Burke, R. and Ng, E. (2006) 'The changing nature of work and organizations: implications for human resource management', *Human Resource Management Review*, 16(2): 86–94.

Canada Employment Insurance Commission (2010) *Monitoring and Assessment Report*, Ottawa: Human Resources and Skills Development Canada.

Cochran, L.R. (1990) 'Narrative as a paradigm for career research', in R.A. Young and W.A. Borgen (eds) *Methodological Approaches to the Study of Career*, New York: Praeger, pp. 71–86.

Corporate Leadership Council (2005) *HR Considerations for Engaging Generation Y Employees*, Washington, DC: Corporate Executive Board.

Dries, N., Pepermans, R. and De Kerpel, E. (2008) 'Exploring four generations' beliefs about career: is "satisfied" the new "successful"?', *Journal of Managerial Psychology*, 23(8): 907–928.

Foot, D.K. (1998) *Boom, Bust, and Echo 2000*, Toronto: MacFarlane Walter and Ross.

Glaser, B. and Strauss, A. (1967) *The Discovery of Grounded Theory: Strategies for Qualitative Research*, New York: Aldine Publishing Company.

Glenn, N.D. (1977) *Cohort Analysis*, Beverly Hills, CA: Sage.

Gower, D. (1992) 'A note on Canadian unemployment since 1921', *Perspectives on Labour and Income*, 4(3): 1–5.

Howe, N. and Strauss, W. (2007) 'The next 20 years: how customer and workforce attitudes will evolve', *Harvard Business Review*, July–August: 41–52.

Lancaster, L.C. and Stillman D. (2002) *When Generations Collide: Who They Are; Why They Clash; How to Solve the Generational Puzzle at Work*, New York: Harper Collins.

Lent, R.W., Brown, S.D. and Hackett, G. (1996) 'Career development from a social cognitive perspective', in D. Brown, L. Brooks and Associates (eds), *Career Choice and Development*, 3rd edn, San Francisco, CA: Jossey-Bass, pp. 373–421.

Lynn, S.A., Cao, L.T. and Horn, B.C. (1996) 'The influence of career stage on the work attitudes of male and female accounting professionals', *Journal of Organizational Behavior*, 17: 135–149.

Lyons, S.T., Schweitzer, L., Ng, E.S. and Kuron, L.K. (2012) 'Comparing apples to apples: a qualitative investigation of career mobility patterns across four generations', *Career Development International*, 17(4): 333–357.

Mannheim, K. ([1928] 1952) *Essays on the Sociology of Knowledge*, London: Routledge and Kegan Paul.

Mitchell, L.K. and Krumboltz, J.D. (1996) 'Krumboltz's theory of career choice and counseling', in D. Brown, L. Brooks and Associates (eds) *Career Choice and Development*, 3rd edn, San Francisco, CA: Jossey-Bass, pp. 233–280.

Moses, B. (1997) *Career Intelligence: Mastering the New Work and Personal Realities*, Toronto: Stoddard.

Ng, E.S.W., Schweitzer, L. and Lyons, S.T. (2010) 'New generation, great expectations: a field study of the Millennial generation', *Journal of Business Psychology*, 25: 281–292.

Niles, S.G. and Harris-Bowlsbey, J. (2005) *Career Development Interventions in the 21st Century*, 2nd edn, Upper Saddle River, NJ: Pearson.

Parry, E. and Urwin, P. (2011) 'Generational differences in work values: a review of theory and evidence', *International Journal of Management Reviews*, 13(1): 79–96.

Sarbin, T.R. (1986) *Narrative Psychology: The Storied Nature of Human Conduct*, Westport, CT: Praeger Publishers/Greenwood Publishing Group.

Savickas, M.L. (2005) 'Career construction: a developmental theory of vocational behavior', in D. Brown, L. Brooks and Associates (eds) *Career Choice and Development*, 4th edn, San Francisco, CA: Jossey-Bass, pp. 149–205.

Shindul-Rothschild, J. (1995) 'Life-cycle influence on staff nurse career expectations', *Nursing Management*, 26(6): 40.

Sullivan, S. and Baruch, Y. (2009) 'Advances in career theory and research: a critical review and agenda for future exploration', *Journal of Management*, 35: 1542–1571.

Super, D. (1957) *Psychology of Careers*, New York: Harper and Brothers.

Twenge, J.M. (2006) *Generation Me: Why Today's Young Americans are More Confident, Assertive, Entitled and More Miserable than Ever Before*, New York: Free Press.

Twenge, J.M., Campbell, S.M., Hoffman, B.J. and Lance, C.E. (2010) 'Generational differences in work values: leisure and extrinsic values increasing, social and intrinsic values decreasing', *Journal of Management*, 36(5): 1117–1142.

Yow, V.R. (1994) *Recording Oral History: A Practical Guide for Social Scientists*, Thousand Oaks, CA: Sage Publications.

11

BEYOND GENERATIONAL DIFFERENCES?

Exploring individual and organizational influences on inter-generational work attitudes and experiences

Jean McCarthy, Jeanette N. Cleveland and Noreen Heraty

Introduction

For the first time in history, there are four generations in the workplace and with this comes a unique opportunity to better understand age diversity at work. The ability to manage an age-diverse workforce towards effective work performance and well-being is a critical issue for leaders and organizations worldwide. It is thus recognized that the manner in which organizations shape this new work environment will require some understanding of the variation in work attitudes and experiences that exist among age-diverse work groups (Bartz *et al.* 1990). Furthermore, this awareness of age variations with respect to work attitudes within organizations is necessary to encourage employees' feeling of being valued organizational members (Armstrong-Stassen and Lee 2009). However, despite the growing body of literature investigating generational differences, the majority of which has been 'based on observation rather than large-scale empirical findings' (Cogin 2012: 2269), and upon work values (such as the PWE scale; Mirels and Garrett 1971), there remains a dearth of reported evidence on actual work outcomes including employees work attitudes about their current working life. Costanza *et al.* (2012: 390) note that 'there is a need for additional, scientifically sound, primary research on generational differences in work-related outcomes … [which] makes more comparisons across cohorts'. Both Dencker *et al.* (2008) and Twenge *et al.* (2010) argue that progress in understanding age diversity is being curtailed by an over-reliance on single assessment research designs that fail to account for a variety of individual and organizational influences on generational comparisons (Benson and Brown 2011). Indeed, reports on generational differences often imply homogeneity within a generation (or little within group variation) (Macky *et al.* 2008), yet it is recognized that generational cohorts are diverse along a number of dimensions (Parry and Urwin 2011).

It cannot be assumed therefore that all members of a generation will experience the workplace in the same way (Giancola 2006), and so a better understanding of the factors that may influence generational variations in work attitudes is required to provide a new perspective on generational cohorts in the workplace. This is our intention in this chapter.

As such, we set out to address two important issues. First, we explore whether generational differences exist in a number of important work attitudes, namely job satisfaction; organizational commitment; and job stress. Second, we seek to identify what specific individual and organizational variables influence intergenerational differences in these important work attitudes. In doing so, we draw on data from two nationally representative surveys (conducted in Ireland in 2003 and 2009) exploring employees' attitudes towards, and experiences of, the changing workplace. Ireland provides a particularly compelling setting for such research because of the timing of these two surveys: the first was undertaken at the height of the so-called 'Celtic Tiger' period of economic boom, while the second was completed two years into the most severe economic recession that has been experienced since the foundation of the Irish State. For this reason, the research setting provides an important opportunity to track changing attitudes towards work and experiences of working life across the generational cohorts.

The chapter is organized around the following sections. Generational cohorts are first defined, and their characteristics and extant evidence on generations and work attitudes are explored in order to contextualize our research objectives. Next, we describe the research setting to provide the reader with an embedded understanding of the Irish labour market. We then discuss our sample frame and analysis, and present our main results. Following an interpretation and discussion of the findings, we consider our limitations and identify possible fruitful future directions for research.

Generations at work

A 'generation' is generally defined as 'an identifiable group that shares birth years, age, location and significant life events at critical developmental stages' (Kupperschmidt 2000: 66). For the first time in history there are now four generations in the workplace (American Association of Retired Persons 2010): Veterans (born 1925–1942), Baby Boomers (1943–1960), Generation X (1961–1981) and Generation Y (1982–2000) (Strauss and Howe 2001: 32). Table 11.1 presents both the work values and the influencing events associated with each generational cohort.

TABLE 11.1 Generational cohorts, work values and influencing events

Generation	*Values*	*Influencing events*
Veterans, also referred to as 'Traditionalists' and the 'Silent Generation' (Andert 2011; Foot and Stoffman 1996; Lancaster and Stillman 2002).	Veterans are inclined to follow the rules (Lieber 2010), value quality and respect (Andert 2011; Houlihan 2007) and are said to believe in traditional values, enacting traditional gender roles (Hankin 2005). At work, Veterans are said to be extremely loyal and patriotic employees (Hankin 2005; Lieber 2010) and build vast amounts of tacit knowledge specific to their organizations (Eisner 2005).	Great Depression, World War II, the 'Golden Age' of radio, emergence of the 'silver screen', the trade union movement and the discovery of penicillin (Cogin 2012; Lieber 2010).
Baby Boomers are the most often studied of the four generations (see, for example, Lieber 2010; Schultz and Adams 2007).	Boomers are said to be self-reliant, individualistic, competitive and often ruthless in the workplace (cf. Cogin 2012; Eisner 2005; Glass 2007), while also being considered loyal to their employers (Smith and Clurman 1997), with some being considered 'workaholics' (Appelbaum *et al.* 2005).	Vietnam War (cf. Callanan and Greenhaus 2008; Hankin 2005), the moon landing, the rise of television, the Cuban Missile Crisis, the Cold War (Lieber 2010), Watergate (cf. Bradford 1993; Smola and Sutton 2002) and 'Woodstock' (Adams 2000).
Generation X	Generation X members are considered to be distrustful of authority, government and even organizations, being more loyal to their profession rather than to their employers (Johnson and Lopes 2008). However, they are perceived to have strong problem-solving skills, efficient communication skills and appreciate freedom (Eisner 2005; Smith and Clurman 1997).	Increase of single-parent homes, economic struggles, the energy crisis and personal computers (cf. Andert 2011; Deal 2007; Zemke *et al.* 2000), rapid change, greater diversity at work and a lack of solid traditions (Smola and Sutton 2002).
Generation Y, also referred to as Millennials, Echo Boomers, Net Generation and the Recession Generation (Lieber 2010).	Generation Y members are believed to be more entrepreneurial than previous generations, work well alone, but better together, but are more likely to 'rock the boat' (Crumpacker and Crumpacker 2007; Martin 2005). Hira (2007) describes Generation Y as needy, impatient and lacking in problem-solving skills, while Smola and Sutton (2002) have stated that Generation Y lack focus and direction, often having high stimulus needs at work (Johnson and Lopes 2008).	Recession of 1990, developments such as computers, schoolyard violence, the Enron scandal, parental unemployment, social networking, 9/11, and an ever-increasing diversity in linguistics, ethnicity, sexual alignment and non-traditional families (Andert 2011; Lieber 2010; Rhodes 1983).

Research questions

Existing literature on the four generations at work is often anecdotal in nature, conflicting and focuses mainly on perceived generational characteristics and work values and, as already indicated, fails to account for generational differences in important individual work attitudes and experiences. We therefore propose the following research question:

> **Research question 1:** Do generational differences exist in employee job satisfaction; organizational commitment; and perceived job stress?

Job satisfaction, organizational commitment and stress among generations

Weiss and Cropanzano (1996: 2) argue that job satisfaction is 'an evaluative judgement about one's job that partly, but not entirely, results from emotional experiences at work ... Together, affective experiences and belief structures result in the evaluation ... *called* job satisfaction.' Job satisfaction thus relates to the feeling that people have about their jobs and the work they do and, as suggested by Lok and Crawford (2001), is reflective of the environment, circumstances, values and expectations associated with the tasks and responsibilities perceived by the employee. Riggio (2003: 214) notes that 'all aspects of a particular job, good, bad, positive and negative, are likely to contribute to the development of feelings of satisfaction'. In their recent meta-analysis, Costanza *et al.* (2012) found a general pattern whereby older generations were slightly more satisfied with their jobs than younger generations, even though the effect sizes were relatively 'small'. It is possible that, as older generations have settled into their organizations and jobs, their durability in terms of life and work experiences may serve to positively influence their perceptions of overall satisfaction levels, or anchor their expected levels of satisfaction. It could also be argued that older workers have gravitated towards work that has more meaning for them, or offers higher possibilities for experienced satisfaction. We therefore propose the following hypothesis for both of our data samples (2003 and 2009):

> **Hypothesis 1:** Older generations will have higher levels of job satisfaction than younger generations.

Organizational commitment has been explicated as an individual's global attitude regarding his/her personal identification with and involvement in an organization. It incorporates a person's 'strong belief in and acceptance of the organisation's goals and values; a willingness to exert considerable effort on behalf of the organisation; and (emphasizes) a definite desire to maintain organisational membership' (Porter *et al.* 1974: 604). Costanza *et al.*'s (2012) meta-analysis demonstrated that, while levels of organizational commitment varied between older and younger generations, generally (and contrary to popular belief) Generation X tended to report the highest levels of commitment. As such, we propose that in 2003 and 2009:

> **Hypothesis 2:** Generation X will report higher levels of organizational commitment than any other generational cohort.

Job stress refers to 'a situation wherein job related factors interact with the worker to change (i.e. disrupt or enhance) his or her psychological and/or physiological condition such that the person (i.e. mind–body) is forced to deviate from normal functioning' (Newman and Beehr 1979: 1). Existing research demonstrates that job stress is associated with negative outcomes such as counterproductive behaviour (see, for example, Lambert *et al.* 2007) and therefore remains an area of considerable interest in organizational research. While little research has been conducted on differences among the generational cohorts in terms of their stress levels at work, Twenge and Campbell (2008) suggest that stressors in the workplace can be particularly potent for Generation Y. In work and career terms, this generation are at a time of significant importance in terms of their developmental trajectory at work, and concomitantly at an age where family considerations are likely to be key influences of life events. We therefore propose the following hypothesis for each of our data samples (2003 and 2009):

> **Hypothesis 3:** Generation Y will report higher levels of perceived stress than any other generational cohort.

Research in this domain has often neglected to consider what particular configuration of individual and organizational variables may affect these differences in work attitudes. While the literature on management sciences and work psychology has established many of the individual and organizational factors influencing job satisfaction (see Kinicki *et al.* 2002), organizational commitment (see Mottaz 1988) and stress (Hansung and Stoner 2008; Martin and Schinke 1998; Toker and Biron 2013), it has not considered whether these factors are more applicable to particular generational groups (Benson and Brown 2011). Given that work attitudes can vary in terms of valence and strength, such that an individual can hold more or less favourable attitudes than others (Eagly and Chaiken 1993), it appears necessary to begin to explore how work attitudes, such as levels of job satisfaction, organizational commitment and stress may differ, not only between but within generations at work. Previous research on work attitudes as they relate with age has suggested that individual level variables such as employee gender and job level, and organizational level variables such as the industry within which an employee works, can influence their attitudes at work (see, for example, Clarke 1997; Kooij *et al.* 2011; Spector 1997). Hence, we formulate the following exploratory research question:

> **Research question 2:** Are generational differences in job satisfaction; organizational commitment; and job stress influenced by employee gender, job level or industry type?

Study context: the Irish labour market

The emergence of the 'Celtic Tiger' in the 1990s showcased Ireland as one of the fastest growing open economies in the world. This incredible growth was in complete contrast to the relative lack of or very slow development of any other industrialized country during the same period. From the late 1980s until the end of the twentieth century, economic growth (GDP) averaged over 5 per cent, while in some years growth was more than 10 per cent (Central Statistics Office 2010). The boom was attributed to progressive industrial policy that boosted large-scale foreign direct investment (FDI), low corporation tax, greater access to third level education and social partnership between the government and trade unions. The drivers of twenty-first-century expansion were primarily construction and consumer spending. From 2003 to early 2007, the Irish economy continued to expand at a steady 3–6 per cent per annum (McCarthy 2010). This unprecedented growth rate reversed the trends of high unemployment and mass migration, and instead attracted an influx of migrant workers; during the 1990s and 2000s Ireland's workforce became significantly more diverse in terms of nationality, language and ethnicity. The roar of the 'Celtic Tiger', however, was weakened when the country fell into recession in the wake of the global financial crisis of 2008. Since 2009, the Irish economy has experienced high unemployment, deflation and a widening government budget deficit.

Age demographics

Trends evidenced globally toward an overall ageing of the population are mirrored in the Irish situation. The 'demographic transition' (Kirk 1996) of declining mortality and fertility rates currently taking place represents a shift toward an ageing society whereby, as the population ages, the workforce ages. These changes to population demographics are well established in most developed countries worldwide, while developing nations are beginning to experience similar transitions (United Nations 2002). The United Nations Population Division (2010: 11) states that 'the number of older persons has tripled over the last fifty years; it will more than triple again over the next fifty years'. The older population is growing faster than the total population. In Europe, it is projected that those aged 65 years or more will account for 30 per cent of the European Union's population by 2060, compared with the current rate of 17.3 per cent (Eurostat 2010). Approximately 11 per cent of the Irish population is now aged 65 and over. Projections forecast that 20–25 per cent of the population will be aged over 65 in 2041. The number of oldest persons (aged 80 and over) is projected to quadruple from 110,000 to 440,000 by 2041 (Central Statistics Office 2011). The age structure of the Irish population, however, is different to most other countries in the European Union. The median age of the population is 35, which is about 10–15 years younger than in the EU 27. Still, by 2050, Ireland's population structure will be quite similar to the rest of Europe and other developed countries (McCarthy 2010).

Method

Sample and procedure

The National Centre for Partnership and Performance in Ireland commissioned two large-scale surveys (in 2003 and 2009) exploring employees' attitudes towards, and experiences of, the changing workplace, in both the public and private sectors.

2003 study

The sample was selected on a random basis from a total of 300 sampling points throughout the country. A set of 100 random telephone numbers was generated in each sampling part and these were used to generate a targeted 20 completed questionnaires from each cluster point. The final report is based on the analysis of 5,189 questionnaires. The fieldwork for the survey was carried out between June and September 2003, using a telephone methodology.

2009 study

The sample was selected in the same way as in the 2003 study, replicating the questionnaire measures used in 2003. The final report is based on the analysis of 5,110 questionnaires. The fieldwork for the survey was carried out from March to June 2009, using a telephone methodology. Table 11.2 shows the descriptive statistics for both the 2003 and 2009 samples.

TABLE 11.2 Sample descriptives

Generation	*Total (n)*	*%*	*Male (n)*	*Female (n)*	*Public sector (n)*	*Private sector (n)*	*Manager or supervisor (n)*	*Rank and file (n)*
2003 study								
Veterans	219	4.2	131	88	96	123	79	140
Baby Boomers	1,835	35.4	862	973	879	956	687	1,138
Generation X	2,663	51.3	1,192	1,471	846	1,817	925	1,706
Generation Y	472	9.1	227	245	42	430	29	438
Total	5,189	100	2,412	2,777	1,863	3,326	1,720	3,422
2009 study								
Veterans	49	1	27	22	45	4	13	36
Baby Boomers	1,209	23.7	619	590	1,136	73	497	712
Generation X	3,020	59.1	1,432	1,588	2,854	166	1,169	1,851
Generation Y	832	16.3	353	479	810	22	145	687
Total	5,110	100	2,431	2,679	4,845	265	1,824	3,286

Note: the age structure of the Irish population, as previously discussed, is different to most other countries in the European Union and in the US. The median age of the population is 35, which is about 10–15 years younger than in the EU 27 and in the US, hence a larger representation of Generation X than Baby Boomers in our sample. Still, by 2050, Ireland's population structure will be quite similar to the rest of Europe and other developed countries (McCarthy 2010).

Measures

The survey instrument used in the 2003 study was designed to capture a comprehensive range of information on the nature of the job and the organization of work, and was replicated in the 2009 study. Variables of interest to the present research are described below.

Generation

Participants were categorized according to their birth date as Veterans (born 1925–1942), Baby Boomers (born 1943–1960), Generation X (born 1961–1981) or Generation Y (born 1982–2000) (Strauss and Howe 1991: 32).

Job satisfaction

Job satisfaction was measured using a four-item scale based on the work of Spector (1997). Participants were asked to what extent they agreed or disagreed with statements describing their current work situation. Items included statements such as 'In general, I am satisfied with my present job', 'I am satisfied with my physical working conditions' and 'I am satisfied with my earnings from my current job'. Each item was scored and measured according to a four-point, Likert-type scale, ranging from 1 (strongly disagree) to 4 (strongly agree). The *job satisfaction* scale yielded a reliability (Cronbach's alpha) of α = .749 in the 2003 study and α = .732 in 2009.

Organizational commitment

Organizational commitment was measured using a five-item scale adapted from the work of Mowday *et al.* (1979) and Marsden *et al.* (1993). Organizational commitment is considered to be an individual employee's psychological attachment and loyalty to their organization. Participants were asked to what extent they agreed or disagreed with statements describing their current work situation. Items included statements such as 'I am willing to work harder than I have to in order to help this organization succeed', 'My values and the organizations values are very similar' and 'I would turn down another job in order to stay with this organization'. Each item was scored and measured according to a four-point, Likert-type scale, ranging from 1 (strongly disagree) to 4 (strongly agree).The *organizational commitment* scale yielded a reliability (Cronbach's alpha) of α = .755 in 2003 and α = .717 in 2009.

Job stress

Job stress was measured using a five-item scale based on the work of Spector *et al.* (2000). Participants were asked how often they experienced stress in their current work situation. Items included statements such as 'How often do you find your work stressful?', 'How often do you come home from work exhausted?' and 'How often do you feel too tired after work to enjoy the things you would like to do at home?' Each item was scored and measured according to a five-point, Likert-type scale, ranging from 1 (never) to 5 (always). The *job stress* scale yielded a reliability (Cronbach's alpha) of $\alpha = .848$ in 2003 and $\alpha = .812$ in 2009.

Results

One of the first things to note is that all of the means for job satisfaction and organizational commitment increased in the five-year interval between measurement, while two of the generations reported less stress in 2009 than in 2003. This is an interesting overall observation, most especially as it occurred during a time of greater economic uncertainty. It is speculated that this economic uncertainty may hold some explanatory power here. As Ireland fell into recession and job losses and likelihood of forced emigration (for employment purposes) were experienced by virtually every household, this may have triggered some 'survivor' instincts among those who remained in employment in 2009. People were glad to have a job, and this may be reflected in marginally higher mean values for satisfaction and commitment. Specific inter-generational comparisons shed greater light on these job attitudes beyond mean values and these are presented against our research questions here.

Research question 1

The means and standard deviations of each generational cohort against the work attitudes of job satisfaction, organizational commitment and job stress are presented in Table 11.3 for both the 2003 and the 2009 study. Two-way analysis of variance was used to test our set of hypotheses.

TABLE 11.3 Means and standard deviations

	Job satisfaction		*Organizational commitment*		*Job stress*	
Generation	*Mean*	*S.D.*	*Mean*	*S.D.*	*Mean*	*S.D.*
2003 study						
Veterans	3.14	.448	2.86	.487	2.38	.837
Baby Boomers	3.05	.482	2.74	.453	2.63	.841
Generation X	3.05	.463	2.70	.464	2.68	.818
Generation Y	3.01	.462	2.62	.487	2.36	.862
2009 study						
Veterans	3.30	.456	2.98	.479	1.94	.813
Baby Boomers	3.15	.514	2.93	.509	2.46	.910
Generation X	3.10	.496	2.87	.471	2.71	.897
Generation Y	3.06	.496	2.84	.464	2.58	.875

Job satisfaction

In 2003, the results indicated that there was a significant main effect for generation. Post-hoc comparisons indicated that Generation Y and Veterans differed in levels of job satisfaction, such that Veterans held significantly higher levels of job satisfaction than Generation Y. In 2009, there was also a significant main effect for generation. Post-hoc comparisons indicated that both Veterans and Baby Boomers held significantly higher levels of job satisfaction than Generation Y and Generation X. The effect size in both samples, however, was weak (.004 in 2003 and .005 in 2009), but the results offer some support to our first hypothesis that older generations would hold higher levels of job satisfaction than younger generations.

Organizational commitment

In 2003, there was a statistically significant main effect for generation, but the effect size was small (.010). Post-hoc comparisons demonstrated significant differences between all four cohorts, where Veterans reported significantly higher levels of organizational commitment than any other cohort, followed by Baby Boomers and Generation X, with Generation Y reporting significantly lower levels of organizational commitment than any other cohort. In 2009, there was also a statistically significant main effect for generation. Post-hoc comparisons indicated that Baby Boomers held significantly higher levels of organizational commitment than both Generation X and Generation Y. Our second hypothesis that Generation X will report higher levels of organizational commitment than any other generational cohort is thus rejected.

Job stress

In 2003, there was a significant main effect for generation, with a small effect size (.015). Post-hoc comparisons demonstrated that Generation Y reported significantly lower levels of job stress than Generation X and Baby Boomers, and Baby Boomers and Generation X reported significantly higher levels of job stress than Veterans and Generation Y. In 2009, again there was a significant main effect for generation, but the effect size for generation was small (.018). Veterans reported significantly lower levels of stress than all other generational cohorts. Baby Boomers reported significantly lower levels of stress than both Generation X and Generation Y, while Generation X reported significantly higher levels of stress than all other generational cohorts. Our third hypothesis, that Generation Y will report higher levels of stress than any other generational cohort, is also rejected.

Research question 2

We used two-way analyses of variance to test interactions between generation and gender; job level; and sector to explore our second research question. These results are presented in Table 11.4.

TABLE 11.4 Two-way ANOVA results

Job satisfaction				
2003	*df*	*F*	*p*	Effect size
Gender	1	.118	.732	.000
Job level	1	.224	.636	.000
Industry sector	1	2.256	.13	.000
Generation X (gender)	3	.924	.428	.000
Generation X (job level)	3	5.520	.001	.003
Generation X (industry sector)	3	1.229	.297	.001
2009	*df*	*F*	*p*	Effect size
Gender	1	2.332	.127	.000
Job level	1	1.101	.294	.000
Industry sector	1	.197	.658	.000
Generation X (gender)	3	.926	.427	.001
Generation X (job level)	3	1.115	.342	.001
Generation X (industry sector)	3	1.19	.309	.001
Organizational commitment				
2003	*df*	*F*	*p*	Effect size
Gender	1	3.250	.072	.001
Job level	1	5.613	.018	.001
Industry sector	1	4.143	.042	.001
Generation X (gender)	3	.797	.495	.001
Generation X (job level)	3	5.613	.781	.001
Generation X (industry sector)	3	143	.191	.001
2009	*df*	*F*	*p*	Effect size
Gender	1	1.285	.257	.000
Job level	1	1.403	236	.000
Industry sector	1	1.193	.275	.000
Generation X (gender)	3	.511	.675	.000
Generation X (job level)	3	.228	.877	.000
Generation X (industry sector)	3	.581	.627	.000
Job stress				
2003	*df*	*F*	*p*	Effect size
Gender	1	675	.410	000
Job level	1	60.898	.000	.012

Job stress				
Industry sector	1	7.332	.007	.001
Generation X (gender)	3	1.583	.191	.001
Generation X (job level)	3	3.586	.013	.002
Generation X (industry sector)	3	.693	.556	.000
2009	*df*	*F*	*p*	Effect size
Gender	1	.245	.621	.000
Job level	1	8.418	.004	.002
Industry sector	1	1.905	.168	.000
Generation X (gender)	3	2.957	.031	.002
Generation X (job level)	3	.803	.492	.000
Generation X (industry sector)	3	1.274	.281	.001

Job satisfaction

In 2003, the interaction between generation and job level was statistically significant. Figure 11.1 suggests that managers and supervisors in Generation Y held lower levels of job satisfaction than Veteran, Baby Boomer and Generation X managers and supervisors. Veteran managers and supervisors held the highest levels of job satisfaction. However, there was no signification generational variation in levels of job satisfaction for those in non-managerial/supervisory positions. There were no significant interaction effects in the 2009 sample.

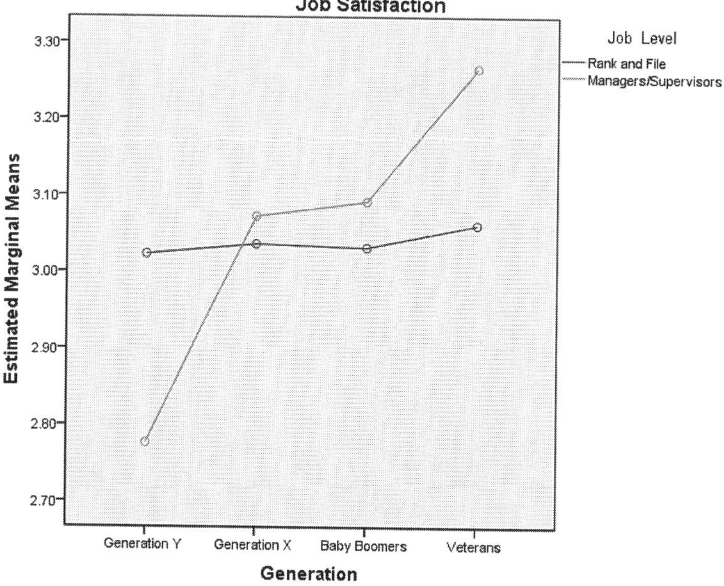

FIGURE 11.1 Interaction between generation and job level on job satisfaction, 2003

Organizational commitment

In 2003, there was a main effect observed between job level and organizational commitment, such that those in managerial positions in general were more likely to have higher levels of organizational commitment. Similarly, there was a main effect observed between industry sector and organizational commitment, such that those employed in the private sector were more likely, in this sample, to have higher levels of organizational commitment than those employed in the public sector. The interactions between generation and job level, and generation and industry sector, however, were not significant. Once again, there were no significant interaction effects in the 2009 sample.

Job stress

In 2003, a main effect was found between job level and job stress, such that those in managerial positions were more likely, in general, to report higher levels of job stress than those in rank-and-file positions. There was also a significant interaction between generation and job level. Figure 11.2 shows that when job level is taken into account, managers and supervisors in all generational cohorts reported higher levels of stress than their rank-and-file counterparts, with Generation Y managers and supervisors reporting the highest levels of stress. Rank-and-file positions in both Generation X and Baby Boomers reported higher levels of stress than Veterans and Generation Y in similar positions, even though the overall effect size was weak. In 2009, the interaction between generation and gender was found to be significant.

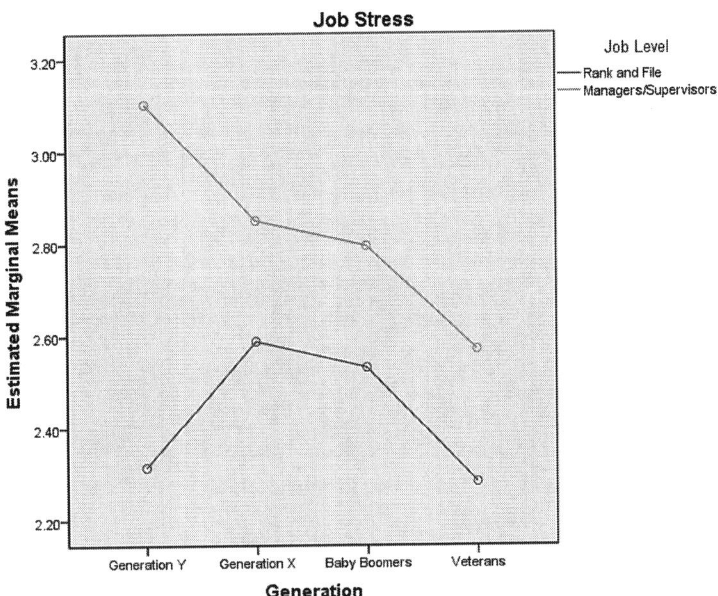

FIGURE 11.2 Interaction between generation and job level on job stress, 2003

Figure 11.3 shows that while male and females in both Generation Y and Generation X reported largely similar levels of job stress, Baby Boomer women reported higher levels of stress than men in this cohort, while Veteran men reported higher levels of job stress than Veteran women, although effect size was weak.

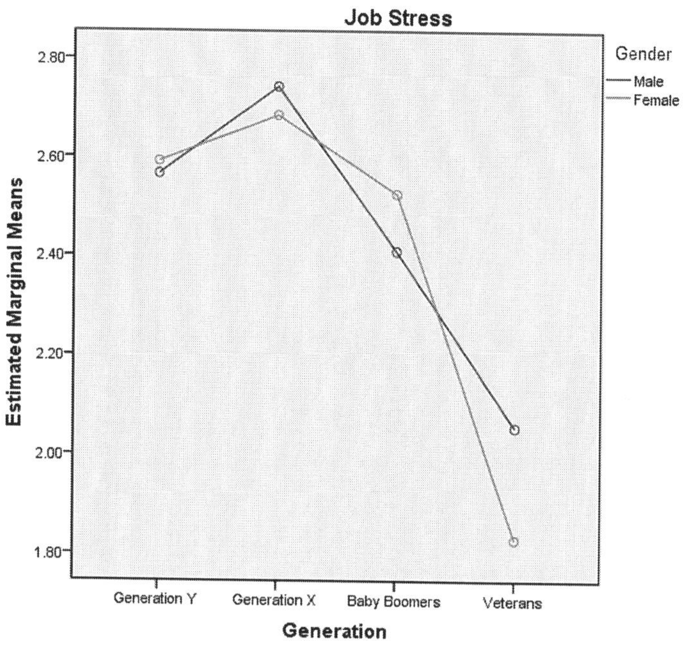

FIGURE 11.3 Interaction between generation and gender on job stress, 2009

Discussion

Our purpose through this research was to determine whether, and what types of, generational variations exist in work attitudes and perceptions among our study population, and to give some consideration to whether within-generation individual and organizational difference variables reveal significant group differences from one another. In so doing we contribute to the literature on generational differences in two particular ways. In the first instance, our evidence points to the existence of generational differences in work experiences and in perceptions about working life. Our results suggest that Generation Y employees report lower levels of job satisfaction and organizational commitment than any other generational cohort. Specifically, managerial employees in this generation cohort report the lowest levels of job satisfaction and ironically the lowest levels of stress also. Conversely, Veterans reported significantly higher levels of organizational commitment, while Veteran managers and supervisors held the highest levels of job satisfaction. The highest stress levels are reported by Generation Xers and, when job level is taken into account, managers and supervisors in all generational cohorts reported higher levels of stress than their rank-and-file counterparts. Generation Y managers and supervisors report the highest levels of stress. Combined, the results point to some generational differences and so add another dimension to the existing body of work which to date has focused almost exclusively on work values, rather than work attitudes and perceptions. However, like much previous work on generational variances, the effects sizes of our results were small.

Second, we show that the generation variable is the most significant predictor of work perceptions, even when controlling for the individual and contextual factors of gender, job level and industry type. This being the case, it is possible that the generation variable could be key to a host of other job factors and outcomes yet to be tested in this way. Next, our results show that interactions between generation and job level appears to hold some explanatory power when it comes to job satisfaction and stress, while the interaction between gender and generations similarly holds explanatory power with job stress levels also. We are thus able to gain some better understanding of this generational phenomenon and the possibilities it offers for reinterpreting the way we structure and organize our workplaces. This is an important factor to be considered by managers and most especially those who are charged with, and mindful of, the requirements for attending to an age-diverse workforce.

Implications, limitations and future research directions

While there is considerable value in the analysis based on the same sampling frame used here, the study is limited by the fact that the data is not longitudinal and so a true tracking of experienced change over the time period is not possible. Moreover, this remains a single country context and it would be especially interesting to compare the results here across cultures and countries. Whether these results are mirrored in other countries experiencing the same recessionary climate around the world remains an interesting avenue for further investigation.

So, while the study here provides an interesting perspective, clearly more work in this area is required. Specifically it would be interesting to take a closer look at generational variations across and within different job contexts, given the effect sizes here. In addition, longitudinal data that could incorporate and test the effect of life cycle on generational differences would yield a better understanding of exactly how generational variables play out in an organizational context and, perhaps more importantly, may pick up on within-generational differences. Here, we also wonder if a more qualitative approach to examining generational differences in future research might help illuminate our results in more depth. This research avenue has remained largely under-investigated to date.

There is a need to delve more deeply into individual differences and their interactions with the generation variable. We take some first steps in this direction here and show that generational differences are clearly in evidence in our data, but additional and more multi-level research methodologies are required to give further credence to generational analysis.

References

Adams, S.J. (2000) 'Generation X: how understanding this population leads to better safety programs', *Professional Safety*, 45: 26–29.

American Association of Retired Persons (AARP) (2010) 'Older workers: the new unemployables', *AARP Bulletin*, 18 November.

Andert, D. (2011) 'Alternating leadership as a proactive organisational intervention: addressing the needs of the Baby Boomers, Generation Xers and Millennials', *Journal of Leadership, Accountability and Ethics*, 8(4): 67–83.

Appelbaum, S.H., Serena, M. and Shapiro, B.T. (2005) 'Generation "X" and the Boomers: an analysis of realities and myths', *Management Research News*, 28: 1–35.

Armstrong-Stassen, M. and Lee, S.H. (2009) 'The effect of relational age on older Canadian employees' perceptions of human resource practices and sense of worth to their organisation', *The International Journal of Human Resource Management*, 20(8): 1753–1769.

Bartz, D.E., Hillman, L.W., Lehrer, S. and Mayhugh, G.M. (1990) 'A model for managing workforce diversity', *Management Education and Development*, 21: 321–326.

Benson, J. and Brown, M. (2011) 'Generations at work: are there differences and do they matter?', *International Journal of Human Resource Management*, 22(9): 1843–1865.

Bradford, F.W. (1993) 'Understanding "Generation X"', *Marketing Research*, 5: 54.

Callanan, G.A. and Greenhaus, J.H. (2008) 'The baby boom generation and career management: a call to action', *Advances in Developing Human Resources*, 10(1): 70–85.

Central Statistics Office (CSO) (2010) *Quarterly National Household Surveys*, Dublin: CSO.

Central Statistics Office (CSO) (2011) *Quarterly National Household Surveys*, Dublin: CSO.

Clarke, A.E. (1997) 'Job satisfaction and gender: why are women so happy at work?', *Labour Economics*, 4(4): 341–372.

Cogin, J. (2012) 'Are generational differences in work values fact or fiction? Multi-country evidence and implications', *International Journal of Human Resource Management*, 23(11): 2268–2294.

Costanza, D.P., Badger, J.M., Fraser, R.L., Severt, J.B. and Gade, P.A. (2012) 'Generational differences in work-related attitudes: a meta-analysis', *Journal of Business and Psychology*, 27: 375–394.

Crumpacker, M. and Crumpacker, J.D. (2007) 'Succession planning and generational stereotypes: should HR consider age-based values and attitudes a relevant factor or a passing fad?', *Public Personnel Management*, 36(4): 349–369.

Deal, J.J. (2007) *Retiring the Generation Gap: How Employees Young and Old can Find Common Ground*, San Francisco, CA: Jossey-Bass.

Dencker, J., Joshi, A. and Martocchio, J. (2008) 'Towards a theoretical framework linking generational memories to workplace attitudes and behaviors', *Human Resource Management Review*, 18: 210–220.

Eagly, A.H. and Chaiken, S. (1993) *The Psychology of Attitudes*, Fort Worth, TX: Harcourt Brace Jovanovich.

Eisner, S.P. (2005) 'Managing Generation Y', *Advanced Management Journal*, 70: 4–12.

Eurostat (2010) *Eurostat Yearbook 2010*, Dublin: European Commission.

Foot, D.K. and Stoffman, D. (1996) *Boom, Bust and Echo*, Toronto: Macfarlane, Walter & Ross.

Giancola, F. (2006) 'The generation gap: more myth than reality', *Human Resource Planning*, 29(4): 32–37.

Glass, A. (2007) 'Understanding generational differences for competitive success', *Industrial and Commercial Training*, 39: 98–103.

Hankin, H. (2005) *The New Workforce: Five Sweeping Trends that will Shape your Company's Future*, New York: Amacom.

Hansung, K. and Stoner, M. (2008) 'Burnout and turnover intention among social workers: effects of role stress, job autonomy and social support', *Administration in Social Work*, 32(5): 5–25.

Hira, N.A. (2007) 'Attracting the twenty-something worker', *Fortune Magazine*, 15 May.

Houlihan, A. (2007) *The New Melting Pot: Leading Different Generations*, Alexandria, VA: Society for Human Resource Management.

Johnson, J.A. and Lopes, J. (2008) 'The intergenerational workforce revisited', *Organisation Development Journal*, 26(1): 31–36.

Kinicki, A.J., McKee-Ryan, F.J., Schriesheim, C.A. and Carson, K.P. (2002) 'Assessing the construct validity of the Job Descriptive Index: a review and meta-analysis', *Journal of Applied Psychology*, 87(1): 14–32.

Kirk, D. (1996) 'Demographic transition theory', *Population Studies*, 50(3): 361–387.

Kooij, D.T., De Lange, A.H., Jansen, P., Kanfer, R. and Dikkers, J. (2011) 'Age and work-related motives: results of a meta-analysis', *Journal of Organisational Behavior*, 32(2): 197–225.

Kupperschmidt, B. (2000) 'Multigeneration employees: strategies for effective management', *The Health Care Manager*, 19: 65–76.

Lambert, E., Hogan, N. and Griffin, M.L. (2007) 'The impact of distributive and procedural justice on correctional staff job stress, job satisfaction, and organizational commitment', *Journal of Criminal Justice*, 35: 644–656.

Lancaster, L.C. and Stillman, D. (2002) *When Generations Collide: Who They Are; Why They Clash; How to Solve the Generational Puzzle at Work*, New York: Harper Collins.

Lieber, L.D. (2010) 'How HR can assist in managing the four generations in today's workplace', *Employment Relations Today*, 36(4): 85–91.

Lok, P. and Crawford, J. (2001) 'Antecedents of organisational commitment and the mediating role of job satisfaction', *Journal of Managerial Psychology*, 16(8): 594–613.

McCarthy, J. (2010) *Republic of Ireland: Workforce Profile*, Workforce Profile No 20, March, Chestnut Hill, MA: Sloan Center on Aging & Work at Boston College.

Macky, K., Gardner, D. and Forsyth, S. (2008) 'Generational differences at work: introduction and overview', *Journal of Managerial Psychology*, 23: 857–861.

Marsden, P.V., Kalleberg, A.L. and Cook, C. (1993) 'Gender differences in organisational commitment: influences of work positions and family roles', *Work and Occupations*, 20: 368–390.

Martin, C.A. (2005) 'From high maintenance to high productivity: what managers need to know about Generation Y', *Industrial and Commercial Training*, 37(1): 39–44.

Martin, U. and Schinke, S.P. (1998) 'Organizational and individual factors influencing job satisfaction and burnout of mental health workers', *Social Work in Health Care*, 28(2): 51–56.

Mirels, H. and Garrett, J. (1971) 'Protestant ethic as a personality variable', *Journal of Consulting and Clinical Psychology*, 36: 40–44.

Mottaz, C.J. (1988) 'Determinants of organisational commitment', *Human Relations*, 41: 467–482.

Mowday, R.T., Steers, R.M. and Porter, L.W. (1979) 'The measurement of organisational commitment', *Journal of Vocational Behavior*, 14: 224–247.

Newman, J.E. and Beehr, T.A. (1979) 'Personal and organizational strategies for handling job stress: a review of research and opinion', *Personnel Psychology*, 32: 1–43.

Parry, E. and Urwin, P. (2011) 'Generational differences in work values: a review of theory and evidence', *International Journal of Management Reviews*, 13(1): 79–96.

Porter, L., Steers, R., Mowday, R. and Boulian, P. (1974) 'Organisational commitment, job satisfaction, and turnover among psychiatric technicians', *Journal of Applied Psychology*, 59(5): 603–609.

Rhodes, S.R. (1983) 'Age-related differences in work attitudes and behaviours: a review and conceptual analysis', *Psychological Bulletin*, 93(2): 328–367.

Riggio, R.E. (2003) *Introduction to Industrial/Organisational Psychology*, Upper Saddle River, NJ: Pearson Education.

Shultz, K.S. and Adams, G.A. (2007) 'In search of a unifying paradigm for understanding aging and work in the 21st century', in K.S. Shultz and G.A. Adams (eds) *Aging and Work in the 21st Century*, Mahwah, NJ: Lawrence Erlbaum, pp. 303–319.

Smith, J.W. and Clurman, A. (1997) *Rocking the Ages: The Yankelovich Report on Generational Marketing*, New York: HarperCollins.

Smola, K.W. and Sutton, C.D. (2002) 'Generational differences: revisiting generational work values for the new millennium', *Journal of Organisational Behavior*, 23: 363–382.

Spector, P.E. (1997) *Job Satisfaction: Application, Assessment, Causes, and Consequences*, London: Sage.

Spector, P.E., Zapf, D., Chen, P.Y. and Frese, M. (2000) 'Why negative affectivity should not be controlled in job stress research: don't throw out the baby with the bath water', *Journal of Organisational Behavior*, 21: 79–95.

Strauss, W. and Howe, N. (1991) *Generations: The History of America's Future, 1584–2069*, New York: William Morrow.

Strauss, W. and Howe, N. (2001) 'The cycle of generations', *American Demographics*, 14(4): 24.

Toker, S. and Biron, M. (2013) 'Job burnout and depression: unraveling their temporal relationship and considering the role of physical activity', *Journal of Applied Psychology*, 97(3): 699–710.

Twenge, J.M. and Campbell, S.M. (2008) 'Generational differences in psychological traits and their impact on the workplace', *Journal of Managerial Psychology*, 23: 862–877.

Twenge, J.M., Campbell, S.M., Hoffman, B.J. and Lance, C.E. (2010) 'Generational differences in work values: leisure and extrinsic values increasing, social and intrinsic values decreasing', *Journal of Management*, 36(5): 1117–1142.

United Nations (2002) *World Population Ageing 1950–2050*, New York: United Nations.

United Nations Population Division (2010) Retrieved from http://www.un.org/esa/population/publications/worldageing19502050/pdf/80chapterii.pdf.

Weiss, H.M. and Cropanzano, R. (1996) 'Affective events theory: a theoretical discussion of the structure, causes and consequences of affective experiences at work', *Research in Organisational Behavior*, 18: 1–74.

Zemke, R., Raines, C. and Filipczak, B. (2000) *Generations at Work: Managing the Clash of Veterans, Boomers, Xers, and Nexters in Your Workplace*, Toronto: Amacom.

PART IV

Generations outside of the Western context

12

GENERATIONAL COHORTS AND PERSONAL VALUES

An exploratory study in the Indian workplace

Vasanthi Srinivasan, Dedeepya Ajith John and Maria Nirmala Christine

Introduction

In recent years, generational differences have received increased media attention. The focus has been on the differences between Gen X and Gen Y related to work values, attitudes to technology, team work, and leadership styles, as well as the challenges that they pose for organizations. However, there are few systematic studies into generational differences in values and behaviors in emerging economies such as India. This chapter presents a report based on a larger study undertaken in collaboration with the Society for Human Resource Management in India, with the objective of understanding multigenerational diversity in the Indian workplace.

The rest of the chapter is divided into four sections. First, we provide an overview and identify gaps in the existing literature on generations; we then describe the rationale, methodology, and analysis of the current study; next we present the findings of the study by using the four generational categories arrived at in the Indian context; and, finally, we highlight the implications for theory and practice in a globalized context.

Literature review

"Generation" as a construct is elusive and multiple attempts have been made by scholars and practitioners to decipher this phenomenon. One commonly used practitioner definition is provided by Kupperschmidt (2000), where a generation is defined as "an identifiable group that shares birth years, age, location and significant life events at critical developmental stages." The dominant literature from the U.S. and parts of Europe assumes that there are four generations in the workforce, namely, Veterans, Baby Boomers, Gen X, and Gen Y. Differences across these generations have been studied in detail by a few authors (see Parry and Urwin

2011 for a detailed review). The academic literature on generations continues to be sparse, even in the Western context.

The conceptual foundations of the notion of a generation, however, are drawn from sociological theory. Mannheim (1952) defined a generation as a group of people "who share a common habitus, nexus and culture, a collective memory that serves to integrate." According to Mannheim (1952), there are two important elements to the term "generation." First, a common location in historical time and, second, a "distinct consciousness of that historical position, shaped by the events and experiences of that time" (Gilleard 2004). Later authors focused on the concept of "collective memories" (Schuman and Scott 1989) or nostalgia (Holbrook and Schindler 1991) to understand generations. Different cohorts recall different events and these memories come specifically from adolescence and early adulthood. Generational effects appear to be the result of the intersection of personal and national history (Schuman and Scott 1989).

Drawing on the marketing literature, research on several entertainment products has indicated that a consumer's early experience plays a significant role in determining subsequent artistic favorites. Similarly, consumers show enduring preferences for movie stars as well as films that they experienced in their youth (Holbrook and Schindler 1994, 1996). This early-experience phenomenon can be considered an example of the influence of nostalgia on consumer tastes (Holbrook and Schindler 1991). This body of work suggests that people are likely to possess a shared memory of a significant national or international event, which affects their future values, attitudes, and preferences; however, these memories are strong only if the individual had actually experienced the events. Other authors have focused on how generations build solidarity through various cultural symbols (Eyerman and Turner 1998) and technology (McMullin et al. 2007). Conceptualizing through collective memories or nostalgia emphasizes the national contextual characteristics that are likely to impact the classification of generations.

Studies undertaken in non-Western contexts were mostly replications of prior research using the four generational categories identified in the Western literature. Using qualitative, in-depth interviews, Lee and Tay (2012) identified three generations in the Malaysian context that were based on the Western classification of Baby Boomers, Gen X, and Gen Y; they also identified unique historical events that characterize the Malaysian context. In their study on personal values across generations in China, Ralston et al. (1999) used three generations of respondents based on significant events in China. They showed that the new generation had higher individualism than the other two groups; they also showed that collectivist as well as Confucian values were lower in the younger group.

By contrasting generations in the U.S. and China, Egri and Ralston (2004) demonstrated that generational characteristics are specific to a national setting rather than being valid globally. The role of socio-cultural, economic, technological, and political influences in the make-up of a national culture is well recognized. Individuals reared in a particular culture share some elements of a common "mental program" (Hofstede 1991). Socio-cultural influences tend to have an impact over generations and centuries. However, the time frames of economic and political influence are usually years or decades, especially in emerging and transitioning economies. Technological change occurs even more rapidly. The last three influences—economic, political, and technological—share a common time horizon that is considerably shorter than the time horizon for socio-cultural change (Ralston et al. 1997). Additionally, all three of these influences are closely related to business activity in a society, whereas socio-cultural influences are more closely related to a society's core social values. This argument fits well in the context of a transitioning society such as India. The present research addresses two gaps in the literature by calling for a deeper understanding of generations from non-Western contexts (Parry and Urwin 2011) and by examining the similarities and differences in values across generations in the Indian context.

Values and generations

A value is defined as an "enduring belief that a specific mode of conduct or end-state of existence is personally or socially preferable to an opposite or converse mode of conduct or end-state of existence" (Rokeach 1973). Values "are initially taught and learnt in isolation from other values in an absolute, all-or-none manner" (Rokeach 1973). That is, rather than placing qualifications on value-related behavior (e.g. being honest some of the time), the social environment teaches individuals that they "should" or "ought to" exhibit such behavior all of the time. As an individual's receptivity to other socialization influences increase, some values get well entrenched while others adapt and change. However, the role of the larger social context in shaping the values of an individual continues to remain significant. Therefore, most individuals develop a value system that is the "organization of beliefs or preferable end-states along a continuum of relative importance" (Rokeach 1973).

Values can be of two types—terminal values and instrumental values. Terminal values are related to goals or "end-states of existence" while instrumental values are related to the means to the goals or "modes of conduct."

Prior research on values across generations showed similarities as well as differences. For instance, a study of public sector and government employees in the U.S. using the Rokeach Values Survey (RVS) found that all three generations of managers—Baby Boomers, Gen X, and Gen Y—valued a sense of accomplishment, family security, intellectual, a comfortable life, and ambition (Gibson et al. 2009). Chen and Choi (2008) found similar results in a study of 398 managers and supervisors across generations in the healthcare industry in the U.S. A comfortable life, a sense of accomplishment, family security, and freedom were ranked important across all three generations in Jurkiewicz and Bradley's (2002) study of the values of healthcare executive in the U.S. A study based in Papua New Guinea, Australia, and New Zealand showed that "true friendship" as a value was rated much higher by the younger generation compared to the previous generation, which rated family security higher (Feather 1986). A preliminary study of respondents from seven countries found that 16 values were ranked similarly across all the countries by generations that were above 40 years of age; 13 values each were similar for those in the age group of 30–39 years and those in the age group of 20–29 years across the countries (Onesimo et al. 2008).

Values impact the attitudes, beliefs, and behaviors of employees. Moreover, values have been linked to a wide variety of work-related constructs, including motivation (Locke 1991), organizational commitment (Meyer et al. 1998), decision making (Meglino and Ravlin 1998), career choice (Judge and Bretz 1992), and organizational citizenship behavior (Feather and Rauter 2004). Therefore, personal values offer an important lens to understand the generational differences in the Indian context.

Understanding the Indian context

Values exist within business as well as social contexts. Since the 1960s, India's regional development has been imbalanced, even for a developing country. The gap in the economic growth of the various states in the country has led to their polarization into high-income states and low-income states. Of the 28 Indian states, some states are worse than sub-Saharan Africa from the perspective of economic development, while others are better than China (Drèze and Sen 1989). Rural India and urban India are at different stages of evolution; even within rural India, there are oases of development (often within the same state) that are poised to leapfrog and become more developed than urban India.

Since the 1990s, India has undergone a significant economic transformation. The liberalization of the economy is still incomplete. Family-owned firms are professionalizing and the emergence of significant multinational players in the Indian market has resulted in a number of global management practices being adopted by local firms. Along with these changes, the exponential growth of information, communication, and technology has meant significant changes in the manner in which careers and work organizations are structured. However, agriculture continues to remain a significant contributor to the GDP of the country. The co-existence of three economies—the agricultural, the manufacturing, and the knowledge/services economy—in significant proportions creates a unique social context, with tensions, contradictions, and challenges in the values that are held by the individuals in the workplace.

The complex dynamics of social, cultural, religious, technological, and economic factors create discontinuities at the level of the individual as well as the group. Chatterjee and Pearson (2000) noted that the radical economic reforms and the imperatives of globalization have impacted Indian managerial mindsets by introducing a set of new values, creating tension between traditional indigenous Indian values and the new values (hybrid values) (Kao et al. 1995). Several researchers (Bedi 1991; Chatterjee and Heuer 2006; Kakar et al. 2002; Neelankavil et al. 2000) have contended that the emerging generation of managers is influenced to a very large extent by the market culture and reforms. Business leaders in India appear to be able to maintain a duality of values—one field of value formation is drawn from their own cultural heritage, while the other impacts on them through the wider forces of internationalization. While a hybrid blending of workplace values is occurring, the exact nature and character of these hybrid workplace values, attitudes, and behaviors require further investigation (Neelankavil et al. 2000). According to the Indian Census data of 2011, 29.7 percent of the population is between 0–14 years of age, 64.9 percent is between 15–64 years of age, and 5.5 percent is over 65. With more entrants into the workforce, differences in values will get accentuated in organizations. Several reports in the business press in recent years have already emphasized the generational challenges to organizations in India (Kelly Services 2012).

To summarize, the Indian context is characterized by contradictions and pluralism; while there is a marked increase in the number of young people entering the workforce, the liberalization process has also unleashed challenges for those already in the workforce. The significant economic and social changes in the past two decades have resulted in a higher performance orientation among corporations to remain globally competitive. However, managerial mindsets and work practices have not altered at the same pace as that which the organizations have changed. We argue that such changes in the economic landscape impact the work as well as the non-work aspects of employment. This study is an attempt to understand the similarities and the differences in values across cohorts of employees, with an attempt to characterize generations based on "collective memories," while recognizing that in a country as diverse as India, collective memories alone would not be adequate to categorize generations.

Framing Indian generations

Research design

A two-phase research design was adopted since the study was exploratory in nature. Prior studies in the Indian context attempted to categorize generations using the widely used four-generation classification from the Western literature and identifying unique historical events in the Indian context (Bijarpurkar 2007; Erickson 2009; Ghosh and Chaudhuri 2009; Parameswaran 2003; Roongrerngsuke 2010). No empirical study has examined whether the identified significant events in the Indian context were perceived by individuals as significant and/or whether the significant events impacted the personal values of individuals.

In the first phase of this study, interviews and focus groups were conducted with 300 respondents from eight Indian cities who were employees in various organizations. The objective of this phase was to identify the key defining events that shape "collective memories" as understood by the respondents. Through unaided recall, participants were asked to remember "significant historical events." Subsequently, a summary of the historical events (provided in Table 12.1) was circulated to the participants, and they were asked whether the events impacted them personally or professionally.

TABLE 12.1 Classification of generations in the Indian context

Pre-liberalization	*Early/liberalization*	*Rapid growth*	*Plateaued growth*
• Soviet Union dominant trade partner • Closed economy • Public sector dominance • Growth rate: 3% • Traditional work cultures, bureaucratic organizations, restricted opportunities, favoritism	• Opening up of the markets, entry of multinational corporations (MNCs) • Penetration of technology, more private organizations being set up, beginning of demand–supply mismatch • Migration from rural areas to urban areas (cities) • Renewed aspirations, need to prove credibility	• Rapid growth: 4–9.5% • Job market at its peak, growth of IT • Rise in education levels, work places representative of both genders • Flexible workplaces, MNC practices deepen	• Economy slowdown • Layoffs, global crisis, cut down on expenditures • Demand–supply gap tapering • Continued uncertainty

During the unaided recall, the geographical diversity and the impact of the events on the respondents began to emerge clearly. For instance, all the respondents from Mumbai mentioned the role of the terrorist attacks on the Taj Mahal Hotel in 2010 as a critical event that impacted their values, but this event was not mentioned by the respondents from Delhi. In the East, the fall of the communist government in the state of West Bengal emerged as a significant event, while this was not mentioned by the respondents from any other part of India. Thus, it became clear that the notions of defining events and collective memories that impact a generation of individuals require further investigation in the Indian context. One significant event that was recalled by all the respondents was the liberalization of the Indian economy. Therefore, for the purpose of this study we chose liberalization as a significant event to define generations.

The four phases of liberalization that emerged from the respondent narratives obtained from the interviews and focus groups were framed. There were differences in how cohorts of respondents described the liberalization process. We used descriptors using "their own words" to define the generations. The respondents who were part of the Pre-Liberalization cohort mentioned that they witnessed significant changes in the manner in which organizations changed—there was a sudden need to become globally savvy, to understand how the private sector worked in other parts of the world, and to have exposure to international quality and trade systems. The employee cohorts from the Early Liberalization period (1991–2001) mentioned corporatization of the public sector, divestments by the government, lack of job security, increased private sector participation, poaching of talent by companies, and a shortage of talent as the significant changes that they had experienced. The employee cohorts from Rapid Growth generation (2002–2008) spoke of the double-digit growth, doubling of employee strength in five years by organizations, boom in the services sector, flow of capital, and FDI (foreign direct investment) (leading to a spurt in economic activities), increased internationalization of human resource (HR) practices and standardization of work processes in organizations, loss of personal touch in organizations, and very high levels of employee turnover. The Plateaued Growth generation (post-2009) cohorts spoke of limited opportunities, the fear of non-performance, the need to keep themselves employable by investing in skills and competences, and the vulnerability of contract jobs with no job security.

The themes that emerged were validated with HR leaders and senior management teams in various organizations, who agreed that the four periods identified by the respondents were indicative of the significant changes in the values of employees that they had observed within their organizational context. The senior leaders mentioned that organizations were confronted with rapid growth, which was defined as the doubling of employee strength in five years (Hambrick and Crozier 1985). This rapid growth required organizations to tap into alternate and diverse talent pools. Gender diversity in the workforce increased from 2002 onwards. More women began to enter the workforce and organizations began to recruit talent from smaller towns rather than from the cities. As one respondent mentioned, "the four generations are not just about organizations and employees; they could also be the generational classification of Indian society." The labels for each generation—Pre-Liberalization, Early Liberalization, Rapid Growth, and Plateaued Growth—were adapted by the authors based on how the respondents described the periods (Table 12.1).

The four generational cohorts that emerged through the qualitative research were used to analyze the survey data. Given the Indian context, where the family has a central and pivotal role to play in the life of an individual, we hypothesized that *Family security* and *A comfortable life* would emerge as important terminal values across generations. Further, we expected *Ambitious* and *True friendship* to emerge as important values for the Rapid Growth generation as well as the Plateaued Growth generation because during this phase, a number of employees migrated from villages and towns to cities to seek employment. As first-time entrants into the workforce, they also moved into a new social context. They had to live up to the expectations of their parents and community back in their towns and villages and yet, at the same time, they would need to forge new relationships and remain effective in their workplaces and, hence, they were likely to rate these values as important.

We also posited that there would be significant differences across generations on the following values: *Freedom*, *Self-respect*, *Sense of accomplishment*, *Social recognition*, and *Independent*. The arguments stem from two reasons. First, these values are acquired through socialization either in school or at the workplace; therefore, the

Rapid Growth and Plateaued Growth generations would be more likely to demonstrate these values when compared to the other generations. Second, given the pervasive impact of liberalization, some of these values would have got entrenched among the new entrants to the workforce, since the larger society and media have begun to mirror some of these values in popular culture, films, and role models.

The objective of the study was to identify the similarities and differences in values across the four generations in the Indian context. The RVS (Rokeach 1973) was the instrument used to gather data. There has been criticism regarding the use of the RVS because of the ranking method, which by its ipsative nature constrains analytic procedures; however, it is a simple instrument, and is easily understood across a wide variety of respondents, and the values measured are universal (Feather 1986, 1991). The RVS assesses the relative importance of different values within a person's total belief system. The respondents were asked to rank 18 terminal and 18 instrumental values in order of importance, as "guiding principles in your life."

The sample for the study consisted of 1,600 white-collar employees from the infrastructure and the information technology sectors. The survey was administered both in paper and pencil mode as well as online, and the reliability was checked. Of the 1,600 respondents, 910 respondents completed the survey, with a response rate of 56.8 percent. The average age of the respondents was 33 years and their average professional experience was ten years. Of the respondents, 22 percent were women; 64.6 percent were married; 60 percent came from an urban background; while the rest were from a rural background. Based on the classifications given in this paper, 11 percent of the sample of 910 belonged to the Pre-Liberalization generation, 31 percent belonged to the Early Liberalization generation, 30 percent to the Rapid Growth generation, and 28 percent to the Plateaued Growth generation. The proportions represented in the sample mirrored the employee composition within the organizations at different levels in the hierarchy.

Analysis

The data analysis consisted of the following steps: rank ordering of the values based on the median scores; identifying the composite rank order; and analyzing for differences in the medians across the four generations. The median scores of the ranks of instrumental values as well as terminal values along with the composite rank order across the entire sample are provided in Table 12.2. The medians across the different generations were analyzed using the non-parametric statistics, Kruskal–Wallis one-way ANOVA and Wilcoxon Mann–Whitney based on the number of groups. The values that emerged with significant p values ($p < 0.05$) across the groups are presented in Table 12.3. Other analyses pertaining to demographics on rural/urban distribution, parental occupation, and family type were done to understand the impact of these factors on values.

TABLE 12.2 Median rank and composite rank order of Rokeach values

Terminal values	*Median ranking*	*Composite rank order*	*Instrumental values*	*Median ranking*	*Composite rank order*
A comfortable life	6	4	Ambitious	6	2
Equality	9	6	Broad-minded	8	4
An exciting life	10	9	Capable	9	5
Family security	3	1	Clean	11	11
Freedom	8	5	Courageous	9	5
Health	4	2	Forgiving	12	15
Inner harmony	10	9	Helpful	9	5
Mature love	11	13	Honest	4	1
National security	12	14	Imaginative	13	18
Pleasure	12	14	Independent	9	5
Salvation	14	16	Intellectual	11	11
Self-respect	5	3	Logical	11	11
A sense of accomplishment	10	9	Loving	11	11
Social recognition	9	6	Loyal	10	10
True friendship	9	6	Obedient	12	15
Wisdom	10	9	Polite	12	15
A world at peace	14	16	Responsible	6	2
A world of beauty	16	18	Self-controlled	9	5

Findings

Four key findings emerged from the study. First, the top four terminal values (based on median rankings; see Table 12.2) across the sample were *Family security*, *Health*, *Self-respect*, and *A comfortable life*. The top four instrumental values were *Honest*, *Ambitious*, *Responsible*, and *Broad-minded*. *Family security* consistently emerged as a high-ranked value among all the generations, with the same composite rank order. Second, we posited that there would be differences in values across the generations based on the unique socio-political and economic developments that characterized the birth years of the generation (Table 12.3). Table 12.4 summarizes the key values that differed across the four generations.

TABLE 12.3 Median rank and composite rank order of Rokeach values across generations

	People entering the workforce in				*Kruskal–Wallis*	*Total*
	Pre-1991	*1991–2002*	*2003–8*	*2008–12*		
Professional experience	> 21 yrs	9 to 21 yrs	4 to 9 yrs	0 to 4 yrs	*p* value sig	910
Sample size	102	285	271	252		
Terminal values						
A comfortable life	8.5 (8)	5 (3)	6 (4)	6 (4)	0.02	6
Equality	9.5 (9)	9 (6)	9 (6)	9 (7)		9
An exciting life	11 (12)	10 (8)	10 (8)	9.5 (9)		10
Family security	3 (1)	3 (1)	3 (1)	4 (1)		3
Freedom	8 (4)	8 (5)	8 (5)	7 (5)		8
Health	4 (2)	4 (2)	4 (2)	4 (1)		4
Inner harmony	8 (4)	10 (8)	10 (8)	11 (10)	0	10
Mature love	11 (12)	12 (13)	11 (12)	11 (10)		11
National security	12.5 (14)	12 (13)	12 (15)	12 (15)		12
Pleasure	13 (15)	12 (13)	11 (12)	11(10)		12
Salvation	13 (15)	14 (16)	14 (16)	14 (17)		14
Self-respect	5 (3)	5 (3)	4 (2)	5 (3)		5
A sense of accomplishment	8 (4)	10 (8)	11 (12)	11 (10)	0	10
Social recognition	10 (10)	9 (6)	10 (8)	9 (7)		9
True friendship	10 (10)	10 (8)	9 (6)	8 (6)	0	9
Wisdom	8 (4)	10 (8)	10 (8)	11 (10)	0.01	10
A world at peace	13.5 (17)	14 (16)	14 (16)	12.5 (16)		14
A world of beauty	16 (18)	16 (18)	16 (18)	15 (18)	0.03	16
Instrumental values						
Ambitious	6 (2)	5 (2)	5 (2)	5 (2)		5
Broad-minded	8 (5)	8 (4)	9 (6)	8 (3)		8
Capable	7.5 (4)	8 (4)	8 (4)	9 (6)	0.02	8
Clean	10.5 (11)	12 (13)	10 (9)	11 (13)		11
Courageous	9 (6)	9 (6)	10 (9)	10 (8)		9
Forgiving	12 (14)	12 (13)	12 (16)	13 (18)		12
Helpful	11 (12)	9 (6)	8 (4)	9 (6)	0.05	9
Honest	3 (1)	4 (1)	3 (1)	4 (1)		4
Imaginative	13 (17)	13 (18)	13 (18)	12 (15)		13
Independent	9 (6)	10 (8)	9 (6)	10 (8)		9

	People entering the workforce in				*Kruskal–Wallis*	*Total*
	Pre-1991	*1991–2002*	*2003–8*	*2008–12*		
Intellectual	12 (14)	10 (8)	11 (12)	10 (8)	0.04	11
Logical	10 (10)	10 (8)	11 (12)	11 (13)		11
Loving	12 (14)	12 (13)	11 (12)	10 (8)	0.01	11
Loyal	9 (6)	10 (8)	10 (9)	10 (8)		10
Obedient	13 (17)	12 (13)	11 (12)	12 (15)		12
Polite	11 (12)	12 (13)	12 (16)	12 (15)		12
Responsible	6 (2)	6 (3)	5 (2)	8 (3)	0	6
Self-controlled	9 (6)	10 (8)	9 (6)	8 (3)	0.03	9

TABLE 12.4 Key values that differed across the four generations

Generation	*High priority terminal values*	*Low priority terminal values*	*High priority instrumental values*	*Low priority instrumental values*
Pre-Liberalization	Inner harmony; a sense of accomplishment; wisdom	A comfortable life; true friendship; a world of beauty	Capable	Helpful; intellectual; loving
Early Liberalization	Comfortable life	True friendship; a world of beauty	Intellectual	Self-controlled; loving
Rapid Growth		A sense of accomplishment; a world of beauty	Helpful; responsible	
Plateaued Growth	True friendship; a world of beauty	Inner harmony; a sense of accomplishment; wisdom	Intellectual; loving; self-controlled	Capable; responsible

The respondents belonging to the Pre-Liberalization generation distinctly prioritized *Inner harmony*, *A sense of accomplishment*, and *Wisdom* as the defining characteristics of their generation. This generation accorded the least importance to *A comfortable life*, *True friendship*, and *A world of beauty*. With regard to instrumental values, *Capable* had a significantly higher priority, while *Helpful*, *Intellectual*, and *Loving* were significantly lower on priority. The possible explanation for this finding is that the respondents were part of the creation of a new era of industrial India. This gave them meaning and a sense of accomplishment. They have held careers spanning over two decades within one or two organizations and had also achieved objective parameters of success in these organizations. Many of them were also first-generation employees in the industrial sector. These aspects could explain the higher importance assigned to *Sense of accomplishment* as a value. The value of *Inner harmony* (defined as freedom from inner conflict) could be a life-stage factor and requires further investigation.

The Early Liberalization generation differed from the Pre-Liberalization generation in giving a significantly high priority to *Comfortable life* and *Intellectual*. The respondents who belonged to this generation were early entrants to the workforce who joined MNCs. Competent professionals during this period would have joined the Government. Given the liberalization process, several of these professionals would have joined the private sector with much higher pay and perquisites.

The Rapid Growth generation ranked *Helpful* and *Responsible* high when compared to the rankings of the other generations. What further differentiated this generation from the rest was the significantly low priority given to *Sense of accomplishment*. One could argue that this generation experienced the real benefits of liberalization with abundant opportunities.

The Plateaued Growth generation was characterized by the significantly high importance ascribed to *True friendship*, *A world of beauty*, *Intellectual*, *Loving*, and *Self-controlled*. This generation accorded low priority to *Inner harmony, Sense of accomplishment*, *Wisdom*, *Capable*, and *Responsible*. The reason for such sharp differences in the priorities accorded by this generation is that several respondents in this cohort were part of nuclear families and they tended to rely on friends for social support. This dimension of *True friendship* is supported by the findings from a study by DeSouza et al. (2009), who found that youth in the age group of 25 and below tended to have a broad-based circle of friends and as the level of education increases, the circle of friends also tended to increase. The benefits of education expose young people to greater opportunities for social interaction. The high median score on *Loving* for similar age groups in India is supported by other studies (see Mulla and Krishnan 2009, for instance).

Our third finding suggests that *Parental occupation* and *Gender* were the two demographic variables that significantly impacted the values within each generation. The *p* values of these two demographic variables are provided in Tables 12.5 and 12.6. *Parental occupation* was divided into four categories for the purposes of this study—agriculture, private sector, government/public sector, and self-employed. The values *Sense of accomplishment*, *True friendship*, *Clean*, *Imaginative*, *Independent*, and *Intellectual* had significant differences based on parental occupation. Table 12.5 shows that there were significant differences in the value rankings of those respondents whose parents were employed in the private sector compared to those whose parents were involved in agriculture. The differences were consistent across all the values, which suggest the co-existence of different values within the same generation. In developing countries such as India, where economic development is still characterized by a significant contribution of agriculture to the GDP, the emergence of the manufacturing, services, and information technology sectors in recent years has meant that the entrants into the workforce continue to be migrants from households where parents are agriculturists or owners of small business. Many of them are from rural households with early education in a town or a village. Access to education and employment is more difficult for such individuals compared to those from towns. These manifest as generational differences in the values and this deep level, class-based difference requires further investigation.

TABLE 12.5 Difference in ranking of values based on parental occupation

Generations	*Agricultural*	*Government/ public sector*	*Private sector*	*Professional/ entrepreneur/ others*	
n = 873 n missing = 37	92	451	136	194	p
	Median (CRO)	*Median (CRO)*	*Median (CRO)*	*Median (CRO)*	
Terminal values					
Comfortable life	6 (4)	6 (4)	5 (4)	5 (3)	
Equality	9 (7)	9 (6)	9 (6)	9 (6)	
Exciting life	11 (11)	10 (9)	9 (6)	9 (6)	
Family security	3.5 (1)	3 (1)	3 (1)	3 (1)	
Freedom	8 (6)	8 (5)	7.5 (5)	7 (5)	
Health	4 (2)	4 (2)	4 (2)	4 (2)	
Inner harmony	11.5 (12)	9 (6)	10 (10)	10 (10)	
Mature love	12 (14)	11 (13)	11 (13)	11 (11)	
National security	11.5 (12)	12 (14)	13 (15)	12 (15)	
Pleasure	10 (10)	12 (14)	12 (14)	11 (11)	
Salvation	13 (16)	14 (16)	15 (17)	14 (17)	
Self-respect	4 (2)	5 (3)	4 (2)	5 (3)	0.05
Sense of accomplishment	12 (14)	10 (9)	9 (6)	11 (11)	0.01
Social recognition	9.5 (8)	10 (9)	9 (6)	9 (6)	
True friendship	7 (5)	10 (9)	10 (10)	9.5 (9)	0
Wisdom	9.5 (8)	9 (6)	10 (10)	11 (11)	
World at peace	13 (16)	14 (16)	14 (16)	13 (16)	
World of beauty	14.5 (18)	16 (18)	16 (18)	15 (18)	
Instrumental values					
Ambitious	6 (2)	5 (2)	5 (2)	5 (2)	
Broad-minded	7 (4)	8 (4)	10 (10)	8 (4)	
Capable	8 (5)	8 (4)	7 (4)	8 (4)	
Clean	9 (8)	11 (13)	12 (15)	11 (11)	0.02
Courageous	10 (9)	9 (6)	9 (6)	9 (6)	

Continued

TABLE 12.5 *Continued*

Generations	*Agricultural*	*Government/ public sector*	*Private sector*	*Professional/ entrepreneur/ others*	
Forgiving	11 (13)	12 (14)	13 (18)	11 (11)	
Helpful	8.5 (7)	9 (6)	9 (6)	9 (6)	
Honest	3 (1)	3 (1)	4 (1)	4 (1)	
Imaginative	14 (18)	14 (18)	11 (13)	12 (17)	0
Independent	10 (9)	10 (10)	7.5 (5)	10 (8)	0.03
Intellectual	12 (15)	10 (10)	10 (10)	11 (11)	0
Logical	12 (15)	10 (10)	10 (10)	11 (11)	0.05
Loving	10 (9)	12 (14)	12 (15)	11 (11)	
Loyal	10 (9)	9 (6)	9.5 (8)	10 (8)	
Obedient	11 (13)	12 (14)	11 (13)	12 (17)	
Polite	12 (15)	12 (14)	12 (15)	11.5 (16)	
Responsible	6 (2)	6 (3)	6 (3)	7 (3)	
Self-controlled	8 (5)	9 (6)	9.5 (8)	10 (8)	

Finally, Table 12.6 shows that there were significant differences in the values such as *Loving*, *Self-respect*, *National security*, *Responsible*, *Equality*, and *Inner harmony* between male and female respondents. However, given the highly engendered work context in India, one could argue that the women's generations would differ significantly since women were late entrants into the workforce.

TABLE 12.6 Median, CRO, and Mann–Whitney Test across gender

Generations	*Male*	*Female*	
n = 910 *n* missing = 0	710	200	P
	Median (CRO)	*Median (CRO)*	
Terminal values			
Comfortable life	6 (4)	7 (4)	
Equality	9 (6)	10 (10)	
Exciting life	10 (9)	11 (12)	0.04
Family security	3 (1)	3 (1)	
Freedom	8 (5)	7 (4)	
Health	4 (2)	4 (2)	
Inner harmony	10 (9)	9 (6)	0.02

Generations	*Male*	*Female*	
Mature love	11 (13)	11 (12)	
National security	12 (14)	13.5 (15)	0
Pleasure	12 (14)	12 (14)	
Salvation	14 (16)	14 (17)	
Self-respect	5 (3)	4 (2)	0.01
Sense of accomplishment	10 (9)	10 (10)	
Social recognition	9.5 (8)	9 (6)	
True friendship	9 (6)	9.5 (9)	
Wisdom	10 (9)	9 (6)	
World at peace	14 (17)	13 (15)	
World of beauty	16 (18)	15.5 (18)	
Instrumental values			
Ambitious	5 (2)	6 (2)	
Broad-minded	8 (4)	9 (4)	
Capable	8 (4)	9 (4)	0.05
Clean	11 (11)	11 (12)	
Courageous	9 (6)	9 (4)	
Forgiving	12 (14)	11 (12)	
Helpful	9 (6)	9 (4)	
Honest	3 (1)	4 (1)	
Imaginative	13 (18)	14 (18)	
Independent	10 (9)	9 (4)	0.04
Intellectual	11 (11)	11 (12)	
Logical	11 (11)	12 (17)	
Loving	12 (14)	10 (10)	0
Loyal	10 (9)	9 (4)	
Obedient	12 (14)	11 (12)	
Polite	12 (14)	11 (12)	
Responsible	6 (3)	7 (3)	0
Self-controlled	9 (6)	10 (10)	

Discussion and conclusions

As is evident from the findings, the definition of a generation in a transitioning context such as India is complex. There are two possible ways to conceptualize generations—through significant events and through socio-economic, class-based variables. In this chapter, we report preliminary evidence of both the conceptualizations. It is clear that historical, political, economic, and social events in critical years impact the manner in which the personal values of individuals and collectives are shaped. Liberalization appears to have been a significant milestone for employee generations. However, other variables such as parental occupation determine access to networks and resources, and the absence of these also plays a dominant role in shaping values. Marketers in India have historically used socio-economic class definitions to define consumer generations. Given the limitations of statistical analysis involving ranked data, more investigation is needed to explore the key variables that would define the generational classes.

The similarity of the ranks across the cohorts can be interpreted using Inglehart's (1997) theory of inter-generational values change. This is based on two hypotheses: the socialization hypothesis and the scarcity hypothesis. Both the hypotheses appear to be relevant in the Indian context. The socialization hypothesis proposes that adults' basic values reflect the socio-economic conditions of one's childhood and adolescence. Longitudinal research has shown that this value orientation remains relatively stable throughout one's lifetime (Inglehart 1997; Lubinski et al. 1996; Meglino and Ravlin 1998). Although societal conditions can change the relative importance that a generation attributes to various personal values, these are only temporary shifts with that generation's value orientations returning to the previous levels once stability is regained (Inglehart 1997). Since the three values pertaining to *Family security*, *Health*, and *Self-respect* were ranked high across the three generations in our study, there is some support for this hypothesis.

On the other hand, Inglehart's scarcity hypothesis proposes that the greatest subjective value is placed on those socio-economic environmental aspects that are in short supply during a generation's youth. Thus, generations growing up during periods of socio-economic and physical insecurity (such as social upheaval, war, and economic distress) learn modernist survival values (such as economic determinism, rationality, materialism, conformity, and respect for authority). Alternatively, generations growing up during periods of socio-economic security learn post-modernist values (such as egalitarianism, individualism, interpersonal trust, tolerance of diversity, and self-transcendence) (Inglehart 1997). The scarcity hypothesis offers a good explanation as to why certain new values emerged for each generation. In the case of the respondents belonging to the Early Liberalization generation, even though they enjoyed economic success, the deep sense of disillusionment and the fear of losing out resulted in them ranking *A comfortable life* and *Intellectual* as key values, while the Pre-Liberalization generation had *Sense of accomplishment* as a significant value. Further research is required to examine which of these hypotheses would provide a more meaningful explanation of the generational differences that were observed.

The findings of our study support the work of other researchers (Bedi 1991; Chatterjee and Heuer 2006; Kakar et al. 2002; Neelankavil et al. 2000) who contended that there is a duality of values in the workforce in India—one field of value formation is drawn from individuals' own cultural heritage, while the other impacts on them through the wider forces of internationalization.

Our study also supports the findings that a blending of values is taking place in India. In the context of the Pre-Liberalization generation, the high ranking of the values of *Inner harmony* along with *A sense of accomplishment* suggest this generation has a need for inner peace along with a need for achievement. In the case of the Early Liberalization generation, the values *Intellectual* and *Comfortable life* were ranked higher and *Sense of accomplishment* was ranked much lower. In the case of the Rapid Growth generation, the values *Helpful* and *Responsible* gained prominence while *Sense of accomplishment* was not ranked as a high priority. With regard to the Plateaued Growth generation, the presence of values such as *Self-controlled* and *Loving* appears to be in dissonance with the values usually attributed to the youngest generation in the workforce. Such hybrid values could be the source of tension and conflict among individuals in organizations; while they provide opportunities for collaboration and creativity, they could also contribute to workplace conflicts. Further research is needed to extricate and exemplify the role of this duality of values in workplace behaviors.

We conducted 50 in-depth interviews to understand how the value *Family security*—which is ranked high not only across different cultures but also across the three generations in India—was interpreted by the respondents. *Family security* was defined in the RVS as "taking care of loved ones." It was interpreted by the Pre-Liberalization generation as "financial stability" and "emotional security," while the Early Liberalization generation interpreted it as "taking care of dependants," "social mobility," and "physical and financial security," and the Rapid Growth generation interpreted it as "providing material comforts" and "providing medical insurance for parents." The Plateaued Growth generation defined it as "giving parents the comfort that they could not enjoy and taking family for vacations." While it can be argued that these interpretations are defined by the life contexts of the respective individuals, it is important to note that the attributed meanings across the different cohorts appear to converge. The centrality of family in the Indian context is well recognized and more research is needed to understand the impact of other demographic variables on the meaning and interpretation assigned to these values by the various cohorts.

Implications

Generational diversity is deep-level diversity in the Indian context. Diversity literatures conceptualize two forms of diversity, namely surface-level and deep-level diversity. Surface-level diversity refers to the almost immediately observable, immutable, and overt attributes of a member such as gender, race, and age which are measurable in simple and valid ways (Harrison et al. 1998). All the variables captured in this study, namely tenure, parental occupation, rural/urban, and education, are all surface-level diversity variables. In contrast, deep-level diversity refers to diversity of thought and attitudes arising out of differences in education, experiences, access, and socialization. Since social and economic development has not occurred uniformly across India, the barriers experienced by those in poorer states, in regional medium of instruction, with limited access to employment, and a first-generation entrant into the workforce will be high. This in turn would determine what values are important to individuals and how they would impact workplace dynamics. Therefore, in a diverse country such as India, surface-level variables reflect a deeper level of diversity in terms of values, attitudes, and beliefs.

It is useful to conceptualize generations as a mosaic in the Indian context. The individual pieces of a mosaic come together to form a whole, but the pieces still remain visible. The mosaics change as the landscape of the organizations change due to growth. Therefore, organizations need to constantly retain the patterns of the mosaic but should be willing to reconfigure the different pieces at the same time. This metaphor of a mosaic poses challenges for HR professionals and line managers. As the HR department copes with the increased size and scope of work, generational diversity and the changes in demographic variables call for innovations in talent management. When a large number of first-generation employees enter the workforce, the induction and socialization systems in the organizations need to be more inclusive. Managers would need to demonstrate higher sensitivity in managing the workforce and the manner in which collaboration is fostered, instructions are given, employees are inducted, and feedback as well as coaching is provided. Talent management therefore takes strategic importance in such contexts.

Line managers require highly differentiated competencies in managing intergenerational collaboration, cross-generational mentoring, relationship building, and conflict resolution. Managers need to identify collaborative spaces that allow for non-threatening conversations. Managers also need to be sensitized to the demographic differences that impact the work behaviors and attitudes of employees. Learning and development therefore is an important element of generational diversity.

Conclusion

While the present study contributes to understanding the generations in India (which is a relatively under-researched subject in literature), the chapter has three key limitations. Since the study used cross-sectional data, it was difficult to segregate the age effects and life-stage effects that have been extensively discussed in the literature on generations. Second, the sample was drawn from two sectors (infrastructure and information technology); therefore, the generalizability of the findings is limited. Finally, since the study used ranking data, statistical analysis (which would allow controlling for demographic variables) could not be attempted. Despite these limitations, the study posits that managers need to be better prepared to manage a workforce that consists of overlapping yet differentiated values. By understanding the differences and the similarities between generational groups, HR professionals and business leaders can communicate values and priorities more effectively and create a more collaborative environment that would allow the organization to leverage its generational diversity.

References

Bedi, H. (1991) *Understanding Asian Managers*, Sydney: Allen and Unwin.

Bijapurkar, R. (2007) *Winning in the Indian Market: Understanding the Transformation of Consumer India*, New Delhi: John Wiley and Sons.

Chatterjee, S.R. and Heuer, M. (2006) 'Understanding Indian management in a time of transition', in H.J. Davis, S.R. Chatterjee, and M. Heuer (eds) *Management in India: Trends and Transition*, New Delhi: Response Books.

Chatterjee, S.R. and Pearson, C.A.L. (2000) 'Indian managers in transition: orientations, work goals, values and ethics', *Management International Review*, 1: 81–95.

Chen, P.-J. and Choi, Y. (2008) 'Generational differences in work values: a study of hospitality management', *International Journal of Contemporary Hospitality Management*, 20(6): 595–615.

DeSouza, P.R., Kumar, S. and Shastri, S. (2009) *Indian Youth in a Transforming World: Attitudes and Perceptions*, New Delhi: Sage Publications.

Drèze, J. and Sen, A.K. (1989) *Hunger and Public Action*, Oxford: Oxford University Press.

Egri, C.P. and Ralston, D.A. (2004) 'Generation cohorts and personal values: a comparison of China and US', *Organization Science*, 15(2): 210–220.

Erickson, T. (2009) *Generational Differences Between India and the U.S.*, http://blogs.harvardbusiness.org/erickson/2009/02/global_generations_focus_on_in.html (accessed 2 September 2011).

Eyerman, R. and Turner, B. (1998) 'Outline of a theory of generations', *European Journal of Social Theory*, 1: 91–106.

Feather, N.T. (1986) 'Human values, valences, expectations and affect: theoretical issues emerging from recent applications of the expectancy-value model', in D.R. Brown and J. Veroff (eds) *Frontiers of Motivational Psychology: Essays in Honor of John W. Atkinson*, New York: Springer-Verlag, pp. 146–172.

Feather, N.T. (1991) 'Human values, global self-esteem and belief in a just world', *Journal of Personality*, 59(1): 83–107.

Feather, N.T. and Rauter, K.A. (2004) 'Organizational citizenship behaviours in relation to job status, job insecurity, organizational commitment and identification, job satisfaction and work values', *Journal of Occupational and Organizational Psychology*, 77: 81–95.

Ghosh, R. and Chaudhuri, S. (2009) 'Intergenerational differences in individualism/collectivism orientations: implications for outlook towards HRD/HRM practices in India and the United States', *New Horizons in Adult Education and Human Resource development*, 23(4): 5–21.

Gibson, J., Greenwood, R.A. and Murphy, E. (2009) 'Generational differences in the workplace: personal values, behaviors, and popular beliefs', *Journal of Diversity Management*, 4(3): 1–7.

Gilleard, C. (2004) 'Cohorts and generations in the study of social change', *Social Theory and Health*, 2: 106–119.

Hambrick, D.C. and Crozier, L.M. (1985) 'Stumblers and stars in the management of rapid growth', *Journal of Business Venturing*, 1(1): 31–45.

Harrison, D.A., Price, K.H. and Bell, M.P. (1998) 'Beyond relational demography: time and the effects of surface and deep level diversity on work group cohesion', *Academy of Management Journal*, 41(1): 96–107.

Hofstede, G. (1991) *Cultures and Organizations*, London: McGraw-Hill.

Holbrook, M.B. and Schindler, R.M. (1991) 'Echoes of the dear departed past: some work in progress on nostalgia', in R.H. Holman and M.R. Solomon (eds) *Advances in Consumer Research*, Provo, UT: Association for Consumer Research, pp. 330–333.

Holbrook, M.B. and Schindler, R.M. (1994) 'Age, sex, and attitude toward the past as predictors of consumers' aesthetic tastes for cultural products', *Journal of Marketing Research*, 31: 412–422.

Holbrook, M.B. and Schindler, R.M. (1996) 'Market segmentation based on age and attitude toward the past: concepts, methods, and findings concerning nostalgic influences on customer tastes', *Journal of Business Research*, 37: 27–39.

Inglehart, R. (1997) *Modernization and Post Modernization: Cultural, Economic and Political Change in 43 Societies*, Princeton, NJ: Princeton University Press.

Judge, T.A. and Bretz, R.D. (1992) 'Effects of values on job choice decisions', *Journal of Applied Psychology*, 77: 261–271.

Jurkiewicz, C.L. and Bradley, D.R. (2002) 'Generational ethics: age cohort and heath care executive values', *HEC Forum*, 14(2): 148–171.

Kakar, S.S., Kakar, M.F.R., DeVres, K. and Vrignaud, P. (2002) 'Leadership in Indian organizations from a comparative perspective', *International Journal of Cross Cultural Management*, 2(2): 239–250.

Kao, H.S.R., Sinha, D. and Ng, S.H. (1995) *Effective Organizations and Social Values*, New Delhi: Sage Publications.

Kelly Services (2012) *Understanding and Leveraging Generational Diversity for Organizational Success*, http://www.slideshare.net/perryky/kelly-services-understanding-generational-diversity-in-workplace (accessed 4 February 2013).

Kupperschmidt, B.R. (2000) 'Multi-generation employees: strategies for effective management', *The Health Care Manager*, 19(1): 65–76.

Lee, S.T. and Tay, A. (2012) Historical moments that are meaningful to the three generations of employees in Malaysia', *World Journal of Social Sciences*, 2(3): 48–56.

Locke, E.A. (1991) The motivation sequence, the motivation hub and the motivation core', *Organizational Behaviour and Human Decision Processes*, 50: 288–299.

Lubinski, D., Schmidt, D.B. and Benbow, C.P. (1996) 'A 20 year stability analysis of the study of values for intellectually gifted individuals from adolescence to adulthood', *Journal of Applied Psychology*, 81: 443–451.

Mannheim, K. (1952) 'The problem of generations', in P. Kecskemeti (ed.) *Essays on the Sociology of Knowledge*, London: Routledge and Kegan Paul, pp. 276–322.

McMullin, J., Comeau, T. and Jovic, E. (2007) 'Generational affinities and discourses of difference: a case study of highly skilled information technology workers', *British Journal of Sociology*, 58: 297–316.

Meglino, B. and Ravlin, E. (1998) 'Individual values in organizations: concepts, controversies, and research', *Journal of Management*, 24(3): 351–389.

Meyer, J.P., Irving, P.G. and Allen, N.J. (1998) 'Examination of the combined effects of work values and early work experiences on organizational commitment', *Journal of Organizational Behaviour*, 19: 29–52.

Mulla, Z.R. and Krishnan, V.R. (2009) 'Do transformational leaders raise followers to higher levels of morality? Validating James Macgregor Burns' hypothesis in the Indian context using Karma-Yoga', *Proceedings of the Annual Conference of the Administrative Sciences Association of Canada*, Niagara Falls (Ontario).

Neelankavil, J.P., Mathur, A. and Zhang, Y. (2000) 'Determinants of managerial performance: a cross cultural comparison of the perceptions of middle level managers in four countries', *Journal of International Business Studies*, 31(1): 121–141.

Onesimo, A., Murphy, E.F., Greenwood, R.A., Ruiz-Gutierrez, J.A., Manyak, T.G. and Mujtaba, B. (2008) 'A preliminary exploration of generational similarities and differences in values between the United States, United Kingdom, Iceland, Japan, Korea, Colombia and the Philippines', *De La Salle University Business and Economics Review*, 18(1): 29–46.

Parameswaran, M.G. (2003) *Understanding Consumers: Building Powerful Brands Using Consumer Research*, Noida, India: Tata McGraw-Hill.

Parry, E. and Urwin, P. (2011) 'Generational differences in work values: a review of theory and evidence', *International Journal of Management Reviews*, 13(1): 79–96.

Ralston, D.A., Holt, D.A., Terpstra, R.H. and Yu, K.C. (1997) 'The impact of national culture and economic ideology on managerial work values: a study of the United States, Russia, Japan, and China', *Journal of International Business Studies*, 28: 177–208.

Ralston, D.A., Egri, C.P., Stewart, S., Terpstra, R.H. and Kaicheng, Y. (1999) 'Doing business in the 21st century with the new generation of Chinese managers: a study of generational shifts in work values in China', *Journal of International Business Studies*, 30: 415–428.

Rokeach, M. (1973) *The Nature of Human Values*, New York: The Free Press.

Roongrerngsuke, S. (2010) 'Attracting and retaining multigenerational workforce in China, India, and Thailand', paper presented at Society for Human Resource Management Annual Conference, USA.

Schuman, H. and Scott, J. (1989) 'Generations and collective memories', *American Sociological Review*, 54: 359–381.

13

GENERATIONAL DIFFERENCES IN THE FACTORS INFLUENCING CAREER SUCCESS ACROSS COUNTRIES

Julie Unite, Yan Shen, Emma Parry and Barbara Demel

Introduction

A growing body of research has explored the career experiences of individuals in different age cohorts or generations (see Dries *et al.* 2008; Strauss and Howe 1991). This work is related to Mannheim's (1952) definition of generations, that suggests members of a generation share common experiences that shape their preferences, attitudes and values towards a number of work-related factors, including that of careers. As such, it is conceivable that different generational groups would have distinct career preferences and attitudes.

Moving on from this, it is also conceivable that, as these common experiences are linked to the context in which these individuals grew up, they are also related to their national culture. Much of the popular literature on generations is based primarily on research from Western cultures such as the USA, UK and Australia. While these Western perspectives are warranted, it is also likely that the experiences or events that individuals in Western and non-Western countries have experienced in their formative years will differ (Parry and Urwin 2011). In this chapter, we investigate career experiences from different generational groups, but we also broaden this investigation by examining career experiences across four countries with different institutional contexts. This allows us to better understand not only the differences between the career experiences of different generational groups, but also to understand how these differences are affected by national contexts.

More specifically, this chapter focuses on the factors that influence career success. Career success is defined as 'the positive psychological or work-related outcomes or achievements one has accumulated as a result of one's work experiences' (Judge *et al.* 1995: 486; see also London and Stumpf 1982). There is a strong multi-disciplinary body of research on career success (Arthur *et al.* 1989a; Dries *et al.* 2008; Dries 2011), including the discussion of the subjective and objective nature of this construct (Gunz and Heslin 2005; Ng *et al.* 2005). Alongside this, there are studies that have identified the factors that influence career success. These include human and social capital variables as well as demographic factors (Judge *et al.* 1999; Seibert *et al.* 2001; Tharenou 1997). There is also evidence that career success is influenced by contextual factors, most notably institutional and cultural contexts, and differs across these factors (Tams and Arthur 2007). However, the extent of comparative studies in this area and particularly from the perspective of generational differences is limited.

With these research gaps in mind, our study begins to address the question of what influences career success for different generations and how this differs by national contexts. We aim to identify which factors influence career success for older and younger age groups across four contrasting countries, the UK, USA, China and South Africa. We also examine how our results relate to current Western career theories and what the implications of our findings are for practice.

Literature review

In order to understand the background to our study, we will briefly examine the research related to career success and its influencing factors. This is followed by a review of the research describing the impact of age and generation on these concepts. Finally, we review the literature exploring both generational differences and national context.

Career success and the influencing factors of career success

Career is defined here as 'the sequence of employment related positions, roles, activities and experiences encountered by a person' (Arnold 1997). Conceptualizations and constituting elements of individual careers are a core part of the career literature (Gunz and Peiperl 2007). As careers unfold, the question of career success and its determining factors becomes salient (Gunz and Heslin 2005). Career success is more generally regarded as 'the accomplishment of desirable work-related outcomes at any point in a person's work experiences over time' (Arthur *et al.* 2005: 178) and is considered to have both a subjective and objective nature.

During the past two decades, intensified globalization and turbulent economic and social environments have influenced how people view careers. For example, organizational change such as restructuring has become more common meaning that job security can no longer be guaranteed. This means that the traditional long-term career, spent working for one or two employers, has declined as workers are forced to change organizations, so workers' willingness to be loyal to a single employer has lessened (Hall and Mirvis 1996; Sullivan 1999). Because of these changes, the focus for career theories and how career success is understood has shifted slightly. Under traditional career theory, career success would be influenced by contextual and organizational factors, such as social background, loyalty to the organization, long service, building good relationships with superiors and advocating for the organization's goals and values (Arthur *et al.* 1999; Hall 2002).

More contemporary career theories however, such as the protean career theory (Briscoe *et al.* 2006; Hall 2002; Hall and Mirvis 1996) and the boundaryless career (Arthur and Rousseau 1996) emphasize the idea of individuals taking more responsibility to direct their own career growth within and across different organizations in a way that is compatible with their values. According to these more contemporary career orientations, success could be affected by personal agency factors such as adaptability, self-awareness and coping skills (Arthur *et al.* 1999). What's more, since the new career unfolds in short 'mini-cycles' or learning cycles (Hall 2002), a person's ability to learn is a critical success factor. Similarly, the contemporary business environment also indicates that work–life integration and balance are key driving factors (Harrington and Hall 2007).

Many studies have investigated the influencing factors of career success (e.g. Judge and Bretz 1994; Judge *et al.* 1995; Mayrhofer *et al.* 2007; Ng *et al.* 2005). Crucial factors identified in these empirical studies include human capital, demographic characteristics, personality, socio-demographic status, and organizational, industrial as well as regional developments (Ballout 2007; Judge *et al.* 1995; Mayrhofer *et al.* 2005; Ng *et al.* 2005). Work–life balance and organizational sponsorship have also been identified as important factors influencing career success (e.g. Aryee *et al.* 1994; Eddleston *et al.* 2004; Ng *et al.* 2005).

Some researchers have also tried to classify the dimensions of career success and its influencing factors and organize these factors into elaborate models (for overviews and comprehensive views see, for example, Arthur *et al.* 1989b; Baruch 2004; Collin and Young 2000; Hall 1987; Holland 1973; Judge and Bretz 1994; Judge *et al.* 1995; Mayrhofer *et al.* 2007; Ng *et al.* 2005; Van Maanen 1977). Heslin (2005: 115), for example, suggests grouping career success criteria into subjective and objective as well as self- and other referent categories.

From the perspective of classifying the influencing factors of career success, attribution theory is useful. A number of variants of attribution theory exist. Both Weiner *et al.* (1972) and Kelley (Kelley 1972a, 1972b) point out that individuals differentiate between two major aspects when explaining behaviour. On the one hand, they distinguish between stable and variable causes. On the other hand, they look for potential causes internally (i.e. within their own person) or externally (i.e. in the relevant environment). Combining these two major dimensions leads to a simple matrix with four quadrants denoting four different types of typical combinations when looking for causality: internal/stable, internal/variable, external/stable and external/variable. Even more simply, one could imagine research classifying influencing factors as to whether they are internally or externally attributed.

While there is a comprehensive array of factors that have been highlighted and attempts to classify these, it is not clear the degree to which these factors differ across generational groups or how national context plays a role. This is what we turn our attention to next.

The impact of age cohorts and generations on careers success

While there has been a growing interest in the differences in career experiences of different age cohorts or generations, to date few scholars have focused specifically on how career success differs for these groups and even fewer have explored the influencing factors related this. Understanding in this area seems important because both individuals and those involved in career management would benefit from knowledge of the factors that shape a particular age group's career and perception of career success. This would support the development and effective management for both the individual and human resource strategies.

Research suggests that career is closely linked with time by definition (Roth 1968). Consequently, one's career or life stage influences one's way of thinking in terms of career success (e.g. Hall and Nougaim 1968; Levinson *et al.* 1978; Schein 1978). According to classic career stage theory for example, what constitutes career success may change over time as individuals experience different career stages (Hall and Mirvis 1996; Levinson *et al.* 1978; Super 1957). Super's Career Stage theory (1957), for instance, suggests that success at the exploration stage may be related to overcoming uncertainties and successfully finding a career niche, while people at the advancement stage may be more concerned about their professional identity or working hard for future promotion and growth (Hall 2002).

Research that takes a generational approach to careers mostly focuses on work values or attitudes (for a review see Parry and Urwin 2011). Most of this literature examines career-related differences between generations and focuses on career preferences and motivations. For example, Wong *et al.* (2008) found differences in the motivations of different generational groups with Generations X and Y being more motivated by career progression than Baby Boomers. A later study by Bristow *et al.* (2011) also suggested that individuals' motivations for careers differed across Generations X and Y, with Generation Y placing more emphasis on security than the older generation. However, other work (see, for example, Appelbaum *et al.* 2005) has failed to find differences in career motivations between generational groups.

One notable exception to this focus on career motivations is the study by Dries *et al.* (2008) which examined whether beliefs about careers differed between Veterans, Baby Boomers, Generation X and Generation Y. Dries *et al.* (2008) found some indications that the different generations did have different career types but were not different in how they evaluated career success, but admitted that their study was somewhat limited in its method and analysis. More recently, Lyons *et al.* (2012) compared the careers of different generations and found that younger generations changed jobs and careers more frequently. In Chapter 10 of this book, Lyons *et al.* build on this work and find further differences in the careers of different generations within the Canadian context.

Despite these studies, the literature in this area is limited. To our knowledge, there is no literature that has focused on generational differences in the factors influencing career success. We will therefore focus on this area in this chapter.

Generations and national context

As discussed above, most of the research on generational differences has been conducted in Western (mostly US) contexts, leading to a tendency for both scholars and practitioners to adopt the American definitions of generations as though they are globally applicable. However, the early theoretical basis (Mannheim 1952) and some current studies (Bennis and Thomas 2002; Parry and Urwin 2011) emphasized the need for individuals to experience historical events in the same way in order to comprise a generation, suggesting that generations should be conceptualized as being within a particular national context. If this is true then, we might assume that generational structures within different countries will not follow the Western model.

Some research has examined generational characteristics in non-Western countries. Ralston *et al.* (1999) created Chinese generations based on events in Chinese history and found clear differences between these age cohorts in individualism, collectivism and Confucianism. Similarly, Whiteoak *et al.* (2006) found differences in values between older and younger UAE nationals. This evidence provides support for the notion that generational groups will differ not only within cultures but also across cultures. More research is needed in order to investigate the differences in the attitudes of age groups and generations across national contexts.

In sum, previous research has established the importance of understanding career success and the factors that influence it, and there is evidence that contextual and cultural factors play a role here. In the context of generations or differing age cohorts, these factors also seem particularly important as what influences a younger or older worker is likely to differ in different cultures. However, the comparative literature exploring these concepts is limited. This study therefore examines two research questions: (1) What are the perceived influencing factors of career success for younger and older individuals? (2) How do these differ at a country level when we look at individuals from China, South Africa, USA and the UK?

Methods

Sample

In order to sharpen the contrast within different age groups and make generational comparisons compatible across countries, we selected two age groups representing the youngest and oldest generations in the workforce. Individuals at or below age 30 (average sample age 27.5 years) and at or over 50 (average age 57) were interviewed. As we are suggesting that generations will differ between countries, we chose not to adopt the Western generations (e.g. Baby Boomers, Generation X and Y) but instead to compare the two most extreme age cohorts in the workplace – the oldest and the youngest.

TABLE 13.1 Sample profile

	English-speaking		*Confucian Asia*	*Africa/Middle East*
Countries	US	UK	China	South Africa
Sample size (n = 89)	20	17	28	24
Female/male	11/9	6/11	15/13	16/8
Older/younger generation	9/11	10/7	16/12	14/10

In total, 89 individuals were interviewed in the four countries and Table 13.1 gives an overview of the samples for each country. Individuals were identified using snowball sampling in each of the countries (more extensive details of the sampling criteria can be seen in Briscoe *et al.* 2012). Table 13.1 provides some details of the sample.

In order to select countries that might best illustrate the comparison of generational differences across national contexts we considered both the national culture and institutional framework of these countries.

National culture

Country cultures have been distinguished for many years by scholars such as Hofstede (1984, 1991), Schwartz (1994, 2006) and Trompenaars and Hampden-Turner (1997). Schwartz defines culture as a 'rich complex of meanings, beliefs, practices, symbols, norms and values prevalent among people in a society' (2006: 3). He organizes similar country cultures into seven clusters based on three bipolar dimensions (Schwartz 1994, 2006): autonomy (freedom and independence to pursue one's own ideas) versus embeddedness (independence and shared collectivism), mastery (assertive actions to change the world) versus harmony (fitting into the world as it is), and hierarchy (ascribed roles and obligations) versus egalitarianism (individuals as being equal). Similarly, Hofstede proposes five dimensions to differentiate country cultures, including individualism versus collectivism, power distance, masculinity versus femininity, uncertainty avoidance and long-term orientation.

Based on Schwartz and Hofstede's frameworks, the four countries explored in this study are located in three different cultural clusters: Confucian Asia (China), English-speaking (the UK and US) and Sub-Saharan Africa/Middle East (South Africa). Each is described in more detail in Table 13.2 and it is clear to see they have distinctive value systems and cultural dimensions, particularly between the developing (China and South Africa) and developed countries (the UK and US).

TABLE 13.2 Cultural dimensions in the four countries

Hofstede cultural dimensions	*China*	*South Africa*	*UK*	*US*
Individualism/collectivism	20	65	89	91
Power distance	80	49	35	40
Uncertainty avoidance	30	49	35	46
Masculinity/femininity	66	63	66	62
Long-term orientation	118	NA	25	29
Schwartz cultural dimensions	*China*	*South Africa*	*UK*	*US*
Autonomy	Low	Low	High	High
Embeddedness	High	High	Low	Low
Egalitarianism	Low	Low	Medium	Medium
Hierarchy	High	High	Medium	Medium
Harmony	Low	Moderately low	Low	Low
Mastery	High	Moderately high	High	High

Note: these cultural dimensions are from Hofstede (2001) and Schwartz (2004)

Institutional context: economic, political and social influences

In addition to the potential cultural influences upon individuals' perceptions about career success, we also assume that the economic, political and social conditions in a country may play a role in shaping how individuals attribute career success. Table 13.3 outlines these conditions for the four countries in our study. A further examination of these four countries clearly shows their differences in terms of economic development, political systems and social conditions, particularly between the developing (China and South Africa) and developed countries (US and UK). Furthermore, the pace of change in each country varies. For example, compared with the UK, there are more recent and dramatic economic, political and/or social changes in China and South Africa. The US is somewhere in between. Since career is socially embedded, the uneven pace of change across the four countries may contribute to some country-specific career patterns, particularly considering the differences between the younger and older generations.

TABLE 13.3 Economic, social and political contexts in each country

Context	*US*	*UK*	*China*	*South Africa*
Economic	• High income[1] • GDP per capita (2008–2012)[2]: USD 46,760–49,965 • Heavy market deregulation • Knowledge economy and outsourcing activities made traditional manufacturing industries fail • Longest economic expansion between the 1990s and 2000s till 2007	• High income • GDP per capita (2008–2012): USD 43,147–38, 514 • Service sector has grown substantially and is now worth over two-thirds of GDP • Highly international with high levels of imports and exports and a large immigrant population	• Upper middle income • GDP per capita (2008–2012): USD 3,414–6,091 • Open-up reform from 1978 aiming to establish a socialist market economy, with an average annual economic growth rate topping two digits • Rapid growth of foreign direct investment and private investment; as opposed to the sharp shrinkage of state-owned enterprises	• Upper middle income • GDP per capita (2008–2012): USD 5,598–7,508 • Economic isolation from the international community due to apartheid laws between 1979 and 1994 • Post-1994, Reconstruction and Development Program initiated to guide government resource distribution, economic policies and employment relations
Social	• Education enrollment (secondary[3]/tertiary[4]): 96%/89% • Public education free through secondary education	• Education enrolment (secondary/tertiary) 102%/59% • Public education free through secondary education	• Education enrollment (secondary/tertiary): 81%/24% • Strong public education, free through the secondary level • Lifetime employment no longer existed and government no longer controlled one's career/job mobility	• Education enrollment (secondary/tertiary): 94%/NA • Segregated education system before apartheid was lifted • Affirmative actions laws favour coloured/black people over white males • The coloured/black people in the older generation had few options except for nursing and blue-collar jobs

Continued

TABLE 13.3 *Continued*

Context	*US*	*UK*	*China*	*South Africa*
Political	• Declaration of Independence from American colonists in 1776 • US Constitution in 1787, emphasizing individual rights and balance of power in government • The end of Cold War in the 1980s made the US the single superpower in the world • A federal democratic republic composed of 50 states	• United Kingdom started in 1707 with political union of England and Scotland to form Great Britain; Ireland added to form United Kingdom in 1800. • Unitary democracy and constitutional monarchy: the Monarch is the Head of State and the Prime Minister the Head of Government • Multi-party system dominated by Labour and Conservative party	• Founding of People's Republic China in 1949, with the Chinese Communist Party as the single ruling party • End of the ten-year Cultural Revolution in 1976, which almost paralysed the national economic development and educational system • Return of HK and Macao to mainland China in 1997 and 1999 respectively	• Racial segregation ('Apartheid') before 1994 • International sanctions and boycotts between 1979 and 1994 against the Nationalist government • The first democratic and non-racial elections were held, with the African National Congress in power in 1994, trying to rectify the devastating effects of racial discrimination and apartheid. A number of laws were promulgated to explicitly prohibit unfair discriminations, regulate employment relations and guarantee fair labour practices

1 This classification is from World Bank listed economies in which countries are classified into high-income, upper-middle-income, lower-middle-income and low-income categories. http://data.worldbank.org/about/country-classifications/country-and-lending-groups#High_income, accessed August 2013.

2 http://data.worldbank.org/indicator/NY.GDP.PCAP.CD, accessed August 2013.

3 http://data.worldbank.org/indicator/SE.SEC.ENRR, accessed August 2013. The percentage can exceed 100% due to the inclusion of over-aged and under-aged students because of early or late school entrance and grade repetition. Since South Africa did not have data for the years 2010 and 2011, we chose the year 2009 as the comparison base for both secondary and tertiary education enrollment.

4 http://data.worldbank.org/indicator/SE.TER.ENRR, accessed August 2013. Data for South Africa are not available.

Data collection and analysis

Data from the US, UK, China and South Africa were obtained from a larger global career study which included 243 interviews (Briscoe *et al.* 2012). Rather than using the entire dataset, for ease of analysis we selected two countries in which the Western generational categories (Baby Boomers, etc.) are generally accepted as being valid (USA and UK) and two other countries that provide a contrast to the USA and UK in relation to national culture and institutional context (China and South Africa).

Qualitative techniques were adopted for this research using semi-structured interviews. A qualitative approach to research is recommended in the early cycles of phenomena investigation (Edmondson and McManus 2007; McGrath 1982) and interviews are considered an especially useful form of data-gathering when flexibility and theory-generation are desired (Patton 1990). Semi-structured interviews were conducted in the respective national languages following an interview guide. On average they lasted for 45 minutes, were tape-recorded and fully transcribed. The interviews were conducted by members of the respective country teams who were very familiar with the purposes of the study and interview procedure. A more detailed outline of the foundations behind the study can be found in Briscoe *et al.* (2012).

The interviews followed a guide that outlined different questions to elicit data about how individuals conceptualize career success and its influencing factors. Sample questions include: (1) Looking back at your experiences and your career thus far, what does it mean for you to have 'career success'? and (2) What do you feel the crucial factors are influencing such career success?

For data analysis we used a variant of qualitative content analysis to extract core categories from individuals' descriptions of careers (Mayring 2003). This was supported by the software tool QSR NVivo 7. In the first round, national research teams coded their individual text materials separately in order to generate culture-specific conceptual categories. After the core categories in the local language were generated, these categories with explanations and illustrative examples were translated into English, using a standard format to display results. Second, a 5C Global Coding Book was created to integrate each country's respective schemes of categories, with detailed definitions for each core category and sub-categories. Intensive face-to-face group discussion and virtual communication were used to ensure a common understanding. Third, each country team recoded all the interview data, strictly following the guidelines in the 5C Global Coding Book and at the same time assuring a better intra-coder-reliability. In terms of the within-team inter-coder reliability, we calculated an agreement rate of coded categories ranging between 85–90 per cent. To provide an example of the Global Coding Book, please see Table 13.6 for the main categories of influencing factors of career success with definitions and representative quotes from the bigger sample of 11 countries.

For generating a framework about the global similarities and differences of core categories within and between countries, the constant comparative method was used (Glaser and Strauss 1967; Strauss and Corbin 1998). The basic goal of this procedure is to construct a reasonably sophisticated picture in each country. Core tools in this process are qualitative data analysis matrix displays that have been effectively used to compare data (Miles and Huberman 1994; see also Briscoe *et al.* 2012). Based on the results of the qualitative content analysis, we compared and contrasted instances within the person, and differences across persons and age groups regarding career success conceptualizations and influencing factors of career success within and between countries.

Results

In the following section, we first outlined the main categories regarding influencing factors of career success identified from the four-country data (Figure 13.1). Then, we took the four countries as a whole and highlighted the top three most important influencing factors for the older and younger groups (Table 13.4). Third, we reported the age group differences and similarities within each country as well as across the four countries (Table 13.5).

Influencing factors of career success: the main categories

Figure 13.1 highlights the influencing factors of career success identified from the four countries (please see Table 13.6 for their definitions and illustrative quotes). As can be seen in Figure 13.1, major influences on career success come from the ***person, one's social and work context***. Factors concerning the person comprise one's *personal history* (e.g. life experiences, educational and job history, family background), *learning and development, traits, skills, motives, gender* and active *career management*. Individuals' social and work contexts such as *support from their family, friends, and colleagues* also influence their career success.

In addition, some macro-level factors, such as ***context of society and culture***, are also identified as important factors influencing career success. The context of society and culture, for example, includes *governmental policies, availability of education, learning and developmental support/barrier* and *discrimination*, etc. The category of ***global context*** comprises *globalization* and *global competition*. The ***generation*** category is seen on a macro-level mirroring the definition put forward by Mannheim (1952) which suggests that members of a generation share common experiences that shape their preferences, attitudes and values. Each 'generation' of individuals defined by each country's context played an important role in influencing career success. Finally, ***luck and contingencies*** are also found to affect one's career success.

Three most important influencing factors of career success

Table 13.4 lists the three most important influencing factors of career success at the aggregated level, i.e. considering the overall sample of 49 interviews for the older group and 40 for the younger group. ***Context of work*** (such as *support from the company, superiors, peers*) and ***Personal history*** (such as *educational history* and *job history*)

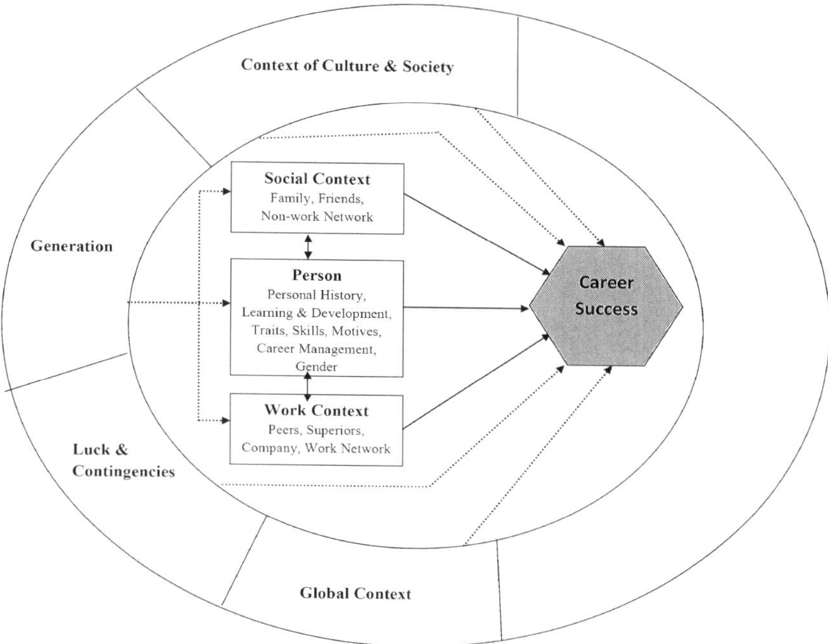

FIGURE 13.1 Framework of career success and its influencing factors

ranked as the two most important influencing factors of career success for both older and younger groups with ***Traits*** (such as *persistence and diligence*) and ***Skills*** (such as *social skills*) being important for the older and younger groups respectively.

As Table 13.4 shows, these major influencing factors vary across the two generations to some extent. Both emphasized personal history and the context in which one works as the most important influences of career success. Younger workers had a slightly greater affiliation for context of work and the older group placed a slightly greater emphasis on personal history.

> I was raised by driven parents. I have got two grannies who are like huge in the community. My granny organizes the old people to get food and organizes fundraisings. Yeah, I have to think it has a lot to do with upbringing and the type of people that have influenced my life.
>
> (*Personal history*, younger person in South Africa)

> You can't get anything done at work without that support. And then there is not a day that goes by that I don't ask one of my co-workers. And that's the other thing, knowing who to go to – there are people I trust and there are people I don't trust, and you ask them you know, 'what do you think about this?' Still having that camaraderie is really important.
>
> (*Context of work*, younger person in the US)

TABLE 13.4 Three most influential factors of career success for younger (n = 40) and older groups (n = 49)

	Influential factors of career success	*Representative quotes*
1	**Younger group:** *Context of work* – Company – Superior – Peer – Work network	You can't get anything done at work without that support. And then there's not a day that goes by that I don't ask one of my co-workers. And that's the other thing, knowing whom to go to – there're people I trust and there're people I don't trust, and you ask them you know what do you think about this? Still having that camaraderie is really important. [Younger interviewee in the US]
	Older group: *Personal history* – Educational history – Family background – Job history	There were also a lot of older nurses who didn't have some of the training, and I don't have that fear of being threatened because I was able to get my degree of Bachelor of Nursing and that gave me a lot of confidence. [Older interviewee in the US]
2	**Younger group:** *Personal history* – Educational history – Family background – Life history	My mom is teacher. She's been teaching long before I was born. She just retired. But I think perhaps the influence came more from my mom because she even used to teach me before even I went to school. [Younger interviewee in South Africa]
	Older group: *Context of work* – Company – Superior – Peer – Work network	People around you, your colleagues wherever that is very important, how you get along with each other. [Older interviewee in South Africa]
3	**Younger group:** *Skills* – Socio-emotional – Task or content related skills	It's the people that you can call upon … when we were bringing people into the corporate development team you think, well you bring an individual in, but you're not just bringing that individual in, you're bringing in the network as well, the people around them, the relationships they have, the people that they can call upon … as you move through your career you start off with a relatively small, inexperienced group of people that you know and relate to and as you move through that, that grows and gets bigger … you talk to some of the senior guys, you know, the networks they have are incredible and that helps you get things done … your network as you move through and how you nurture those relationships going forward because you … can't become an effective business leader on your own. It's about you and the people that you know and work with. [Younger interviewee in the UK]

Influential factors of career success	*Representative quotes*
Older group: *Traits* – Work ethic – Persistence-diligence – Character	I think the most important contributor is my personality. My mom died when I was quite young, which made me very independent and tried to do everything well. [Older interviewee in China]

Interestingly, younger people placed more weight on the skills necessary for career success than the older group. Older people felt that traits or one's personality were more important. This partly reflects current career environment characterized by increased national and global competition and the emergence of boundaryless and protean careers where skills and employability are critical for individuals' career development and success.

Similarities and differences across generation and country

Callanan (2003) summarized three general categories in prior studies that were found to influence career success: demographic and human capital characteristics (e.g. level and quality of education), personal traits (e.g. motivation and proactive personality) and organizational contexts (e.g. human resource development strategies). As we saw from Table 13.4, the interview data revealed a similar pattern. However, our research also showed other categories unique to age group and country, particularly regarding a country's macro-environment. Turning our attention to some of these patterns, Table 13.5 shows the most frequently mentioned career success categories across both age and country.

If we first look at some of the differences between the two age groups, we can see in both China and South Africa, context of society and culture (e.g. government policy) is a factor considered as crucial to one's career success among the older generation. In these cases, the government policies were perceived as barriers or facilitators to this generation's career development and success. Looking first at China, for example, one migrant worker emphasized this factor throughout the entire interview, including China's open-up policy since 1978, the famous Southern tour led by Deng Xiaoping in 1992 when 'Guangdong became the hot spot within the reform blueprint', and bias against rural migrant workers due to the household registration system. The interview data suggest that the older generation's career path was shaped by the evolution of government policies at various periods. This quote by an older Chinese interviewee describes this influence clearly:

> At that time, we didn't have the freedom to find our own job, all were assigned by the government. I wanted to leave the countryside and work in cities when I was young. However, it was not allowed by the government policy at that time. We could only stay home working on the farms.
>
> (Older interviewee from China)

TABLE 13.5 Three most frequently mentioned influencing factors of career success across age group and country

Country	*Younger age group*	*Older age group*
China	Personal history 91% educational history; general educational history Skills 91% task and content skills Context of work 83% superior psychosocial support; company support; job opportunities	Personal history 81% educational history; general educational history Traits 69% persistence and diligence Context of society and culture 56% resource barrier; government policies
South Africa	Traits 50% persistence and diligence Motives 50% goal-related drivers; effort Context of work 40% company support	Motives 50% goal-related drivers; doing what you love Traits 43% good work ethic Context of work 29% superiors; resources support Context of society and culture 22% resource barrier; government policies
US	Context of work 36% peers; psychosocial support Social environment 36% family psychosocial support Personal history 27% personal history; job history; educational history and life and family influence Career management 27% setting career goals and identifying new career opportunities	Personal history 56% job history; work experience Ongoing learning and development 56% continuing formal education; learning through job experience Traits 44% character Context of work 44% peers; psychosocial support
UK	Context of work 86% peers; psychosocial support; company learning and development support; key assignments Personal history 71% educational history; general educational history Skills 29% socio-emotional skills; social and networking skills	Personal history 70% educational history; general educational history Context of work 70% company; resource support Skills 20% task and content skills; general know-how Social environment 20% family and friends; psychosocial support

The role of institutional contexts, particularly government regulations and policies, cannot be underestimated when discussing older generation's career success in China. Since they had little control over the type of work they wanted to do, they did not have much expectation about their career development. For them, career management such as setting career goals and securing person-organization or person-job fit was meaningless, and possibly unheard of. In addition, life-long employment was the norm in state-owned enterprises and promotion was based on seniority rather than merit and individual competence. Therefore, lack of market competition made skill development less relevant in the work context.

Similarly, in South Africa, government policies prohibited equal educational and employment opportunities for certain racial groups. This restricted job choice and progression for many of the older interviewees and significantly shaped what influenced their career success. A good example of this is the story of Mary who started working as a bank teller in the early 1970s. She describes how as a woman of colour, she faced a number of stumbling blocks to her career progression and success but also how things changed post-Apartheid in the early 1990s:

> Well when I started at the bank in 1974 I'd been working for about a year and I was the first person of colour who was allowed to interact with the public. Back then we still experienced quite a bit of discrimination between male and female and there were certain distinctions made due to colour. It was quite difficult and certain roles were not open to women or to people of the racial group that I came from. That changed over a period of time and there were quite a lot of changes before 1994. We were really gearing up towards an acceptance of all races. While there is still an element of discrimination, there is now a lot more opportunities for previously disadvantaged individuals, especially if you are willing to work hard.

When we look at the younger generations from these two countries we can see that in China the younger generation attributed their career success more to individual factors than to institutional contexts. They paid more attention to their educational background (a university degree as a 'must have'), life experiences, task and socio-emotional skills, active career management and work/non-work contexts (support from their superiors, peer colleagues and family/friends). Compared with their parents, the younger people have the freedom to choose their careers and design their own career path. The fast-changing economic landscape has helped enhance individuals' confidence in securing their perceived career success through continuous individual efforts – including getting a university degree, accumulating necessary hard and soft skills, building personal supportive networks and taking the initiatives in their career development. The role of institutional factors such as government policy played a much less salient role in one's career success in today's context.

Similarly in South Africa, the pattern for the younger generation does not show the negative extent of government policies to that of their parents. Interestingly for the younger group in this country, personal history is not an influencing factor as it is in the younger generation for the other countries. This could be interpreted by cultural patterns in which the younger groups from previously disadvantaged groups do not have familial role models to look up to. Similarly the relevance and place for education is still developing for the younger people in this country, so its importance in shaping career success is not as significant as that in other countries. Instead, some traditional influencing factors such as persistence and diligence and effort turned out to be more important.

More generally, we saw that in China, South Africa and the US, older interviewees talked about 'traits' such as 'persistence', 'diligence' and 'having good work ethics' – 'No matter what you do, you should love it and try your best to perform it well' (quote from an Chinese older interviewee) – as important influencing factors. This was seen less so in the older generation in the UK, which fits with the idea of the decline of the protestant work ethic. The younger generation seemed to put emphasis instead on 'skills' particularly in China, UK and the USA as an emerging influence on career success. These included a range of things such as socio-emotional skills (social and networking), and task and content-related skills.

The context of work generally is important across all countries and to both generations, however, in some cases, there was a shift in the emphasis placed for each age group. In the UK for example, for the older generation it is more about support from the company and superiors whereas for the younger workers, it is more about peer support. This supports current career theories such as the protean career theory in which younger workers are less reliant on the company for their career development and show more evidence of career self-direction.

Related to this, career self-management was also talked about in the US as an important influencing factor of career success in the younger generation. More generally, our research also showed evidence that career self-management strategies such as setting career goals and identifying new career opportunities was also important to the younger generation in the other countries too, and mentioned more so than that of the older generation.

Discussion

The results from our research provide an outline of the factors that individuals from older and younger generations perceive as influencing their career success. The results showed that one of the most common influencing factors for both older and younger generations was the *Context of work*, particularly the support from one's company, superiors and peers. This highlights the necessity to take a relational perspective when examining individuals' career success (Fletcher 1999; Hall *et al.* 1996; Kram and Hall 1996). *Personal history* was another common influencing factor for both the older and younger groups. This could be related to what Bourdieu (1977) called the *habitus*, the person's phenomenological response to the objective structural context.

In general, the younger employees in all four countries embraced many ways to influence their career success, from one's human capital to more self-directed career management, such as setting clear career goals and identifying new opportunities. They also paid more attention to skill development rather than relatively static traits. This evidence not only reflects the current turbulent career environment in which one's employability is directly related to one's career success (De Vos *et al.* 2011), but also supports current career theory including boundaryless and protean career orientations in that the younger generation focuses more on actively managing their own careers.

Our results also indicated that social capital has become a more salient factor influencing the younger generation's career success, particularly in the US, UK and China. When the fast-changing career landscape requires individuals to draw career and psychosocial support from multiple developers rather than one formal mentor (Higgins and Kram 2001), it is not surprising that both intra- and extra-organizational relationships, including those with one's colleagues, family and friends, have become more critical in shaping one's career success (Cotton *et al.* 2011). In addition, some of the stereotypes commonly placed on the younger generation such as their emphasis on work–life balance seemed to be less significant factors in shaping their career success in comparison to work context and personal history.

Despite these generalizations, when we look at the specific picture for each country, we can see the effect of the institutional context on generational characteristics in each case. Though culture may influence how people attribute their career success, our findings suggest that its role is very limited in comparison to institutions, particularly when considering the generational differences within and across countries. For example, one may expect that 'context of work' (e.g. support from one's supervisors and peers) as well as 'social environment' (e.g. support from one's family and friends) play a more salient role in China and South Africa where collectivism or embeddedness is the cultural norm. But as Table 13.5 indicated, these two factors are equally or even more important in the US and UK where individualism is a much more prevalent cultural value.

We argue that in terms of how people attribute their career success, the pace of economic and political change in one country tends to provide a more reasonable explanation for generational differences within and across countries than national culture does. Some of the differences between age groups in one country are not as significant as we may have imagined, particularly when the country has not experienced dramatic change in its economic and political landscape. The UK, for example, had fewer differences between older and younger groups. By contrast, in countries where there has been significant change in the macro-environment, such as South Africa and China, we saw relatively big differences in the profile between the two age groups. As the younger generations move away from the difficulties faced by the older generations in these countries and adjust to their new career environment, we are able to see the effects of this 'local context' on their career perceptions. In these situations, the local economic and political contexts supersede the national cultural context and the global context.

From a theoretical and practical perspective, our results raise a number of important points. Theoretically, it brings into question the notion of generations that are universally applicable across countries and suggests that institutional contexts play a significant role in shaping career success in different generations. In particular, our study suggests that differences between generations are larger in countries that have undergone significant institutional change. This supports Mannheim's (1952) original theorization of generations as being related to the 'social space' that an individual operates within, rather than simply to birth year. Future research should build on this chapter and other work (e.g. that by Hui-Chun and Miller 2003, 2005) to examine generational differences in non-Western countries. In addition research is needed to more closely examine the historical events that shape individuals' experiences during their formative years and therefore also lead to distinct generational characteristics.

Similarly, comparative studies across the four countries highlight the difficulties of applying some of the contemporary career theories in all contexts. While, for example, the sample in the US provided evidence for the emergence of boundaryless and protean careers, many of the more traditional factors are still being retained and the older generation are still emphasizing or valuing many of these factors as well as embracing the new ones.

Drawing from this, future research would benefit from further development of a theoretical model underpinning the influencing factors of career success. While we suggested a simple model here in Figure 13.1 as a possible framework for categorizing the influencing factors we found from this qualitative research, further quantitative work could be useful. The differential effects of various perceived influencing factors, whether they are more internal factors such as personal history or external factors such as affirmative action, on an individual's perceptions of career success could provide insight into a more comprehensive framework. This chapter was not able to explore in detail the effects of such things as gender or more diverse age groups, and these could be interesting moderators in these career success relationships.

From a more practical perspective, this study suggests that a one size fits all approach to human resource strategies across generations might not be sufficient when managing the workforce. For example, companies, regardless of where they locate, should try to cultivate a developmental culture that facilitates the building of high-quality relationships (Higgins and Kram 2001). However, when building such a culture, one needs to consider the local contexts and such things as the degree of power distance and collectivism. Moreover, for companies in countries with dramatic social and economic changes such as China and South Africa, they should take a more strategic and differentiated approach when dealing with different age groups since they may have very different perceptions of what influences their career success.

TABLE 13.6 Perceived influencing factors of career success: major categories, definitions and representative quotes

Main categories (internal/individual level)	*Definition*	*Representative quotes*
Personal history	Aspects of the interviewees' history that they see as influencing their career success, such as one's family background, life experience, educational history and job history.	I would say that I am successful today because of my basic education from the primary school. Without that, I wouldn't be who I am now. I mean that is the base. The education I got when I was at SM Agama Persekutuan Kajang. What I got there gave me the knowledge and faith that I have now. [Younger person in Malaysia]
Learning and development	Formal and informal learning and development after interviewees' usual training or education period required to enter career, such as continuous formal education, company-sponsored training and learning through jobs and/or relationships.	And I love school, I love to learn and like I said before I have so much support in going back to school that it actually was fairly easy to decide. [Younger person in the US]
Traits	Prominent personal aspects enduring across situations that interviewees see as influencing their career success, such as persistence and diligence.	You have to create the good in all you do. Not always what you plan comes true but even if not, you have to make the best out of it that is easy for me to do. I am a very optimistic person, I have a good basis. [Older nurse in Israel]
Skills	A skill is an ability, usually learned and acquired through training, to perform actions that achieve a desired outcome, such as social skills.	You will succeed if you have strong competences you learned from the job. [Older person in Serbia]
Motives	Factors that drive interviewees' motivation, which, in turn, influences their behaviour, such as one's career ambition, commitment and enthusiasm.	Through my daily activities I would like to show my subordinates how much I love my job and how much I enjoy helping people. [Older person in Mexico]

Continued

TABLE 13.6 *Continued*

Main categories (internal/individual level)	*Definition*	*Representative quotes*
Career management	Interviewees take an active role in evaluating, planning and pursuing their careers, such as setting career goals, identifying new career opportunities and managing work–life balance.	I have planned for my career in a way that children are already included… When I plan my career I also think how those plans interact or synergize with other life priorities. [Younger person in Spain]
Context of work	Aspects of the interviewees' work contexts that they see as influencing their career success, such as support from their peers, supervisors and companies.	[My] social network outside the company did not help my career, but my network within this company did. Having a personal connection with workers in other factories [of this company] influenced my career success. [Younger person in Japan]
Social environment	Aspects of the interviewees' immediate social (non-work) environment that they see as influencing their career success, such as support from their family and friends.	I have friends that are very knowledgeable and successful and they definitely contributed to connecting me to the right people and giving me good advice. [Younger person in Israel]
Context of society and culture	Aspects of the interviewees' country contexts that they see as influencing their career success, such as cultural and societal barriers, government policies and priorities, etc.	Career success depends upon the change of relevant regulations … When I first came to this city, I was not accepted by the local government. But now, migrant workers have not only been accepted but also encouraged. [Older person in China]
Global context	Dynamics at the global level that impacts interviewees' careers and career success, such as globalization and global competition.	Career success is about family and work balance. I was involved in the 9/11 attacks and as we started walking away from the buildings I just kept thinking 'I don't wanna like die now and not experience children with my husband, and life is not about just this.' [Younger person in the US]

Main categories (internal/individual level)	*Definition*	*Representative quotes*
Luck and contigencies	Random and contingent influences upon interviewees' career success.	Starting my own business was like causality. My first client was the concessionaire of cafeterias in the company. He asked me to design a human resources system for his company and once finished he also asked me to implement it. I took that opportunity to start my own consultancy business. [Older person in Mexico]

References

Appelbaum, S., Serena, M. and Shapiro, B. (2005) 'Generation X and the Boomers: an analysis of realities and myths', *Management Research News*, 28(1): 1–33.

Arnold, J. (1997) *Managing Careers into the 21st Century*, London: Sage.

Arthur, M. and Rousseau, D.B. (eds) (1996) *The Boundaryless Career: A New Employment Principle for a New Organizational Era*, New York: Oxford University Press.

Arthur, M.B., Hall, D.T. and Lawrence, B.S. (1989a) 'Generating new directions in career theory: the case for a transdisciplinary approach', in M.B. Arthur, D.T. Hall and B.S. Lawrence (eds) *Handbook of Career Theory*, Cambridge: Cambridge University Press, pp. 7–25.

Arthur, M.B., Hall, D.T. and Lawrence, B.S. (eds) (1989b) *Handbook of Career Theory*, Cambridge: Cambridge University Press.

Arthur, M.B., Inkson, K. and Pringle, J.K. (1999) *The New Careers: Individual Action and Economic Change*, London: Sage.

Arthur, M.B., Khapova, S.N. and Wilderom, C.P.M. (2005) 'Career success in a boundaryless career world', *Journal of Organizational Behavior*, 26(2): 177–202.

Aryee, S., Chay, Y.W. and Tan, H.H. (1994) 'An examination of the antecedents of subjective career success among a managerial sample in Singapore', *Human Relations*, 47(5): 487–509.

Ballout, H.I. (2007) 'Career success: the effects of human capital, person-environment fit and organizational support', *Journal of Managerial Psychology*, 22(8): 741–765.

Baruch, Y. (2004) *Managing Careers: Theory and Practice*, Harlow: Pearson Education.

Bennis, W.G. and Thomas, R.J. (2002) *Geeks and Geezers*, Boston, MA: Harvard Business School Press.

Bourdieu, P. (1977) *Outline of a Theory of Practice*, Cambridge: Cambridge University Press.

Briscoe, J.P., Hall, D.T. and DeMuth, R.L.F. (2006) 'Protean and boundaryless careers: an empirical exploration', *Journal of Vocational Behavior*, 69: 30–47.

Briscoe, J.P., Hall, D.T. and Mayrhofer, W. (2012) *Careers Around the World: Individual and Contextual Perspectives*. New York: Routledge.

Bristow, D, Amyx, D., Castleberry, S.B. and Cochran, J.J. (2011) 'A cross-generational comparison of motivational factors in a sales career among Gen-X and Gen-Y college students', *Personal Selling and Sales Management*, 31(1), 77–86.

Callanan, G.A. (2003) 'What price career success?', *Career Development International*, 8: 126–133.

Collin, A. and Young, R.A. (eds) (2000) *The Future of Careers*, Cambridge: Cambridge University Press.

Cotton, R.D., Shen Y. and Livine-Tarandach, R. (2011) 'On becoming extraordinary: the content and structure of the developmental networks of Major League Baseball Hall of Famers', *Academy of Management Journal*, 54(1): 15–46.

De Vos, A., De Hauw, S. and Van der Heijden, B.I.J.M. (2011) 'Competency development and career success: the mediating role of employability', *Journal of Vocational Behavior*, 79: 438–447.

Dries, N. (2011) 'The meaning of career success: avoiding reification through a closer inspection of historical, cultural and ideological contexts', *Career Development International*, 16(4): 364–384.

Dries, N., Pepermans, R. and De Kerpel, E. (2008) 'Exploring four generations beliefs about career: is "satisfied" the new "successful"?', *Journal of Managerial Psychology*, 23(8), 907–928.

Eddleston, K.A., Baldridge, D.C. and Veiga, J.F. (2004) 'Toward modeling the predictors of managerial career success: does gender matter?', *Journal of Managerial Psychology*, 19(4): 360–385.

Edmonson, A.C. and McManus, S.E. (2007) 'Methodological fit in management field research', *Academy of Management Review*, 32(4): 1155–1179.

Fletcher, J.K. (1999) *Disappearing Acts: Gender, Power, and Relational Practice at Work*, Cambridge, MA: MIT Press.

Glaser, B. and Strauss, A.L. (1967) *The Discovery of Grounded Theory: Strategies for Qualitative Research*, Chicago, IL: Aldine Transaction.

Gunz, H.P. and Heslin, P.A. (2005) 'Reconceptualizing career success', *Journal of Organizational Behavior*, 26: 105–111.

Gunz, H. and Peiperl, M. (eds) (2007) *Handbook of Career Studies*, Thousand Oaks, CA: Sage.

Hall, D.T. (1987) 'Careers and socialization', *Journal of Management*, 13(2): 301–321.

Hall, D.T. (2002) *Careers In and Out of Organizations*, Thousand Oaks, CA: Sage.

Hall, D.T. and Mirvis, P. (1996) 'The new protean career: psychological success and the path with a heart', in D.T. Hall (ed.) *The Career is Dead: Long Live the Career*, San Francisco, CA: Jossey-Bass, pp. 1–12.

Hall, D.T. and Nougaim, K.E. (1968) 'An examination of Maslow's need hierarchy in an organizational setting', *Organizational Behavior and Human Performance*, 3: 12–35.

Hall, D.T. and Associates (eds) (1996) *The Career is Dead: Long Live the Career: A Relational Approach to Careers*, San Francisco, CA: Jossey-Bass.

Harrington, B. and Hall, D.T. (2007) *Career Management and Work–Life Integration: Using Self-Assessment to Navigate Contemporary Careers*, Beverly Hills, CA: Sage.

Heslin, P.A. (2005) 'Conceptualizing and evaluating career success', *Journal of Organizational Behavior*, 26(2): 113–136.

Higgins, M.C. and Kram, K.E. (2001) 'Reconceptualizing mentoring at work: a developmental network perspective', *Academy of Management Review*, 26(2): 264–288.

Hofstede, G. (1984) *Cultures Consequences: International Differences in Work Related Values*, 2nd edn, Beverly Hills, CA: Sage.

Hofstede, G. (1991) *Culture and Organizations: Software of the Mind*, London: McGraw-Hill.

Hofstede G. (2001) *Culture's Consequences: Comparing Values, Behaviors, Institutions and Organizations across Nations*, 2nd edn, Thousand Oaks, CA: Sage Publications.

Holland, J.L. (1973) *Making Vocational Choices*, Englewood Cliffs, NJ: Prentice-Hall.

Hui-Chun, Y. and Miller, P. (2003) 'The generation gap and cultural influence: a Taiwan empirical investigation', *Cross-Cultural Management*, 10(3): 23–41.

Hui-Chun, Y. and Miller, P. (2005) 'Leadership style: the X Generation and Baby Boomers compared in different cultural contexts', *Leadership and Organisation Development*, 26(1/2): 35–50.

Judge, T.A. and Bretz, R.D. (1994) 'Political influence behavior and career success', *Journal of Management*, 20(1): 43–65.

Judge, T.A., Cable, D.M., Boudreau, J.W. and Bretz, R.D.J. (1995) 'An empirical investigation of the predictors of executive career success', *Personnel Psychology*, 48(3): 485–519.

Judge, T.A., Higgins, C.A., Thoresen, C.J. and Barrick, M.R. (1999) 'The big five personality traits, general mental ability, and career success across the life span', *Personnel Psychology*, 52(3): 621–652.

Kelley, H.H. (1972a) 'Attribution in social interaction', in E.E. Jones, D.E. Kanouse, H.H. Kelley, R.E. Nisbett, S. Valins and B. Weiner (eds) *Attribution: Perceiving the Causes of Behavior*, Morristown, NJ: General Learning Press, pp. 1–26.

Kelley, H.H. (1972b) 'Causal schemata and the attribution process', in E.E. Jones, D.E. Kanouse, H.H. Kelley, R.E. Nisbett, S. Valins and B. Weiner (eds) *Attribution: Perceiving the Causes of Behavior*, Morristown, NJ: General Learning Press, pp. 151–174.

Kram, K.E. and Hall, D.T. (1996) 'Mentoring in a context of diversity and turbulence', in E.E. Kossek and S.A. Lobel (eds) *Managing Diversity: Human Resource Strategies for Transforming the Workplace*, Cambridge, MA: Blackwell Business, pp. 108–136.

Levinson, D.J., Darrow, C.N., Klein, E.B., Levinson, M.H. and McKee, B. (1978) *The Seasons of a Man's Life*, New York: Ballantines.

London, M. and Stumpf, S. (1982) *Managing Careers*, Reading, MA: Addison-Wesley.

Lyons, S.T., Schweitzer, L., Ng, E.S. and Kuron, L.K. (2012) 'Comparing apples to apples: a qualitative investigation of career mobility patterns across four generations', *Career Development International*, 17(4): 333–357.

Mannheim, K. (1952) 'The problem of generations', in P. Kecskemeti (ed.) *Essays on the Sociology of Knowledge*, London: Routledge and Kegan Paul, pp. 276–322.

Mayrhofer, W., Meyer, M. and Steyrer, J. (2005) 'Karrieren: eine Einführung', in W. Mayrhofer, M. Meyer and J. Steyrer (eds) *Macht? Erfolg? Reich? Glücklich? Einflussfaktoren auf Karrieren*, Vienna: Linde Verlag, pp. 12–24.

Mayrhofer, W., Meyer, M. and Steyrer, J. (2007) 'Contextual issues in the study of careers', in H.P. Gunz and M.A. Peiperl (eds) *Handbook of Career Studies*, Thousand Oaks, CA: Sage, pp. 215–240.

Mayring, P. (2003) *Qualitative Inhaltsanalyse: Grundlagen und Techniken*, 8th edn, Weinheim: Beltz.

McGrath, J. (1982) *Judgement Calls in Research*, Beverly Hills, CA: Sage.

Miles, M.B. and Huberman, A.M. (1994) *Qualitative Data Analysis: An Expanded Sourcebook*, 2nd edn, London: Sage.

Ng, T.W.H., Eby, L.T., Sorensen, K.L. and Feldman, D.C. (2005) 'Predictors of objective and subjective career success: a meta-analysis', *Personnel Psychology*, 58(2): 367–408.

Parry, E. and Urwin, P. (2011) 'Generational differences in work values: a review of the evidence', *International Journal of Management Reviews*, 13(1): 79–96.

Patton, M. (1990) *Qualitative Evaluation and Research Methods*, Beverly Hills, CA: Sage.

Ralston, D.A., Egri, C.P., Stewart, S., Terpstra, R.H. and Kaicheng, Y. (1999) 'Doing business in the 21st century with the new generation of Chinese managers: a study of generational shifts in work values in China', *Journal of International Business Studies*, 30(2): 415–427.

Roth, J.A. (1968) 'The study of the career timetables', in B. Glaser (ed.) *Organizational Careers: A Sourcebook for Theory*, Chicago, IL: Aldine, pp. 35–49.

Schein, E.H. (1978) *Career Dynamics: Matching Individual and Organizational Needs*, Reading, MA: Addison-Wesley.

Schwartz, S.H. (1994) 'Beyond individualism/collectivism: new dimensions of values', in U. Kim, H.C. Triandis, C. Kagitçibasi, S.C. Choi and G. Yoon (eds) *Individualism and Collectivism: Theory Application and Methods*, Newbury Park, CA: Sage.

Schwartz S. (2004) 'Mapping and interpreting cultural differences around the world', in H. Vinken, J. Soeters and P. Ester (eds) *Comparing Cultures, Dimensions of Culture in a Comparative Perspective*, Leiden, The Netherlands: Brill.

Schwartz, S.H. (2006) 'A theory of cultural value orientations: explication and applications', *Comparative Sociology*, 5: 136–182.

Seibert, S.E., Kraimer, M.L. and Liden, R.C. (2001) 'A social capital theory of career success', *The Academy of Management Journal*, 44(2): 219–237.

Strauss, A. and Corbin, J. (1998) *Basics of Qualitative Research: Techniques and Procedures for Developing Grounded Theory*, London: Sage.

Strauss W. and Howe N. (1991) *Generations: The History of America's Future 1584–2069*, New York: William Morrow.

Sullivan, S.E. (1999) 'The changing nature of careers: a review and research agenda', *Journal of Management*, 25(3): 457–484.

Super, D.E. (1957) *The Psychology of Careers*, New York: Harper & Row.

Tams, S. and Arthur, M. (2007) 'Studying careers across cultures: distinguishing international, cross-cultural and globalization perspectives', *Career Development International*, 12(1): 86–98.

Tharenou, P. (1997) 'Managerial career advancement', *International Review of Industrial and Organisational Psychology*, 12: 39–80.

Trompenaars, F. and Hampden-Turner, C. (1997) *Riding the Waves of Culture: Understanding Cultural Diversity in Business*, Boston, MA: Nicholas Brealey Publishing.

Van Maanen, J. (ed.) (1977) *Organizational Careers: Some New Perspectives*, New York: Wiley.

Weiner, B., Frieze, I., Kukla, A., Reed, L., Rest, S. and Rosenbaum, R.M. (1972) 'Perceiving the causes of success and failure', in E.E. Jones (ed.) *Attribution: Perceiving the Causes of Behavior*, Morristown, NJ: General Learning Press, pp. 95–120.

Whiteoak, J.W., Crawford, N.G. and Mapstone, R.H. (2006) 'Impact of gender and generational differences in work values and attitudes in an Arab culture', *Thunderbird International Business Review*, 48(1): 77–91.

Wong, M., Gardiner, E., Lang, W. and Coulon, L. (2008) 'Generational differences in personality and motivation: do they exist and what are the implications for the workplace?', *Journal of Managerial Psychology*, 23(8): 878–890.

INDEX

Note: Page numbers followed by 'f' refer to figures and followed by 't' refer to tables.